Theoretical Introduction to Programming

Bruce Mills

Theoretical Introduction to Programming

With 29 Figures

 Springer

Bruce Mills, BEng, BSc, PhD

British Library Cataloguing in Publication Data
A catalogue record for this book is available from the British Library

Library of Congress Control Number: 2005926335

ISBN-10: 1-84628-021-4   Printed on acid-free paper
ISBN-13: 978-1-84628-021-4

9 8 7 6 5 4 3 2 1

Springer Science+Business Media
springeronline.com

Preface

This book is organised into a large number of brief, self-contained entries.

Admittedly, there is no such thing as a *self-contained entry*. For example, you need some knowledge of English to understand this paragraph. But, the principle is that each entry, of one or two pages, is a conceptual whole as well as a part of a greater whole (see note 20) in the same way that a car has four whole wheels, and not eight half wheels.

Some entries are intended to demonstrate a technique, or introduce an historically contingent fact such as the actual syntax of a contemporary language, or in this case, a specific issue regarding this book. Others are intended to illustrate a more eternal truth. They may be about a contemporary language, but stress a philosophical position or broadly based attitude. Both of these I have called *notions*. Finally, there are entries that are intended to cause the reader to do something other than just nodding their head as a sign of either agreement or an incipient dormant state. These are the exercises.

The distinction can only be arbitrary; the classification is merely a guide to suggest the sense in which the pages are intended.

In many cases, entries that are not specifically labelled as exercises involve generic opportunities for self-study. As this is a book on computer programming, it is natural and strongly advised that the reader try implementing each concept of interest as it arises. With this in mind, I have tried hard not to leave out pragmatic details whose omission would leave the reader with nothing but the illusion of understanding. Nevertheless, actually cutting practice code makes a big difference in the ability of the programmer to use the concepts when the need arises.

At the end of the book are the notes explaining short and simple issues or (paradoxically) issues that are too complex to explain in this book. If a note became too lengthy while being written it was converted into a notion or an exercise.

Contents

Preface v

Chapter 1. The Abstract Rational Outlook 1
    Abstract Computation...2
    Rational Thought...4
    Human Psychology 6
    Mythological Language 8
    Literate Programming..10
    Hand-Crafted Software 12
    Technical Programming.......................................14

Chapter 2. A Grab Bag of Computational Models 17
    Abstract and Virtual Machines 18
    State Machines..20
    State Machines in Action 22
    Turing Machine 26
    Non-Deterministic Machines 30
    Von Neumann Machine 34
    Stack Machine...36
    Register Machine..38
    Analogue Machine..39
    Cellular Automata...40
    Unorthodox Models 41
    The Game of Life..42
    The Modern Desktop Computer 44
    Aspects of Virtual Machines 46
    Aspects of Programming......................................48
    Register Indirection 50
    Pure Expression Substitution 52
    Lists Pure and Linked 54
    Pure String Substitution...................................56
    The Face Value of Numerals 58
    Solving Equations 62
    Pure Unification...64
    Equality of Expressions....................................66
    Equational Reasoning 68

Unification Reduction 70
Code Reduction 74
Programming With Logic 76
Negation in Logic Programming 78
Impure Lambda Calculus 80
Pure Lambda Calculus 82
Pure Lambda Arithmetic 84
Pure Lambda Flow Control 86
S-K Combinators 90

Chapter 3. Some Formal Technology 92
The Ellipsis Is Not a Definition 93
The Summation Operator 95
Propositional Calculus 97
Boolean Algebra 99
Predicate Calculus 101
Formal Mathematical Models 102
The Formal State Machine 103
Several Types of Networks 105
Informal Petri Nets 107
Formal Turing Machine 109
The Table-Driven State Machine 110
Factors of Graphs 111
Products of Graphs 113
Constructive Numerics 115
Prime Programs 117
Showing that Factorial Works 119
Reasoning About Code 123
Logical Conditions 127

Chapter 4. Limitations on Exact Knowledge 131
Finite-State Limitations 132
N log N sorting 133
Russell's Paradox 134
Pure Lambda Paradoxes 136
Godel's Theorem 138
Non-Computability 140
Solving Polynomials 142

Churche's Thesis 143
Algorithmic Complexity 144
P and NP 146
NP completeness 148
Turing Test 149
Natural Language Processing 150
The Computable Reals 151
The Diagonal Argument 152

Chapter 5. **Some Orthodox Languages** 154

C Pointers to Functions 159
Taking C on Face Value 161
Functions and Other Data in C 163
The C Preprocessor 166
C Functions are Data Again 167
Java Code 169
Pointer Casting 171
The Object Data Type 177
Manual Objects 179
Inheritance and Dynamic Type 181
CODASYL and Objects 183
Typecasting 185
The Concept of Type 187
Type-Checking 188
Subtypes and Programming 189
New Datatypes 190
Scheme Code 193
Declarative and Imperative 195
Sorting with Pure Substitution 197
Fast Sorting in Haskell 199
Logic in Prolog 201
Functions in Prolog 204
Arithmetic in Prolog 205
Meta-Logic in Prolog 207
What Is HTML Code? 209
Illogical markup language 211
HTML Forgive and Forget 212
Expanding Beyond Recognition 213

Chapter 6. **Arithmetic Computation**....................214
  Natural Arithmetic...215
  Modulo Arithmetic...217
  Integer Arithmetic..219
  Rational Arithmetic.......................................221
  Complex Arithmetic..223
  Exact Arithmetic..225
  Showing That a Power Loop Works...........................227
  When Is a Proof Not a Proof?..............................229
  Real-Valued Memory..231
  Cellular Matrix Multiplication............................232

Chapter 7. **Repetitive Computation**.....................235
  The Use of Recursion......................................236
  Doing Without the While Loop..............................238
  Defining the Generic While-Loop...........................240
  Design of the Power Function..............................244
  Powers by Multiplication..................................246
  Computing Powers by Squaring..............................248
  Language or Algorithm?....................................250
  Repetitive Program Design.................................253
  Recursive Code Compilation................................254
  Functions as Data...256
  Lambda Expressions in Java................................258
  The Y-combinator definition.............................260
  Y-combinator factorial..................................263
  Y-combinator Fibonacci..................................264

Chapter 8. **Temporal Interaction**.......................265
  Virtual Interaction.......................................266
  Incorruptible Operations..................................268
  Temporal Computing..270
  Multi-Threaded Code.......................................272
  Graphs of State Machines..................................273
  Direct Thread Composition.................................274
  Concurrent Thread Interference............................276
  Control Structures..278

Thread Point of Execution 280
The Transition Network 281
High-Level Interference.................................... 285
Incorruptible Commands Again.............................286
Thread Interaction 288
Pure String Interaction 292
Showing That a Parser Works 295
Mutual Exclusion 296
Good Mutual Exclusion 298
A Partial Mutex Protocol 299
Guarded Commands...300
Blocking Commands..306
Hardware Assistance 307
Proving That a Protocol Works............................308
Two Partial Exclusion Protocols...........................309
The Peterson Protocol.....................................310
The Decker Protocol 312
Proving That a Protocol Works............................314

Chapter 9. Container Datatypes 315
Abstract Arrays..316
Pure Containers..318
Generic Maps 322
Showing That Infinite Lists Work..........................325
Generic Lists.. 326
Computing with Infinite Lists 328
Sequence Builder 330
Infinite Lists in Haskell................................... 333
Infinite Lists in Scheme...................................334
Primitive List Recursion...................................336

Appendices 339
End notes... 340
Bibliography 351
Glossary 353

Index 355

Chapter 1

The Abstract Rational Outlook

In which we discover that programming is about being human. That to truly master a technology we must first master ourselves. That philosophical esoterica will bite us on the backside if we do not pay them enough attention. We discuss the effect that eternal truth, pure science, rational thought, group behaviour, and contemporary fashion have on our daily programming activities. We discover that identification of computation is a matter of opinion, that programming is an outlook on life in general, that the task of a programmer is to add a little wisdom to the inanimate.

In short, this theme contains the bulk of the material that most readers will pay scant attention to, until it is too late.

You may now skip to the next theme.

Notion 1: Abstract Computation

This book promotes the pragmatic use of computational theory in technical programming, providing a compact discussion of and a practical guide to its use. But theory is merely organised compound abstraction. So why should the *practical* programmer be concerned? Well, arithmetic, variables, procedures and functions are all abstractions and vital to the contemporary practical programmer. The universe is complex and an abstraction is a simplification that enables correct reasoning (see note 7). By its very nature, programming requires computational abstraction. But, like a martial arts practitioner, we must be able to push techniques to their limit and frequently learn new techniques to help us to solve new problems, or to solve old problems more efficiently.

This book expounds fundamental and generic abstractions of computation that have been developed, tested, and debugged by many people over the course of the twentieth century. At one time complex and esoteric, these ideas can now be well learned by an individual with only a few years of effort. Circumstances in which these abstractions can be used are common, but it requires a deft touch to recognise the right moment. This skill can only come from practice. If you do not consciously practice this until it becomes second nature, then the concepts will forever elude you, and you might not even realise your loss.

Traditional logic is a study of rules that enable *humans* to reason correctly. Classically, the humanity of the reasoner was implicit. Humans were viewed as the only non-trivial reasoners. With computers, a technical constraint in the complexity of the rules in a logic system was lifted. However, technical logics are only of use on computers. In practice, a human is incapable of reasoning with these logics due to mistakes. Human logic needs cross-checks and intuition. Technical logics are not logic in the traditional sense. They do not enable a *human* to reason correctly. Our need for human-oriented rules of reasoning has been obscured by computers, for which it is easier to make rules. Developing rules for human reasoning can be very difficult, but it is of vital importance to humans.[1]

---

[1]With apologies to any non-human readers, I will assume from now on that the reader is human.

Today, more than ever, we ask for human meaning in technology. We expect software to respond to us in a human manner. Without an abstract notion of software, we will fail in this aim. To tame the complexity we must instill a human literary component in specification and code (see note 17). To be portable means to be abstract. A truly concrete program runs on only one machine. But, even working on a singular low-level machine, instilling a human meaning requires an abstraction.

Abstraction is modularity and re-usability in one package.

When the same abstraction applies to physically distinct cases, we can save time and effort by applying the same reasoning to both. We cannot understand the machine in detail, so we must collect situations together into abstractions that enable us to write larger programs with some certainty that they will function. By viewing the program as an abstraction, we can be certain, without referring to the details, that our program will work. We can conceptualise and even literally visualise our program by means of simplifying abstractions. Recognising the points at which the intended abstraction breaks down is a good way to debug.

But abstraction should not be too rarefied or pedantic. It should be clean, clear and practical. Good theory is theory that helps clarify the code, not obscure it. Without abstraction, our code is a jumble of meaningless symbols. With the right human level of abstraction, it becomes a unified comprehensible whole. But with the wrong abstraction, or one that is too technical or too formal, once again our code becomes meaningless symbols.

Code written by a human is never truly written *for a computer*. To use that idea as an excuse to produce meaningless code is inexcusable.

This book is about literate theory, human theory intended for human understanding, decisive theory that works in practice where it has to be both robust and rigorous.

This theory is a software upgrade for the human brain.

Notion 2: Rational Thought

It has been said; man is a rational animal.
All my life I have searched for evidence of this.
Bertrand Russell.

Your mind is the software running on your brain (see note 12). Uniquely, programming requires the transfer of a part of the operation of your mind to another medium. In detail, it can be difficult to separate the creator from the created. In accomplishing this transfer your brain is your primary tool. It thus helps to understand that tool. In particular, this book is about rational programming, about making the thought processes involved in programming available to the conscious mind, and thus to introspection and adjustment. This requires effort, practice and discipline.

The human mind is made from conscious and subconscious parts. The subconscious has the greater capacity and speed. It provides the high-level simulation of the universe that is the environment of the conscious mind. The conscious mind would be completely unable to operate if fed the raw sensory input that is normally feeding through the subconscious. The subconscious, however, is subject to instability, catastrophic loss of learning, and a tendency to settle into pathological limit cycles or self-perpetuating habits of thought. This seems to be an unavoidable property of complex systems rather than bad design in the human mind. But, whichever it is, it is what we are. The purpose of the conscious mind is to act as a moderator, to provide introspective feedback to stabilise the subconscious mind.

Unfortunately, however, at each moment it is easier for the conscious mind to dump the processing and guess. This is not a magic solution, nor a mystical connection to the great sea of universal knowledge, but simply an inappropriate demand that the subconscious do the processing. In order to allow the subconscious to perform correctly at high speed, the conscious mind must delay the transfer of processing until that processing is well organised. This debugging is not unlike using a computer except that it requires conscious introspection.

We have the ability to observe, think, and act. Self-evident logical truth is observation. To think is to compute, to build truth into greater truth or actions into greater actions. The ability to act, to control the environment, is as vital as truth and thought but it is often neglected in discussions. To operate we must know that something is true, decide what we need to do and act on this decision. The scientific outlook is that we have a model (which is a creature of thought with a formal structure) and we have a correspondence of this model with reality, which cannot be formalised. This correspondence tells us how the model relates to our observations and actions. Together, this is abstraction.

So, abstraction has pre-conditions. To apply arithmetic validly to counting trees, we must be able to determine the number of trees. We must also have a way of combining trees through which the corresponding numbers combine according to arithmetic. Counting waves is harder because they merge and split, and it is unclear where one stops and another begins.

Abstractions never apply precisely in practice, but they may apply sufficiently well while we have the power to maintain their pre-conditions. If the pre-conditions are violated, then the conclusions from the abstraction may be invalid. For example, if we count rabbits and combine them in a box, some may be born, and some die and we might or might not be left with the sum of the number of rabbits. But for as long as we can prevent the rabbits from breeding or dying, we can validly apply integer arithmetic. Knowledge of abstraction tells us where best to concentrate our limited ability to control the environment.

An abstraction should be learned with a clear understanding of the environmental control required for its application. Thus, Euclid begins with *we can draw a line and a circle*. As long as this holds, Euclidean geometry applies. Once it no longer holds, the use of Euclidean geometry is no longer justified. But good abstractions such as Euclidean geometry are robust. Often, when the original conditions are violated, related conditions may be substituted, leaving intact the overall theory. While justification of theory depends on the details, practical use depends on the overall intuitive impact. When conditions fail, it is worthwhile to hunt for others that will sustain the theory. But we must check the details.

Notion 3: Human Psychology

It has been well said by Edsger Dijkstra —

Computer Science is about computers
only as far as Cosmological Science is about telescopes.

But more needs to be said.

Cosmological models have been built to help humans understand the cosmos. The models reflect the nature of the human mind, not the nature of the cosmos; at most, they reflect the interaction between the human mind and the cosmos. The strongest constraint on these models is the human mind.

Even more so with computer science. Computer theory and computer languages are designed for humans. Although they often reflect, more than is admitted, the Von Neumann architecture, their nature is human; their reason for existence is the limitations of the human mind.

People do not, and most likely cannot, understand computers. Computer languages exist because we need to impose a much simpler virtual environment on top of the ones that we can create as artifacts. When a person claims to understand computers, at best they are familiar with one of these virtual environments.

Imagine that the computer revolution had not occurred. The typical computer has a maximum of 1,024 bytes of memory, and runs on a one-second clock cycle. Programming as we know it today would not exist. Writing in machine code is best done by simply understanding the exact effect that each instruction has on the total state of the machine.

In 1986, I worked as a machine code programmer. One microprocessor had 1,024 bytes, paged at each 64 bytes. The first problem I solved was why none of the software worked on the machine at all. Because I had memorised the machine code in binary, I recognised in the output of a logic analyser that the data lines had been switched around. *Hey, the binary for that instruction is written backwards.* Later I wrote a multiplication routine when I had only a few bytes of space left. I knew I had no room for Booth's algorithm, so I went home and read the opcode definitions again, several times. The next day I wrote a sequence of instructions that would produce, for no reason, the right answer on each multiplication that could actually occur in the execution of the program. I could do this because I knew the details of exactly what was required and how the machine responded at the bit-level.

A creature that fully understood our desktop computers would not need any high-level computer language to program it.

Further, many aspects of computer science owe very little to any eternal truths. They are matters of fashion. If everyone writes programs in a particular way, using particular constructs, mythos, and culture, then it behooves the novice to follow likewise.

Computer languages change, as word usage does in natural language, without rhyme, reason, or advance. This is human nature. Arbitrary changes are often promoted as being deep and significant progress. This promotion is aided by the cognitive illusion which causes a person taught in one system to believe another system to be intrinsically more difficult and awkward, regardless of whether it really is or not. The familiar is erroneously believed to be *intrinsically* easier and more natural.

Further, old ideas are often repackaged with a new name and new jargon, alienating the older system and gaining promotion for the organisation that invented the new jargon. The roots of many concepts go significantly much further back than is often admitted. The tragedy is that these psychological factors have led to more, rather than less, complex computer environments.

To understand truly how to program, in practice, here and now on this planet, is to understand, pay attention to, and keep abreast of developments in the culture, politics, and fashion of computing environments. But keep in mind that these are contingencies, not eternal truths. If we confuse the contingent with the eternal, then we will have to constantly re-learn. If we do know what is eternal, we can adapt to changes in contingencies by a superficial change in form.

For the most part this book is intended to be about eternal truths.

Notion 4: Mythological Language

Language has syntax, semantics, pragmatics, and mythos.

Syntax is the mechanical form of the language, semantics is the meaning based solely on the syntax, pragmatics is meaning or purpose in the broader context, and mythos is the body of stories people tell each other about the language.

Consider this C code: x=6;

The syntax is the literal sequence of characters,

'x' followed by '=', followed by '6' followed by ';'.

The semantics is that

'x' stores value '6', so that '6' may be retrieved from 'x' later.

The pragmatics might be that

'x' is the number of people coming to dinner.

The mythos is that 'x' represents an integer.

In reality, it does nothing of the kind.

The common truth of the **int** datatype in many languages is that it is n-bit arithmetic, meaning that it is arithmetic modulo 2^n. If we keep adding 1, we get back to 0. This is a perfectly respectable arithmetic itself, and can be used, if used carefully, to determine integer arithmetic results. But to say that **int** is integer arithmetic with bounds and overflow conditions is to say that it *is not* integer arithmetic. Similarly, to say that **float** is real arithmetic, with approximation errors, is to say that it *is not* real arithmetic.

This is not to say that mythos is *by definition* false, but typically if mythos was true, it would be semantics or pragmatics. Mythos is the collection of comfortable half-truths that we programmers tell each other so that we do not have to handle the full truth. Mythos helps us to communicate with other programmers who subscribe to the same mythology. Mythos simplifies the programming of familiar tasks, restricting usage to a subset of the possibilities. Mythos helps us to feel comfortable with our environment. Mythos is very human, and most likely unavoidable.

But *truly believing* (not just on Sundays) in a mythos can cause difficulty when something does not fit. A software bug does not typically fit the mythos. This is partly what makes it a bug. To debug you need to understand more of the nature of what the language *really is* rather than what we pretend it to be. If you believe the mythos, it is easy to jump to unjustified conclusions about the code behaviour without even realising consciously that you have done so — or worse, to believe that you have justified the conclusion. If you know it is only mythos, you can step outside its bounds for a while to find the bug. You might even search deliberately for something that does not conform to the mythos as a possible location for the bug.

Further, believing in a mythos makes it much harder to communicate with programmers who believe in a different mythos, makes it much harder to program an unfamiliar task, and makes it easy to miss a shorter or faster code option. Believing in a mythos is a form of blinkered specialisation.

I can think of four distinct mythological systems that compete with each other in the computing arena: Engineering, Management, Book-keeping, and Mathematics. Correspondingly, the computer is a: piece of electronic machinery, virtual office environment, data storage device, or corporeal reflection of eternal concepts. But of course this is just an exercise in classification, and in detail we have many different combinations, and permutations and subsystems.

In my use of the terms, a *paradigm* is an outlook that contains unjustified existential ideas, while a *mythology* is an outlook that contains unjustified empirical ideas.

We should use as minimal a mythos as possible, and we should be aware, and gain experience in, several distinct and conflicting mythologies.

Notion 5: Literate Programming

Donald Knuth once said,

... when you write a program,
think of it primarily as a work of literature.

To program in computing is to prove in mathematics: both in syntax and in semantics. The formal structure of a program is identical to that of a formal constructive proof. To write a routine is to assert the theorem that *the code performs to specification.*

Although there are errors in mathematical works, the density is much lower than in contemporary programs. In the mythos, this is due to a greater complexity or urgency of software. The truth is, mathematics was designed to be understood. A mathematics book does not just prove, it also motivates, justifies, and discusses. This human nature makes it easier to follow, detect errors, use elsewhere, or extend.

The larger part of the life of a piece of software is maintenance. The code is modified to suit new specifications, conceptual errors are identified and corrected, and typographical faults removed. This is also the life of a mathematical proof.

A mathematical proof can be lengthy, technical, complex, obscure and urgent; and yet it will not be left without justification. The mathematical community would not accept it if it was. The fact that much code is written without proper contemplation today is related to market forces. But, whatever excuse we give for why there is this lack, this means (very) low-quality code.[2]

There are good proofs and there are bad proofs. A good proof conforms to both logic and intuition. A bad proof might give no clear concept of why the result is true or might be difficult to follow. A flawed proof with good discussion may be of more use in the development of related correct material, than a technically correct proof that has no explanation.

Code should be written to be clear by itself, but also with good com-

---

[2]Actually I do not see, *To make more money,* as a socially acceptable response to, *Why do you write bad code?*

ments. More than just a cursive phrase stating *this variable stores the number of hobos found in Arkansas*. It should contain discussion, explanation, and justification.

The natural language in a mathematics book is like the comments in a program and is typically more extensive than the formal language. We can compute $f(n) = \sum_{i=1}^{n} i$, by a loop. The loop is "self-commenting" because it reflects the original specification. But it is better to compute this as $f(n) = n(n+1)/2$, relying on the series identity $\sum_{i=1}^{n} i = n(n+1)/2$, which is by no means obvious. In the code, we need a non-trivial comment to explain why what we are doing works.

A program should be developed with a coherent theory of its operation. Clearly defined data structures, with explicit axioms, greatly ease the use and re-use of the code. If each item has a clearly explained purpose and a distinct, justified, and discussed property, if each item is a whole as well as a part (see note 20), then it is much less likely that a later programmer will accidently misuse it.

Consider a program to be written primarily to explain to another human what it is that we want the computer to do, how it is to happen, and why we can believe that we have achieved our aim. Do this even if you write code for yourself. The "other" human being might be you in a few month's time when the details have escaped your mind.

I have found it advisable that, in selecting what to write in comments, if you have just spent a lot of time writing a routine, you should write down what is obvious. Because it is likely that it is only obvious to you now because you are steeped in the problem, next day, next week, or next month, when you come back to modify it, the operating principle might not be obvious at all.

Literate Haskell style is supported by typical Haskell environments. In this approach, the code–comment relation is reversed. Normally the code has primacy, and the comments are introduced by a special syntax, as if in afterthought. In the literate approach, the comments are primary. By default, text is comment; the code must be introduced by a special notation stating that it is code.

Notion 6: Hand-Crafted Software

Technical programming is a craft, a combination of art and science intended to create aesthetic, functional artifacts. A person well versed in this craft can use a variety of media. Their skill is not limited to a particular computer, language or paradigm. To be a virtuoso you must learn to feel down through the superficiality of the outward appearance toward the computational fundamentals below.

The three R's of programming[3] (see note 21) are to be *robust, rigorous* and *reasonable*. Software should be robust, meaning that it is not easily broken by changes in the conditions under which it is used; rigorous, in that it should be constructed on solid logical foundations; and reasonable, in that it should be readily understandable by those who try (as distinct from those who do not). First and foremost, a program is a literate work, from one human being to another, even if only from you to yourself.

Technology should be made human, and yes, it is possible, but we have stopped trying, and stopped promoting this attitude. This book emphasises the idea that software is primarily a work of literature and science, like Euclid's *Elements of Geometry*, or Dante's *Divine Comedy in Three Parts*. It is an attempt to make sense of the universe and to make the future a nicer place to live in.

This book contains a collection of entry points to fundamental skills. Skills that if practised by a programmer until they are second nature can form the foundation of a pragmatic ability to rapidly construct software that is robust, rigorous and reasonable. Based in abstraction the discussion is primarily intended to encourage quality software in realistic environments.

Like any craft, there are tools of the trade that the practitioner carries with them physically, and techniques carried mentally. The programmer may have their favourite compiler, editor, or operating system on disk. The programmer will have various tools they have built themselves, some of which they keep hidden. They will also have standard approaches to problems, techniques to break the problem into parts similar to problems

---

[3]Sorry, no wordplay here.

they have seen before. Michaelangelo is famous for solving a technical problem in the shape of a block of marble for the statue of David, this is not so very different from what programmers do today.

One technique, and a common theme in this book, is that we have an initial state, a body of code that is applied repeatedly to the state, a test that indicates when the computation is complete, and a method for extracting the desired information from the final state. The distinction between iterative, recursive, logical, machine and combinator code is merely in the way in which this theme is expressed. The concept is the same, regardless of the specific language or paradigm.

Another technique, and universal implicit theme, is the repeated replacement of equals for equals within a pure expression, an expression which may be taken on face value alone. This is the foundation of all of formal human science. As in the graphic arts, to see exactly what is there is a skill that takes much effort to develop. In Zen style, paradoxically, the explorer may not comprehend because the truth is too simple.

Although you can buy curry paste at the shop, a good cook makes their own from the basic spices. Once the art is learned, and with the spices on hand, the paste is made with little loss of time, and the result is of higher quality and well fitted to the specific occasion.

Likewise, the programmer should practise constructing basic computational machinery from scratch in multiple languages. In this way, the techniques are never used in exactly the same way in any two programs, but always styled to suit the task. A higher quality of code is the result.

Understand, cut, paste, and edit, is still the best way to reuse code.

It is my fervent hope that you will take what is presented here as a clue to where to begin a trip that could take a lifetime, with the recognition that there is far more to it than you have already seen, no matter how much you have seen.

Notion 7: Technical Programming

This is a book about technical programming.

What exactly is technical programming? And what is not? It is hard
to define exactly. As a quick guide, most hard-science applications are
technical, but not all. Technical programming is about defining a specific
problem as clearly as possible, and obtaining a clear solution. It is about
logical modularity and giving structure to the problem domain. Perhaps
the problem can't be defined formally; for example, *find the centre of the
drawing pins in an image*. But this does not mean it is a non-technical
problem.

Technical programming is engineering. It is most like electronic engineering because of its lack of physical intuition, but it has much in
common with the technical (rather than bureaucratic) aspects of all engineering disciplines. The engineering of non-trivial software[4] should
not be attempted without a good grounding in logical, mathematical,
and scientific methodology.

While a technical programming problem might not have an exact definition as a whole, we still find as much precision as possible. Precise
subproblems are identified. Tasks such as sorting a list, finding an average, solving linear equations, etc., all have formal specifications, and
precise provable solutions exist. They are wholes in themselves as well
as being parts of the solution to the larger problem. This is an approach rather than an application domain. Technical programming is
far broader than just hard-science software.

Some areas of programming lend themselves more easily to technical
programming. An area that has been known for a while may well become
technical, just because the techniques accumulate over time. An area of
cutting edge research might be technical, while an old area might still
have little technical content. What is, or is not, technical depends on
the techniques available. An area is non-technical if there is little in the
way of help from specific models.

Software modelling physical systems may be very technical because phys-

---

[4]As opposed to *software engineering*, which is a business subject.

ical scientific theory is very highly developed and reliable. Thus, programmers are in some peril if they ignore the transmitted wisdom. Predicting the stock market used to be very non-technical — there were relatively few models, they were simple, and they did not work. Now, the models are highly sophisticated, and regardless of whether they work or not, to be seen as a viable builder of stock-market-predicting software, the programmer would have to be well versed in these models. A lot of current web programming, however, is almost completely non-technical.

A core theme in technical programming is the promotion of the rational approach, the conscious awareness of the human thought processes involved in programming. A sub-theme is that every interactive program defines a language. The execution of a program is a discourse with the universe.

What is not technical programming? Because it is a matter of approach, it is impossible to exclude any application domain. But, graphical aesthetics, menu design, programs that produce art, web pages, and word processors are all examples of application areas that tend to be non-technical.

What might someone be dealing with for this book to be helpful?

CAD programs, network diagrams, circuit diagrams, pipeline flow, solid modelling, fluid flow, sketch input, architectural software, geometric computing, structural analysis, statistical analysis, parsing, natural language processing, compiler writing, computer language translators, graphics files, and sound files, language design, file compression, computer algebra, embedded software design, multi threaded real-time code, calculators, ATM machines, EFTPOS, cash registers, microwave ovens, security protocols, simulation software, graphics games, networked software, industrial control.

If I have left out your area please write it in below.

Chapter 2

A Grab Bag of Computational Models

In which we take the view that designing software is the technological aspect of computer science in analogy to the designing of hardware being the technological side of electronic science. We find that there is a smooth shift from one to the other, with firmware in the twilight zone.

Knowing that a hardware engineer or technician requires a grab bag full of formal models of the material at hand, small enough and simple enough to submit to analysis, realistic enough to be relevant, we admit that a programmer likewise needs a collection of software models: pure archetypical computational mechanisms that assist analysis and design of practical software in the real and very impure world.

We recognise that every piece of software is a virtual machine. And so, study a collection of specific abstract models, including Turing machines, state machines, Von Neumann machines, s-code reduction, lambda calculus, primitive recursive functions, pure string substitution expression reduction, etc.

We learn about unification-reduction, which has been rightly referred to as the arithmetic of computer science, acting both as a low- and high-level concept. It is a first model of every computer language so far devised. The substitution of equals for equals is a beguilingly simple concept; we learn that it is a deeply powerful representation of computation itself. Computation is constructive logic, the propositional and predicate calculi being the foundational material.

Notion 8: Abstract and Virtual Machines

We do not know how the universe actually works.

Through whatever process pleases us, scientific or otherwise, we decide to act on incompletely justified assumptions about the possible effects of our actions. A physical machine, be it a can-opener or a computer, is always designed as an idealised conception in our minds. For digital computers, we construct small component machines whose behaviour may be finitely described.

The nand gate takes two inputs, whose values may only be 0 or 1, and so the output can be listed explicitly for each of the four possible input combinations.

a	b	a nand b
0	0	1
0	1	1
1	0	1
1	1	0

We may also conceptualise a component as a physical device.

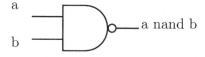

While this might (or might not depending on your background) appeal more strongly to your intuition, it is still a virtual machine, an abstract construction, or an idealised conception of our minds.

Inspired by this concept, we build a physical device that is supposed to work in like manner. In reality it never does. If we are smart then we know that it does not. But it works correctly, under the right conditions, to sufficient accuracy, with sufficient probability, to make it practical to assume that it will work.

Abstract devices abound. They include everything from idealised can-openers to spacecraft complete with navigational software and zero-gravity toilet. But, in this discussion we concentrate on abstract *digital computational* machines. Generically this will involve a finite symbolic state that changes in time.

Any computer language defines an abstract machine.

The distinction between an abstract machine and a virtual machine is that we have an implementation of the virtual machine.

Pragmatically, there is little to distinguish the nature of the firmware or hardware virtual machine from the pure software virtual machine.

For example, Java is said to operate on the Java Virtual Machine or JVM, which is typically implemented in software. But we could equally build a JVM chip. The JVM is just an orthodox Von Neumann architecture, and would be easy to design and manufacture. We could also build a CVM to run our C programs. In a strong sense that is exactly what the compiler is.

Micro-coded machines have machine code in which each instruction is actually a small program written in a simpler lower-level machine code. Thus, the supposed hardware, the target for an assembler, is actually being emulated on even lower level-hardware.

Software is easy to modify; firmware can be modified with moderate effort; and hardware is typically difficult to change. As components become smaller towards the size of atoms and electrons, we find less ability to control them directly via high-level software in our machine, but there is no precise cutoff.

The difficulty of modifying hardware is contingent. Programmable gate arrays can be modified in normal operation. Research is ongoing into ways in which the arrangement of transistors on the chip may be dynamically modified. In the longer run, hardware may be just another form of software.

Conceptually, they are all virtual machines.

Notion 9: State Machines

The interactive state machine concept is central computational technology. To apply this concept we first identify its four components. The device must be distinct from its environment. A wristwatch, for example, is distinct from its wearer. The device must internalise information. A wristwatch stores the time. The device must act externally. A wristwatch may display the time, or sound an alarm. The user must act on the device. The wearer may push buttons or turn knobs on the watch. Finally, the device must exist in time, responding to actions of the environment by actions of its own, and by modifying its stored information. Any computer, analogue or digital, is a state machine.

Discreteness is definitive of digital technology. Quantities are discrete if each may be distinguished by a definite amount from all others. The display of a digital watch is discrete because the numerals are distinct from each other. In contrast, the possible positions of the second hand of an analogue watch form a continuum. No matter how good our eyesight, there are always two locations so close together that we cannot tell them apart. Pushing a button is a discrete action — we either manage to push the button, or we do not. Turning a knob is continuous; we may turn the knob a little or a lot, with indefinite shades in between. A digital watch might act only ten times a second, it operates at discrete times. An analogue watch responds continuously to the continuous turn of the knob. The state of the analogue watch is a continuous voltage or position, while the digital watch stores only a collection of discrete symbols.

On closer examination, most analogue watches are discrete state. The second hand moves by distinct jumps. But looked at even more closely, the jumps of the second hand are fast, but continuous. So are the changes in the display of a digital watch. It is an open question whether the universe is ultimately discrete or continuous. In practice, the question is resolved by asking which model most simply describes the interesting behaviour to the desired accuracy. In programming, we model a digital computer as having a discrete state, display, input and action. This is referred to as a discrete state machine. If the states, display, input, and actions performed in a finite time are all finite, we refer to this as a finite state-machine.

Another example of a discrete-state machine is a video cassette player interface. Each step is discrete. As we operate the machine we switch it from one state to another. The validity of an input varies from state to state. The video player responds by showing information on its display and updating the information that it stores.

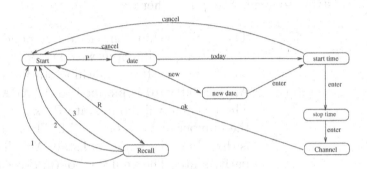

As above, we can draw a diagram, a network of nodes and links that represents the states and transitions of the state machine. The input is written on the links, and the output (not indicated in the above diagram) may be thought of as being dependent on the state. This notion may be given a much more precise formalism. (see page 103).

A state machine may be used to map input strings to output strings (see page 22). This can either be used as a program, mapping an input question to the output response, or as a temporal interaction for interactive systems such as communication protocol implementation, and user interface design.

Explicit use of state machines is most important for embedded controllers and communication devices. Often such a machine is written up as an array of transition and state information (see page 110). State machines can be implemented easily by a microprocessor, but also rather nicely by regular arrays of logic gates.

Notion 10: State Machines in Action

State machines (see page 20) can operate on symbolic strings in a variety of ways. Fundamentally, it maps a symbolic string to a sequence of states and transitions. If we associate a symbol with the state (a Moore machine) or transition (a Mealy machine), then we have a string-to-string map. Alternatively, by taking the last symbol of the output string, we obtain a string to symbol map in either case.

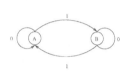

The state machine on the left responds to a {0,1} string on its input with an {A,B} string on its output. If the machine starts in state A, then 0011010 is mapped to AAABAABB. The machine will be in state B exactly when the number of 1s so far is odd. Thus, state B is the odd parity state, and state A is the even parity state. The final symbol (in this case B) shows us the parity of the whole input string.

Indicating state A as the starting state, this machine is said to recognise, at state B, even parity strings. The final state, A or B, classifies the input string as even or odd parity.

For a Moore machine the output string is one symbol longer than the input string. For a Mealy machine the lengths are the same. Sometimes, since the starting symbol does not depend on the input string, the starting symbol is ignored in a Moore machine. But in the above example the parity of an empty string is even, and the output "A" is correct. A Mealy machine would not provide this output, but we can fix this by providing a *start of string* indicator. By using these and similar tricks, either machine can be used equally.

In the parity example, there is an output symbol for every state. We may relax this condition so that some states, or transitions, do not generate an output symbol. In this case, the string mapping behaviour of the Moore and Mealy machines is identical.

Explicit coding of state machines is most typically advisable in temporal interaction. User interfaces, communications systems, parsing of languages, and embedded control code all can benefit from this approach.

A state machine may be hard-coded by a systematic use of nested conditionals, with a variable storing a state number. The state number is tested and set to the new state. Procedural code and state machine code tend to fight each other. It is still possible for them to coexist, even call each other. But they should normally be written separately, and from a different point of view.

```
state = 0;
while(state<2)
{
    putchar(state==0?'A':'B'));
    c = getchar();
    if(state==0 && c=='0') state=0; else
    if(state==0 && c=='1') state=1; else
    if(state==1 && c=='0') state=1; else
    if(state==1 && c=='1') state=0; else
    state=2;
}
putchar(state==0?'A':'B'))
```

Rather than hard-coding the machine, an array can store output for given state. Another array can store new state versus old state and input. Generic code can then be used for the heart of the machine.

```
state = 0;
while(putchar(output[state]))
{
input = parse(getchar());
if(input==error) break;
state = next[state,input];
}
```

In some cases, it is best for the arrays to be replaced by functions, since either the size of the state machine or a lack of knowledge of its structure may prevent explicit listing of the states and state transitions.

Typically, the table driven approach (see page 110) to implementing a state machine is the most practical, as well as being the closest to the formal algebra (see page 103). This close association between the most formal and the most pragmatic approach to a datatype is very common, more than is often realised, and should be design focus.

Exercise 1: Virtual Machines

Design a pneumatic digital computer. (See hints below.)

Separate in your mind computers from electronics. The first fully fledged digital computer designed (by Charles Babbage) was mechanical, and was largely the same as the modern electronic digital computer. Pneumatics has many advantages over mechanics, e.g., an air hose can be bent around easily, while rods and wheels need careful alignment. Pneumatic computers are less affected by the environment and were used for industrial control into the 1980s.

The basic element in many computers is the nand-gate. It has two signal inputs and one output. If both inputs are active, then the output is inactive, otherwise the output is active. It computes "not both".

The simplest place to start is to design an inverter. It has one hose connector for input and one for output. If there is high pressure on the input then there is low pressure on the output; low pressure on the input means high pressure on the output.

In principle, an inverter can use an input to slide a block to shut off a high-pressure bias intake. If the input is low-pressure the bias escapes to the output, otherwise the output is low pressure. The one on the right is not practical because of difficulties such as sealing the sliding surfaces. For simplicity we can ignore this, but your solution is better if you consider the mechanics.

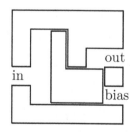

Two pressures can be used for each signal. A hi-lo combination means a logic 1, and a lo-hi means 0. An inverter might just swap the hoses. This is simple, but loses signal strength. The output should mainly be driven by a separate bias intake, which you can assume to be provided globally. Springs can also be used, from which a valve may be built.

Experiment and use your imagination.

Exercise 2: Finite State-Machines

A finite state-machine (see page 20) classifies strings (see page 22).
Design finite state-machines that classifies strings according to —

1. whether it ends in the substring 1010, or not;

2. whether it contains the substring 1010, or not;

3. whether it is a binary number greater than 1010, or not;

4. its remainder after division by 4. (so, four categories).

In a standard msb first binary numeral, $x_3x_2x_1x_0$, x_3 is the most significant bit. The reverse order is lsb first, and is more natural for finite state-machines. To store two binary numbers we can use an infix $x_3x_2x_1x_0 + y_3y_2y_1y_0$, or spliced $x_3y_3x_1y_2x_1y_1x_0y_0+$, format.

A finite state-machine (see page 20) maps strings (see page 22).
Design state machines that map strings to the effect —

1. of incrementing an lsb first binary number;

2. of adding two spliced lsb first binary numbers;

3. of multiplying an lsb first number by 3;

4. of adding two msb first binary numbers;

5. of adding two lsb first infix binary numbers;

6. of multiplying two lsb first spliced binary numbers.

Some of the above operations are impossible for a finite state-machine — which ones and why?

Notion 11: Turing Machine

As a physical intuition, the definitive Turing machine is built from an infinite tape of discrete memory cells, together with an interactive cpu that moves along the tape reading and writing the cells. The cpu moves at a finite speed and has a finite number of states. Each cell contains one (at a time) of a finite collection of symbols. The choice of action, writing a symbol, moving to the left or right, or halting, is determined by a lookup table from the current tape symbol and cpu state.

The classic view is that each Turing machine computes a natural number function. The n symbols may be taken as the digits of a base-n natural number. At startup, all cells to the left of the cpu are 0, and only a finite number to the right are non-0. The initial tape represents a natural number. If the machine halts after a finite time, the tape will still only have a finite number of non-0 cells. The input number has been mapped to the output number. Generically, a Turing machine defines only a partial map, since the output is undefined if the machine never halts.

By finitely placing non-0 symbols to the left, we can program a Turing machine. For each program, the machine computes a potentially distinct function. But it is a generic limitation of effective computational devices that not all natural functions can be thus computed.

Other encodings can allow a Turing machine to solve problems on other domains. For example, a universal Turing machine takes a pair (m,d) of a Turing machine table m, and input data d, and emulates the machine operating on the data. Oddly, universality is subjective. Marvin Minksky's classic 7-state universal Turing machine works, but the "proof" is mainly a subjective justification of the encoding.

To illustrate this point, consider the machine M that increments each even number, and deliberately does not halt on odd numbers. For each input (m,d) there is a unique output r. If the machine m does not halt on the data d, then we want the universal machine to not halt. If m halts on d, then encode (m,d) as an even number and encode r as the next odd number. Otherwise encode (m,d) as an odd number. Thus, M is universal. True, from any standard description of a Turing machine it is a non-computable problem to determine what to feed this universal machine. But logically, the representation is valid.

There are many Turing variations. Some have a lesser computational ability, but none have more. A one-way (single-pass) Turing machine moves only in one direction. Increment in binary can be performed by one pass, but this is so strong a restriction that this variants ability is reduced.

There are multi-tape and multi-cpu versions, as well as a two-dimensional one that can move north, east, south, and west. Trying to envisage this physically can lead to tangles of tape all over the floor. For simplicity, assume that the tapes and cpu's pass through each other.

The tapes may be fed around in circles, forming limited storage; and the surface may be a cylinder, a sphere, a torus, or something topologically more interesting. The cells might be connected to five neighbours, or more, or less, or form an irregular graph. Any number of dimensions can be used.

A continuous version might be a linear filter in which the speed of the interactive head depends on an output computed from the input read on the tape, and an internal state in the head.

Non-deterministic Turing machines are also possible, as are versions in which the head can cut and splice pieces of tape. However, once it is generalised too far, like any other model, it becomes something other than what was envisaged by the creator and is more of an outlook on computation than a particular device.

Exercise 3: Design a Turing Machine

You do not understand a virtual machine until you have written several
programs for it. In this exercise, we try to understand Turing machines.
One direct way to specify a Turing machine is a transition table. The
columns are old-state, old-symbol, new-symbol, new-state, and movement, where L means go left, R means go right, and H means halt. The
starting state is s, and the halting state is h.

For example, given a tape that contains only 0's except for a single run of
1's, we can make the run an even length by overwriting the first 0 on the
right with a 1, if required. A Turing machine might do this by starting
on the leftmost 1 and then moving to the right, switching between two
states to keep track of whether the run of 1's is so far even or odd in
length.

$$
\begin{array}{ccccccc}
s & 1 & \rightarrow & 1 & b & R \\
b & 1 & \rightarrow & 1 & s & R \\
s & 0 & \rightarrow & 0 & h & H \\
b & 0 & \rightarrow & 1 & h & H \\
\end{array}
$$

The machine switches between states s and b at each occurrence of the
symbol 1 on the tape. Thus, s is the even parity state, and b is the odd
parity state. When a 0 is found, the appropriate symbol is written and
the machine halts. Even if the tape symbol is unchanged, we still fill in
the entry in the table explicitly.

It is fairly easy to write a simple Turing machine simulator in a finite
array, and it is recommended that you do so to help with these exercises.

The state of the Turing machine is easy to represent as a single finite
string of tape symbols with an extra symbol, T, for the cpu; we assume that the final character on either end is repeated indefinitely. So,
00001T000 represents a tape full of 0's except for a single 1, and the
Turing head is currently located on the cell containing the single 1.

The tally system of representing numbers just means to represent 1 as 1 and 2 as 11 and 3 as 111 and so on, with an arbitrary amount of padding with 0s on either side, so 0111000 also represents 3.

1. We write the addition 4+2 as 0001111011T000 in the tally system, where the T represents the Turing head initial position.

   Write a machine that moves only to the left, and changes this into a single equivalent tally base number.

2. In the binary system, we can increment a number by moving to the left, changing 1 into 0, until we find a 0. Write such a Turing machine.

3. Write a machine that converts tally to binary, by repeated use of an incrementing state on a binary number, and decrementing the tally number.

4. Write a machine that adds two numbers in binary. This time we include three symbols on the tape, so that the initial state might be sss10010s101sss, where s represents a space character. The desired output in this case is sss10111sss, where the original numbers have been erased.

5. Different Turing machines behave differently to the same input, such as an initially blank tape. Given a two-symbol tape, we can ask, how many 1's will Turing machine T write before halting (assuming it does halt). Since there are only a finite number of machines of a given number of states, there must be a maximum number of 1s that can be written. Such a maximal Turing machine is a *Busy Beaver*.

   Write a 1-, 2-, and 3-state Busy Beaver.

6. Determining that an n-state machine is a Busy Beaver, or just how many 1's an n-state Busy Beaver will write is very difficult, and the number rises rapidly, in the manner of Akerman's function.

   Can you work out any conclusions?

Notion 12: Non-Deterministic Machines

By an engineering definition, a *state* of a machine is some information which determines the machine's future behaviour. Strictly, it is tautologous that every state machine is deterministic. Any other machine does not have a state. It is unknown whether the universe as a whole has a state. But, even if a state exists, often only a part can be measured. The rest is hidden. Observing only the measurable part means that for each (observable) state there may be multiple possible futures.

For a discrete deterministic machine, each state leads to a unique next state. The next state is a function of the current state. Such a machine is characterised by a space of states equipped with a next-state function. It is natural to describe a non-deterministic discrete machine by a next-state *relation*.[5] Each state has a *collection* of next states.

Given a collection of (observable) states in which the machine might be, the set of states it might be in next is the union of the sets for each of the states in the collection. Thus, a non-deterministic machine is a special case of a deterministic machine on the power set of the states of the original machine. The final value returned by the non-deterministic machine is the value returned by the *first* deterministic machine to terminate. Of course, in general, this is a *collection* of values.

The power set of the states of a finite machine (see page 20) is also finite. So, a non-deterministic finite machine is still a finite machine, just on a larger state space. However, a finite machine viewed as a non-deterministic machine may be easier to design or modify than if viewed as deterministic. The non-deterministic machine has a special structure, admitting direct parallel implementation.

For Turing machines (see page 26), the machine state is the state and location of the cpu together with the state of the tape. This can be encoded as a finite integer. A Turing machine is a *countable state* machine. The set of subsets of a countable state space is uncountable, which takes us outside the scope of the modern desktop computer entirely. For this reason, the subsets will be restricted to be finite. The set of *finite* subsets of a countable state space is also countable.

---

[5]Sometimes referred to as a multi-valued function.

It is true, but not immediately clear, that a non-deterministic Turing machine can be emulated by a deterministic one. By using the Hanoi sequence (see note 22) we can splice a countable number of virtual tapes into one single tape. With one virtual tape used for scratch space, a deterministic Turing machine may simulate a non-deterministic Turing machine.

The true non-deterministic machine might compute more than, the same as, but never less than, the deterministic machine. Similarly, it is typically faster but never slower. However, this speed-up might be only in *time used*, since we really should count the steps of *every* one of the deterministic machines involved.

In practice, the overhead of emulating n machines on 1 is roughly proportional to n; the slowdown is about n as well. So it is a contradiction to have a greater than n times speed-up using a parallel machine. In practice, the speed-up may be much less. Logical dependencies between intermediate results computed during an algorithm can make it tricky at best to split it into parallel threads.

Many variations of this idea are used. In the Communicating Sequential Process [10] approach, the non-deterministic version acts in all ways that the hidden version can, but may also act in ways that the hidden version does not. A non-deterministic Turing machine might duplicate only the state of the cpu, becoming a shared memory device. A stochastic machine can be developed by introducing the probability that a machine will progress to a given state.

The full details of some of these models are complicated, and require great deals of theory to justify. However, the starting point of a set of states replacing a singular state is simple and foundational, finds many uses on its own, and has the merit of assuming very little about the nature of the non-determinism.

The question of whether there are problems for which a polynomial time algorithm exists on a non-deterministic Turing machine, but not on a deterministic Turing machine, is currently a (im)famously open problem in theoretical computer science (see page 146).

Exercise 4: Non-Deterministic Machines

A deterministic Turing machine can emulate a non-deterministic Turing machine (see page 30) and the principle is relatively straightforward. But the technical details require some work. Also, there is more than one way to complete the task. In practice, writing a Turing machine emulator would be a good idea before attempting this exercise.

Go through the details of making this work.

A couple of clues follow.

For the Hanoi sequence 1 2 1 3 1 2 1 4 1 2 1 3 1 2 1 5, notice that every second entry is 1; and if you ignore 1's then every 2nd entry is 2; and if you ignore 1's and 2's, every 2nd entry is 3. In this way, we see that finding the elements of a specific tape is in principle straightforward. If you are on tape 1, skip 1 space, on tape 2 skip 3, and so on. But in order for this to work with a finite cpu, we need to store the info on tape. So we might put a tape number marker cell next to each virtual tape, but knowing which tape you are on cannot be stored in the cpu, or in a single cell (since there is an infinite number of virtual tapes). Of course, a Turing machine with an infinite number of tapes is different, like a register machine with an infinite number of registers. It could just use location 0 on each tape as an infinite random access memory.

A deterministic single-tape Turing machine simulating a non-deterministic Turing machine is ok, even for an infinite number of Turing machines, because we are simulating completely separate machines of which we have only a finite number at any one time, and each one has a finite description at all times. We could store the ones we are not using to the left, and fold the full tape over so that odd means negative and even means positive to get a full tape into one-half a tape to run the active Turing machine. However, this does require a lot of shifting machines around, and it does not enable us to determine which machine finishes first (once one machine finishes at n steps, how do we know that not one of the infinite number we have stops at, say, $n - 1$ steps).

Exercise 5: Quantum Computing

Ignoring the physics, a quantum computer inputs a complex vector representing qubit logic values which is multiplied by a hermitian matrix, which is then projected onto a subspace, and the magnitude gives the result. We will not duplicate this exactly. We take logic inputs as being just $(1, 0)$ to represent a logic 1 and $(0, 1)$ to represent a logic 0.

The following has the flavour but not the detail of designing quantum algorithms.

This is the identity logic function: $\begin{bmatrix} 0 & 1 \\ 0 & 0 \end{bmatrix} \begin{bmatrix} 1 & 0 \\ 0 & 1 \end{bmatrix} = \begin{bmatrix} 0 & 1 \\ 0 & 0 \end{bmatrix}$

This is negation: $\begin{bmatrix} 0 & 0 \\ 0 & 1 \end{bmatrix} \begin{bmatrix} 1 & 0 \\ 0 & 1 \end{bmatrix} = \begin{bmatrix} 0 & 0 \\ 0 & 1 \end{bmatrix}$

This is exclusive-or:

$$\frac{1}{2} \begin{bmatrix} 1 & 0 & -1 & 0 \\ 0 & 1 & 0 & -1 \\ -1 & 0 & 1 & 0 \\ 0 & -1 & 0 & 1 \end{bmatrix} \begin{bmatrix} 0 \\ 0 \\ 1 \\ 1 \end{bmatrix} \begin{bmatrix} 1 \\ 1 \\ 0 \\ 0 \end{bmatrix} \begin{bmatrix} 0 \\ 1 \\ 0 \\ 1 \end{bmatrix} \begin{bmatrix} 1 \\ 0 \\ 1 \\ 0 \end{bmatrix}$$

$$= \frac{1}{2} \begin{bmatrix} 0 \\ -1 \\ 1 \\ 0 \end{bmatrix} \begin{bmatrix} 0 \\ 1 \\ -1 \\ 0 \end{bmatrix} \begin{bmatrix} 0 \\ 1 \\ -1 \\ 0 \end{bmatrix} \begin{bmatrix} 0 \\ -1 \\ 1 \\ 0 \end{bmatrix}$$

The principle of operation is that the input logical data is presented in 01 or 10 form for 0 and 1, respectively. So one logic input is two dimensions, two logic inputs is 4, and so on. The output of the function is determined by taking the magnitude of the output vector, which must be either 0 or 1. The matrix must be symmetric.

Find as many of the 16 two-input logic functions as you can.

Find a system for determining matrices for logic functions.

Notion 13: Von Neumann Machine

The Von Neumann machine is traditionally described as being distinct from the Turing machine. It has a linear array of memory cells, each with a non-negative integer index, called its address. The memory array is read and modified by the central processing unit, or cpu. The cpu is an otherwise finite state-machine that can access several cells simultaneously. The location of the cells being accessed can be changed arbitrarily, a behaviour referred to as random access into memory.

But the memory array is simply half a Turing machine tape, and the cpu a Turing cpu. The multi-access aspect is identical to the multi-tape Turing machine in which the multiple tapes are just the same tape folded over and fed back into the cpu.

The mechanism for the random access is the pointer, which is a register that contains the address of a memory cell. However, unrestricted access to the pointer, as an indefinite precision integer, would completely change the character of the machine, and admit general-purpose programming within the cpu itself (see page 38).

In practice, the infinite memory array is addressed by a sequence of smaller moves, which could be simulated by having a stepping register in the Turing machine. The machine could then continue to step as long as the register was non-zero. Adding a finite capacity register to the Turing head does not change it from being a finite state-machine.

Thus, the Von Neumann machine is essentially a multi-tape Turing machine with a long-jump instruction to help speed things up. And, just as for the Turing machine, it is assumed that the Von Neumann machine memory begins with a finite amount of information, possibly in a finite number of non-zero cells.

The reasons for distinguishing the Von Neumann machine from the Turing machine are contingent, partly, on the politics of their invention. More significantly, the Von Neumann machine was designed to be implemented, and is the machine most implemented in desktop hardware, by a very wide margin. The Turing machine is simple and easy to implement, and while not intended to be used this way, would be perfectly serviceable. But the limitation in movement to a single step is in practice very constraining, and easy to improve on in hardware.

A Turing machine storing its program in one part of its tape and the data in another has to move constantly between the two in order to determine what to do next, and then to do it. The ability of the Von Neumann machine to refer to two locations at once means that one can be the program and the other data, allowing the machine to execute program on data without the constant shuttling. However, this is almost identical to the 2-tape Turing machine, storing program on one tape and data on the other.

Further, the Turing machine has no problem with data overrun errors destroying the program. Memory protection mechanisms, both in hardware and software, are typically based around partitioning the memory into virtual distinct tapes in order to avoid memory clash.

The often-heard phrase *Von Neumann bottleneck* is a somewhat unfair reference to the fact that there are very few pointers into memory compared to the number of memory cells. In principle, if we could open this up so that a vast number of the cells could be processed at the same time, then we could speed up processing. But, in practice, (except in special cases often involving vector and matrix operations) there has been little prospect of an alternative. Further, if Von Neumann was not the most common hardware, we would no doubt hear about the register machine bottleneck, or the stack machine bottleneck, or something similar.

The fact is, the situation could be improved, but it is not easy to do so, and this is not specific to the Von Neumann machine. Ultimately the fact that the information needs to be sent across space would lead to the geometric bottleneck.

Technologically, the Von Neumann machine has been a very serviceable abstraction that has allowed the construction of practical, though conceptually "dirty", digital machines. The actual architectures are typically much more complicated to describe than is apparent in the above discussion, and involve many specific concepts, such as memory protection, indirection tables, memory mapped interaction, and so forth.

Notion 14: Stack Machine

Many abstract devices are expressed as a finite state machine cpu operating on a potentially infinite memory whose initial state contains only a finite amount of information. The volition is intrinsic to the cpu. The memory is used only as a scratch pad, remembering what the cpu cannot, analogously to a human computing with pencil and paper. But, curiously, it is in the memory that different devices differ, rather than in the cpu.

The symbolic stack machine memory is, naturally, a finite collection of stacks of symbols. Each individual stack is finite, but there is no finite upper bound to the possible stack size. The symbols are drawn from a constant finite alphabet. Each row in the table defining the cpu gives the current state, the stack to pop, the symbol popped, the stack to push, the symbol to push, and the new state. A halting state may be included.

A cpu augmented by a finite register storing a fixed-length integer is still a finite state-machine. The natural state space is the direct product of the states of the original cpu with the states of the register (see page 113). It is common to describe the nature of the cpu in the language of registers rather than directly in the primitive concepts of the state machine (see page 50).

To perform a binary operation the cpu can copy one symbol into an internal register first and then perform the correct unary operation on the other symbol. The register may be larger than the stack cells. Such a register can be pushed onto and popped from the stack, taking multiple cells and multiple steps. A common approach is to pop two arguments from a single stack, compute internally, and then push the result onto a (possibly different) stack.

A one-stack machine is limited by having to remember within its own state anything popped from the stack or lose the information forever. Such a machine cannot count the number of open brackets seen preceding a close bracket, and thus cannot compute whether brackets are matched. It is not a general-purpose computer. The simplest general-purpose case is the two-stack machine.

Stack machines have been implemented within compilers to convert in-fix expressions into postfix expressions, and within compiled code to evaluate the resulting postfix expression. Using an expression stack and a result stack, each expression symbol is popped in turn, and used to determine the action to take on the result stack. For example, a + symbol could cause the top two elements to be popped and their sum pushed. Data symbols in the expression are pushed directly onto the result stack. It is usually very easy to convert these actions into Von Neumann machine code.

Pure postfix numeric expressions do not need any brackets and are easy to evaluate. Repeatedly take the leftmost operator whose arguments are all known numbers and evaluate it. Reverse polish calculators are built on this principle. They typically have only one stack, the other stack is in the head of the person using the calculator.

The two-stack stack machine is almost identical to the one-tape Turing machine. The memory of the Turing machine is like two stacks of paper. The cpu views the top element of one of the stacks. To write is to pop and push a different symbol on the same stack, and to move is to pop and push the same symbol on different stacks.

In this analogy, the stack machine has the option of adding and deleting cells on the tape, which is one variant of the Turing machine. This approach has the philosophical advantage of needing only an Aristotelian *potential infinity* rather than the Cantorian *completed infinity*. More pragmatically, the entire Turing machine is at all times a finite structure. Related formal constructive definitions of Turing machines are neater than their infinite counterparts are.

Stack machines are a good basis to implement lambda calculus. Since the essential data structure in lambda calculus is a computed function, and the action is to call it, a stack machine can fairly naturally execute a lambda expression directly. This has been suggested as a practical way of building a computer. However, there are some issues with the building of large stacks, and the Von Neumann architecture is well established. There would have to be a major reason to change.

Notion 15: Register Machine

Instead of unlimited memory cells (see page 26) that store a limited range of integers, the register machine has a limited number of cells that store an unlimited range of integers. The register machine is analogous to the stack machine (see page 36); the stack is replaced by an integer. The standard constraint (starting with only finite information) is satisfied. The memory is a finite collection of finite integers.

The numeral "123" is not just a notation. It is an expression involving digits and an implicit operator. Let $a \circ b = 10a+b$. Then $(1 \circ 2) \circ 3$ is $(1 \times 10+2) \circ 3$, which is $(1 \times 10+2) \times 10+3$, which is $1 \times 100+2 \times 10+3 \times 1$. $123 = 1 \circ 2 \circ 3$ is an integer valued expression not a syntactic primitive.

The remainder from 123 after division by 10 is 3. That is, the digits of the integer do not disappear after the integer has been constructed, but can be determined arithmetically. An integer is a stack of base 10 digits. To read the top digit take the number modulo 10, to push a digit, multiply by 10 and add the digit.

More precisely, given b symbols to store, use

$$\text{push}(s, e) = s \times b + e$$
$$\text{top}(s, e) = s \bmod b$$
$$\text{pop}(s, e) = s \text{ div } b$$

An integer storing a collection of Boolean flags is the same situation.

From   `step(n) = if n<0 then 0 else 1,`

form   `m = step(n) * A + (1-step(n)) * B`

which sets m to two distinct values depending on the sign of n. This is one of a vast collection of useful arithmetic conditional constructions.[6] No Booleans need apply.

Two integer-registers equipped with arithmetic allows general-purpose computing.

---

[6]Similar constructs can be useful C and Java.

Notion 16: Analogue Machine

Most of the abstract machines considered in this discussion are digital; they have discrete states that change discretely in time. However, in the earlier part of the 20th century, analogue machines were more common.

Analogue originally meant *by analogy*. Many physical systems can be modelled by differential equations. Two distinct systems having the same equations are *analogues* of each other. For certain differential equations, especially (but not only) linear ones, it is easy to set up a system of electronic components that behave as specified by the equations. A collection of such components constitutes an electronic analogue computer [13]. It could print out directly a waveform from within the system being modelled, something that could be very difficult to determine experimentally.

Digits are the symbols used in enumeration systems. Originally, computers that explicitly did arithmetic with digits were unable to compete with analogue computers for speed and adaptability. Such *digital* computers were promoted through their use in combinatorial problems such as breaking foreign encryption systems before and during the Second World War.

However, since the most obvious difference between digital and analogue computers is that the digital ones are discrete, and the analogue ones continuous, this has become the use of the word today.

An analogue computer is one that takes in a collection of continuous functions of time, and outputs likewise. The obvious application is in solving differential equations (but there are others). We feed in the forcing function for an ordinary differential equation, and the machine feeds out the solution to the equation. More generally, it might solve partial differential equations. There might also be auxiliary functions that are entered to assist the computation.

However, by interpreting ranges of real numbers as coding discrete symbols we can input and output discrete information. This is actually how digital computers are designed at a low level.

Notion 17: Cellular Automata

The input of a finite machine (see page 20) can be the output or state
of another machine. Compounds built from a finite number of finite
machines are still finite. However, the compound structure gives them
an intuitive aspect that would not be apparent in a direct listing of the
states.

The component machines of a *cellular automata* are typically arranged
into a regular grid. Most often they are square 1-, 2-, or 3-dimensional
(see page 42) but hexagonal grids are also common. At each clock-tick,
every machine undergoes one transition, inputting the current state or
symbol of the neighbouring machines. Less synchronous behaviour may
also be considered.

Hexagonal grids have proved better than square grids for simulating
physical systems such as two-dimensional fluid-flow. Artifacts of square-
ness often persist at a large scale, while the hexagonal grids discrete
nature rapidly becomes unobservable.

Machines may also be built on other surfaces, such as spheres or toroids.
However, regular grids on a sphere cannot be scaled. Irregular grids
must be used. Common examples of simulated cellular automata are
the numerical models for solution of partial differential equations. This
merges seamlessly with finite element analysis.

By including states indicating *the cpu is here*, a one-dimensional cellular
automata can easily emulate a Turing machine (see page 26). This leads
naturally to a Turing Machine that wanders around on a surface. Often
such a device is called an ant. One famous ant is Langton's ant — if
on a white cell turn left, if on a black cell turn right, as you leave a
cell, toggle the colour. It is famous for the complexity of behaviour it
generates from such a simple rule, and in particular because it tends
eventually to spend all its time building highways of regular pattern, no
matter the (finite) pattern on which it was originally placed.

In biology, a developing embryo can be viewed as a solid cellular automaton able to change its underlying topology.

Notion 18: Unorthodox Models

This is a collection of special-purpose mechanical devices that appear to have an order of complexity advantage over the best digital techniques. They are selected partially for aesthetics, but also to emphasise the broad search space available for computational solutions. No discussion of the foundation of computation should ignore these options. Programming is about finding the desired computation within the given environment.

To sort a list of numbers, cut spaghetti into lengths proportional to the numbers (a linear time operation), thump them on a table (a constant time operation) and then pick the longest one, and the next longest, and so on (a linear operation). This is a linear time sorting routine.

To find the point whose weighted total distance to a set of other points is minimal, drill a hole through a board at the location of each points, put a rope through each hole with weighted proportionaly to the point, tie all the ropes together, and release.

To find out the shortest road network joining a collection of points, place a nail between two boards at the location of each point, dip into soap water. Shake it a bit to be more certain of a global rather than local minimum.

To find the convex hull of a set of points, drive nails into a board at required locations and stretch an elastic band around them. Alternatively, put a ruler against the nails (to find a single point on the hull) then wrap string, or just walk the ruler around. The ruler will make exactly one full rotation.

To find the shortest path in a network, make a string and beads model. The beads are nodes and the connecting strings have length proportional to the length of the corresponding edge. Grasp the points you want the shortest path between and try to pull the points apart; then the shortest path is the one that goes tight first. The longest path is found by constantly cutting the shortest path.

Notion 19: The Game of Life

Although it is a specific machine, the modern desktop computer may be used to simulate a multitude of other architectures. Thus, an awareness of other virtual machines can be a boon to the practical programmer. Finite state-machines, for example, are often useful in the construction of protocols for security, cryptography, communications, or parsing of input. It has already been mentioned that a cpu machine has a compound of state machines as memory; however, the way in which these state machines receive their input and output means that they might as well be randomly scattered. An alternative is to stitch the finite state-machines together into a fabric called a cellular automaton. Cellular automata whose states are integers (or floating-point numbers) can be used for doing matrix multiplication in parallel (see page 232), in time proportional to the side, instead of the area, or the matrix. The numerical integration of partial differential vector equations is typically achieved using cellular automata.

A conceptually and historically significant exemplar is Conway's *game of life* (see note 8). Intuitively, Conway's life represents a population of stationary creatures analogous to coral or plants. In an infinite chessboard garden, each square either contains a plant, or it does not. At each clock-tick, every square is updated. If the square is occupied and has two or three occupied neighbours, then it survives into the next generation, otherwise it dies (of loneliness or overpopulation). If the square was vacant, but has three occupied neighbours, then a new plant is born into this square. The interest, however, is not with the individual cells, but the emergent phenomena.

Some patterns are stable — they do not change under the transformation — for example, a 2×2 black square, the *block*. Any larger or smaller square is not stable.

Some patterns repeat themselves periodically — for example blinkers, which cycle between two states. (A row of three blinkers is called *traffic lights*.)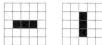

More interesting behaviour is shown by the glider. It moves. After four iterations it reappears in a different location looking the same.

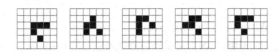

Many moving patterns exist; gliders move diagonally, space ships move horizontally, some leave debris behind as they move. The speed of light is one cell per clock-tick.

There are also *Garden of Eden* configurations, which have no precursor pattern, they must be explicitly entered into the grid.

The vast array of behaviours that this simple model produces is significant. In particular, there are very large structures with complex properties, such as reproduction and general-purpose computation. Some require millions of cells. Although the rules generalise in obvious ways, most variants tend to lead to uninteresting universes. However, two variants in particular, *high life* (survive — 2 or 3, birth — 3 or 6) and *night and day* (survive — 3 4 6 7 8, birth — 3 6 7 8) have been found to have interesting properties.

Can life evolve in Conway's life? The restriction to two dimensions is a severe restriction, sometimes thought to be completely prohibitive. However, some interesting work has been done on this (see note 9). Studies have also been made in higher-dimensional life (see note 11). Of central interest is the question of how to get the computer to recognise life forms, should they evolve. Rapid exact cycling is fairly straightforward to check. But recognising that something kept its general appearance is an open problem on which a lot of work has been done (in vision research).

Notion 20: The Modern Desktop Computer

Almost all computers in use now, at
the dawn of the 21st century, are cpu
machines. A state machine (see page
20) called the cpu is augmented by
a compound of state machines called
memory cells that provide the input
and record the output of the cpu. At
each moment the cpu access to memory (see note 5) is limited in scope
or in nature. But the resulting feedback expands the power above that
of the cpu alone in a manner which
may reasonably be emulated in our
technology. Examples include the
stack (see page 36) and register (see
page 38) machines.

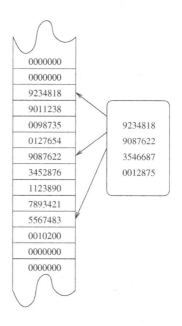

The standard modern desktop machine, regardless of brand, is inspired
by the Turing (see page 26) or Von Neumann machines, in which the
memory is a belt of cells, each of which contains a single symbol from
a finite collection, and the cpu is a finite state-machine augmented by
special pointers into memory. When the machine is started, the memory
contains only a finite amount of information (see note 6). At each tick of
the clock, the the memory is written, and the internal state of the cpu is
updated. This simple cycle of computation is repeated indefinitely. Only
a finite number of clock-ticks occur in a finite time. Only a finite amount
of information is in the memory at any point in time. The machine,
however, is potentially infinite. The memory and time available for the
computation is indefinitely extensible. This subtle balance between finite
and infinite has made this type of machine a very useful abstraction of
computation.

Despite the utility of a potentially infinite model, any physical computer
we can build has a finite number of states. Taking all the bits in the

memory (including disk storage) of a hundred million interconnected modern desktop computers, we still have less than 10^30 bits. So, the complete state of all these computers is a single finite integer in the range from 0 to 2^(10^30)-1 inclusive. If the machine does not suffer a hardware error, then, knowing the input (the key press or mouse click), the next state of the machine is determined uniquely by the current state. Thus, a finite list expresses the complete behaviour of the machine. Such an abstraction is called a finite state-machine.

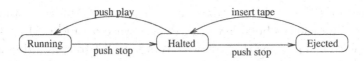

A state machine may be in one of several conditions, called *states*. The state affects the way the machine responds. An example is an audio recorder with a red button that stops the tape if it is running but ejects the tape otherwise.

A desktop computer is a device that accepts a sequence of input events, acts in a manner dependent on its state, changes its state, and then awaits another input event. The number of states is astronomical, but finite.

The cpu of the desktop machine is a finite state-machine whose input is from, and output to, a potential infinity of information in memory. The design of the cpu-on-a-chip of the modern desktop computer is explicitly an exercise in the construction of a finite state-machine. The memory belt is implemented by the indefinite memory and disk resources. Many limitations proved for finite state-machines cannot be applied directly to the desktop machine because there is no hard limit to the resources (memory and time) available. It may be expanded indefinitely subject to vague economic and physical constraints.

Notion 21: Aspects of Virtual Machines

Digital machine: *a physical limit of discrete technology.* Although there are other things that may be said to compute, the basic idea of the modern digital computer can be nicely abstracted by saying that it is a state machine, whose states are countably many (may be numbered by the integers) and so are the transitions. Further, in any run of the machine, there are a countable number of clock-ticks.

Universal machine: *acts like every other machine.* It is possible to program some computers to simulate others. For example, you may be aware of PC simulators that were written for Macs, a number of years ago, in order to be able to run PC software on a Mac. I personally worked with a simulator that allowed Windows 3.1 to run under another operating system (RMX) as an application. In practice, any sufficiently complex computer can run a simulation of any other, with typically no more than a low-order polynomial slowdown.

General purpose machine: *to do anything that can be done.* It is a curious implication of the idea that any sufficiently complex machine can simulate another that the set of things that each can compute is the same. Indeed, there seems to be a natural boundary to digital computation. Problems that fall inside this boundary are called computable. All "reasonable" models of computation turn out to be able to compute exactly this set, the same set, no matter what type of digital computer we are talking about. There is a connection between this and constructive logic. There is a strong sense in which this limit is the limit of certain knowledge. It is the limit of those things that can be worked out, or known, in a finite amount of time, using discrete and definite steps.

Quantum computing: *A current research topic, but is it different?* Quantum computing is essentially analogue, a qubit encodes a continuous phase. The evolution of a quantum computer is related to multiplication of a vector by a matrix. This type of programming is difficult. The only good algorithms so far are of the Shor or Grover type. But it might be possible to implement these algorithms directly in nano-technology, and thus have a very fast solution to things that are currently outside the capacity of our computational technology. Whether a quantum computer can compute anything that is classically non-computable is an open theoretical question. This is essentially a question about the relation between a continuous- and discrete-state machine. It might be possible, but it would require the precision of variable storage to be able to be increased without bound, making any solution physically meaningless. Any realisation to a bounded precision (and accuracy) would be equivalent to some digital machine. This is no more than the admission that a single real number contains an infinite amount of information, a fact that is of theoretical interest, but, due to finite signal-to-noise ratios, of no practical consequence.

Implementation: *Can we build it?* The idea of a finite state-machine is powerful and forms the heart of all our computational machinery. The memory structure used in each of the different digital computers has a potential infinity of information. This allows us to implement limited extensible versions of many types of machine, with the idea that it will run all those programs that do not require more than a certain amount of information storage. All the various discrete-state machines mentioned in this book have been implemented in this sense.

The register machine is essentially the same as the stack machine in realisation, and the Von Neumann machine has the advantage of speed and cost in most implementations. This would be reduced by the economies of scale, or the use of different compilation technology. Along these lines, multi-stack machines have been suggested and built which use lambda calculus as machine code.

Analogue computing was more common in the first half of the 20th century. But analogue signals are inherently hard to correct, while digital signals can be checked and corrected. In addition, digital computers can be easily adapted to other tasks, such as symbolic processing. These two factors lead to the demise of the analogue computer.

Quantum computing is in many ways a return to analogue computing, based on the behaviour of certain nano-technology. But, researchers are having a very hard time implementing anything non-trivial in quantum technology.

Notion 22: Aspects of Programming

Programming: Many abstract machines (see page 18) have a state which can be divided into a product of a processor state and a memory state. The pure use of this machine is to encode the input value into the memory and start the processor in its distinguished starting state. Later the output value is retrieved from memory. This encodes a function $F(problem) = solution$. But a new machine is required for each new class of problem. An alternative is to allow another part of memory to be used to record information that tells the computer how to solve the class of problem it has been given. In digital computers, this extra information is a sequence of symbols. In an analogue computer, it might be the interconnections between the analogue elements. This extra information is called a program. Technically this means that the problem is specified as the union of the two sections of memory, but the outlook is very different. $F(program, problem) = solution$. Given the machine, the task is to find the program that will solve the problem. We view each program as producing a new virtual machine.

Real programming: Programming is not menu-lookup. Certain program code can be written by checking which library call performs the required action and providing the correct arguments. This is not the type of programming discussed in the book, and in fact does not satisfy the intention of the word as used, except in a trivial sense. Real programming means to increase the computational capacity, to begin with a set of operations, and develop them into new operations that were not obviously implicit in the original set. To borrow an economics term, real programming is computational value-adding, i.e., providing new capacity in a non-trivial manner.

Algorithmic computation: In the strict sense, an algorithm for determining a result is a process that has discrete, exactly defined steps and is sure to terminate after a finite number of steps, producing as a result the required result. Precisely when a step is exactly defined is actually a philosophical matter, but in practice it appears that exactly defined means expressible by formal, unification production (see page 64), axioms. For an ongoing process that has no natural termination, the requirement is that the steps are exact and correctness is certain.

Heuristic computation: When no algorithm is available, or those that are available are too slow, a heuristic might suffice. A heuristic generally has precise, uniquely determined discrete steps, but it is not certain to produce the right result. It is often considered acceptable for a computer to be right only a certain fraction of the time if this results in a lower use of resources.

Stochastic computation: An alternative approach related to heuristics is a computation in which random choices are made at certain points. The curious character of these computations is that they can be developed so that there is a tweaking parameter (such as how long a loop runs) that can push the probability of a correct answer toward certainty. Once a process produces the right answer with a chance of 1,000,000,000:1, we would start to worry about hardware failure before worrying about the process going wrong. Many computations in theorem proving, group theory, prime factorisation, and cryptological work are stochastic these days.

Another curious character of stochastic computation, in practice, is that the asymptotic correctness is established on the assumption of the use of a true random number. But, in a typical computer, this is implemented as a pseudo-random number, generated by a computation with extremely erratic, but deterministic, behaviour. The resulting patterns can break the computation. In particular, some attacks on certain encryption systems involve locking onto the pseudo-random computation. This would not be possible if the encryption was based on a truly random number.

This is a pragmatic computational problem. But it leads us immediately into the deeply philosophical problems of what a random number is, and whether there really is such a thing. One suggestion for getting around this is to use physical noise sources, especially ones based on quantum mechanical principles. However, whether that will remove the correlation with other factors remains to be seen. A device sitting inside a computer is subject to many influences and might not be random even if the truly isolated device would be. Perhaps randomness in isolated quantum systems actually comes from that isolation, leading to true lack of information.

Notion 23: Register Indirection

A typical contemporary desktop computer is built on a collection of low-level storage cells. Each cell contains at each instant a single symbol from a finite alphabet (see page 44). Each cell is referred to via an address which is unique to that cell. Each of these identical cells is called a *register* (see note 15). We assume that the address space and the alphabet are the same (see note 14) so, any register may be interpreted to contain the address of another register.

It is common to use numerals from 1 to m as the symbols. Parentheses refer to content. So (123) means the symbol contained in the register with address 123, or more briefly (123), is the contents of 123. If x and y are symbols, then $x \leftarrow y$ is the command to place the symbol y in the register at address x. This is similar to assignment in many common languages, but there is no implicit indirection. What you see is what you get. This is best understood by interpreting all symbols in register language to be *constant* symbols. That is, $x \leftarrow y$ does not affect x any more than M[1]=5 affects the number 1. There are no variable symbols in register language. Everything dynamic is stored in the registers.

In C, a variable symbol is a constant pointer, an address. The assignment x=y is implemented as $x \leftarrow (y)$. Implicitly the symbol y is treated as an indirect reference to its contents. So if x has (or is) the address 123 and y is the address 64, then x=y in C causes the contents of location 64 to be placed into location 123. In register indirection, this is $123 \leftarrow (64)$. The command $x = y$ has one level of indirection on the right, and none on the left. The automatic de-reference can be prevented in C by using the form x=&y, which means $x \leftarrow y$. The & quotes the variable name. In C, $*x$ is largely the same as (x) in register indirection. In C, $*x = y$ is $(x) \leftarrow (y)$.

Any occurrence of the symbol x in C means (x). C expects an l-value[7] to have parentheses, and removes them. Sometimes an error occurs, *l-value expected*, exposing this behaviour. In register indirection, $123 \leftarrow 5$ is valid, but in C, $123 = 5$ generates an error because the compiler tried to remove one level of indirection. This is the meaning of &. The term $*x$ means (x) but $\&*x$ means x. Thus, $\&\&x$ is often an error. A

---

[7]Left hand side of an assignment.

constant value has no address. But **&&x has the intuitive meaning of x, even though by strict application the second & was an error. Some C compilers allow compound expressions such as **&&x with any number of * and &. Occurrences of & and * cancel. This is useful in association with #define directives.

Each machine code instruction has an address. The program counter pc is a register that stores the address of the current instruction. Thus, $pc \leftarrow 123$ is a jump. Also if sp is the location of a stack in memory, then $(sp) \leftarrow (x); sp \leftarrow (sp) + 1$ pushes the value of variable x onto the stack, while $sp \leftarrow (sp) - 1; x \leftarrow (sp)$ pops the value from the stack. This introduces $(sp)-$, which is a post-decrement operation. Obtain the value and then decrement the register. So the pop is $x \leftarrow (sp)-$ and the push is $+(sp) \leftarrow (x)$.

Something very similar was used on the PDP series of machines, and it is likely that this is where C obtained its ++ and -- operators.

Register indirection is supplemented by at least one conditional form, such as "f x then $x \leftarrow 23$". With only these elements in the language it is typically possible to give a simple formal specification of each assembler instruction in a machine. The C language can also largely be defined in these terms.

Register indirection is a good concrete model for an understanding of the operation of pointers. All abstract pointer algorithms can be cleanly expressed in this manner. It is a high-level generic method for understanding many specific Von Neumann machines, and machine codes.

Caveat: it is common to find register language in which $(x) \leftarrow y$ means *the contents of x becomes y*. That is, what we are notating as $x \leftarrow (y)$. This leaves the requirement for getting at the actual value of y, which is done by an *immediate* reference, denoted typically $\$y$ or #y.

Notion 24: Pure Expression Substitution

Given that $x = 6$, we deduce that $x + y = 6 + y$ by replacing the symbol
"x" by the symbol "6" in the expression "$x + y$". This replacement of
equals by equals is deeply fundamental to all formal reasoning and may
be performed in an entirely mechanical manner.

The environment of an expression such as "x+y" is the set of values of
the symbols it contains. Not all symbols need to be given a value. A
symbol is *bound* if it has a value, and *free* if it does not. An environment
is a partial function whose domain is the set of symbols. An environment may be naturally represented as a set of ordered pairs. Thus,
$\{(x, 5), (y, 6)\}$ acting on "x+y" produces "5+6". The value might also
be an expression, in the environment $\{(x, (a+b)), (y, 23)\}$, the expression
"x+y" becomes "(a+b)+23".

An environment $E = \{(x_i, y_i) : i \in I\}$ is a function taking a primitive
expression, and returning an expression. The action A of E is a natural
extension of E to compound expressions.

1. $\forall i \in I : A(x_i) = y_i$
2. $\forall x \notin \{x_i : i \in I\} : A(x) = x$
3. $A(a_1, .., a_n) = (A(a_1), .., A(a_n))$

Although it is non-trivial to prove, A is a function. As a set of ordered
pairs A includes composite expressions on the left, if we allow composite
expressions in E, then the action may become a more general relation
than a function. For example, starting with $E = \{(xy, w), (yz, w)\}$ we
get $A(xyz) = wz$ or xw.

A substitution system $S = \{(x_i, y_i) : i \in I\}$ is a set of ordered pairs of
expressions. A substitution is a relation. The action of S is the closure
of S under composition of its elements.

1. $\forall i \in I : (x_i, y_i) \in A$
2. $\forall x \notin \{x_i : i \in I\} : (x, x) \in A$
3. $\forall (a_1, b_1)..(a_n, b_n) \in A : ((a_1..a_n), (b_1..b_n)) \in A$

Generically, an inductive definition of a set will include a number of
clauses of the form *if x,y,z are elements then C(x,y,z) is also.* From this

we derive the induction if A includes $(x_1, v_1), .., (x_n, v_n)$, then A also includes $(C(x_1, .., x_n), C(v_1, .., v_n))$.

The action of an environment is a special case of a substitution system, a simple substitution system. If $S_1 = \{x_i \rightarrow y_i : i \in I\}$ is a simple substitution and S_2 is any substitution system, then relation composition $S_1(S_2(E)) = \{(x_i, (S_1(y_i)) : i \in I\}$. This is a fairly natural result but is not generically true. If compound expressions exist on the left of S_1, then it is possible for a rule in S_1 applied to $S_2(xy) = S_2(x)S_2(y)$ to match on a subexpression that overlaps the two pieces. But this does not occur in the case of a simple substitution system, derived from using only primitive symbols on the left.

The composition equation was determined using the assumption that the left-hand sides were primitive symbols. The rule does not cover all cases with a composite left-hand side. But if there is no instance of an entities on the left overlapping, then it does still work. Intuitively we could replace each instance of the composite symbol by a single primitive one.

Each pair (x, y) stands for a logical equality. One substitution is *more general than* another if, treated as a collection of equalities, the latter implies the former. A term is *primitive* with respect to a substitution if the substitution leaves it unchanged.

By allowing a substitution to be applied in the reverse as well as forward sense, we can use it to generate a concept of equality very similar to a Prolog program. If, however, we allow substitutions to be applied only in the forward direction, then we have a model of computation very similar to a Haskell program.

One aspect not covered here, but of significance in lambda calculus, is the concept of locally bound variables. If our expression is $(sum(n = 1to10)n)*n$, then substituting $n = 2$ would produce $(sum(2 = 1to10)2)*2$, which is not quite what we intended. The n used as an index for the summation is distinct in intention from the free occurrence of n. The idea of substitution can be modified by allowing local bindings to be recognised, and to avoid substituting in this case.

Notion 25: Lists Pure and Linked

A singly linked list allows us to put something on the head of the list and find it there again later. Abstractly it is identical to a stack. To look down the list we have to move past all the earlier elements. An abstract list datatype is a tuple (List,Item,head,tail,cons,empty), such that —

empty is a List
for each Item a, and List b : head(cons(a,b)) = a
for each Item a, and List b : tail(cons(a,b)) = b

This can be constructed by the following substitutions:

empty = ()	By inspection ...	
head((a,b)) = a .	head(cons(a,b)) = head((a,b)) = a	
tail((a,b)) = b	tail(cons(a,b)) = tail((a,b)) = b	
cons(a,b) = (a,b)	So, the axioms are satisfied.	

The (Haskell/Prolog style) list [1,2,3] is (1,(2,(3,()))).

It is good, if possible, to implement an abstract type so that there is a natural correspondence between the code and the axioms. This helps to prove, technically and intuitively, that the code conforms to the axioms.

Firstly, the type definitions:

```
struct pair {item x; list *next;};
typedef pair *list;
pair newPair(item x, list l){pair p={x,l}; return p;}
```

Now the definitive code:

```
item empty = 0;
item head(list l){return l->x;}
item tail(list l){return l->next;}
list cons(item x, list l){return newPair(x,l);}
```

This code is so close to the substitutions that it is almost just a syntax change. Thus, we have a rigorous implementation.

Pragmatically, these axioms are incomplete.

Firstly, there is no way to compute head(empty) and tail(empty). In principle, the attempt to do so is an error, and we could insist that any system that satisfies the axioms must assure that these terms are never evaluated. Technically, this is a valid solution, with rigorous logical justification. But in practice, it puts too heavy a load on the user of the abstract type. What we need is error handling. A simple option is ...head(empty) = tail(empty) = error = head(error) = tail(error). The full study of pure error handling is non-trivial.

Secondly, they are satisfied by this trivial construction:

head(empty) = empty
tail(empty) = empty
cons(empty,empty) = empty

The generic way out to state that the system must not satisfy any equality involving head, tail and cons, other than those implied by the original axioms. This amounts to such things as cons(a,b) $\neq$ empty. But negative axioms are more difficult to deal with.

Pure expressions are naturally interpreted as trees. The nodes are weighted by operators, and the subtrees are arguments. Recursion scans down the tree. But the only way back is to return from the recursion. Generic networks have no natural counterpart in pure expressions. A network can be a list of pairs of nodes, but a constant time search for neighbours does not exist. Contrast this with back pointers in doubly linked lists. Or, perhaps, it does not exist for pointers either; rather, pointers are fast hardware assistance for random lookup limited to the machine memory. Severe slow-down occurs once disk or network storage is required. Pointers are a fast hardware implementation of a network. With an in-built fast network type included, pure expressions can match the impure performance. Haskell, which is very pure, has array and network types available if required.

However, reorganisation of the details of the software can often achieve the same aim. The programming required in the pure case is for sorting, for example, is different, rather than less efficient.

Notion 26: Pure String Substitution

Pure substitution into expressions (see page 52) respects the bracketing. Acting on $x \times y$ with $\{(x, a + b), (y, 23)\}$ produces $(a + b) \times 23$, not $a + b \times 23$. The latter, using implicit bracketing, would standardly be interpreted as $a + (b \times 23)$. Expression substitution software based on trees would not typically make this sort of mistake. But it is a very common mistake among teenagers learning algebra in secondary school. Partly, this is because the student is dealing with the expression as a pure string, an otherwise unstructured sequence of characters on the page. If we literally replace "x" by "$a + b$" in the string "$x \times y$", then we get "$a + b \times y$", resulting in a change in semantics.

With this rather dubious beginning,[8] we enter the world of pure string substitution. We can act on a string s using a pair of strings (s_1, s_2). Find a decomposition (by catenation) of $s = as_1b$, and construct the string $s' = as_2b$. We have replaced an instance, in s, of the substring s_1 by an instance of s_2. The decomposition might not be unique, so there are multiple possible resulting strings. String substitution does not inherently respect the structure of the expression that the string might happen to represent.

String substitution is a special case of replacing one directed subgraph by another (see page 117). In the simplest case, replace a subgraph by another with the same number of terminals. In the string case, we replace a compound directed link by another in the same direction.

A string is *primitive* with respect to a substitution if the action of the substitution is sure to leave it unchanged. For example, $zxzx$ is primitive with respect to $xx \to y$. A string reduction machine repeats the action of a substitution on a state string until a primitive string is produced. The string machine includes in a natural way parallelism and non-determinism. Two substitutions working on non-overlapping pieces of the string may act at the same time, when there are multiple options at one location a non-deterministic choice is made.

---

[8]I have found that often advanced study in mathematics or computation is a casebook of things you were told not to do in secondary school.

A string reduction machine is a general-purpose computer. $0c \to 1$
The substitutions on the right define an operator I that $1c \to c0$
increments a binary number enclosed in brackets. The use $[c \to [1$
of c forces the computation to be local. $]I \to c]$

An example shows its action. Although the brackets do actually delimit the binary number, this is an emergent property; in detail they are treated as any other character. DNA computing works this way. The string of symbols is the sequence of bases, and the substitutions are performed by the various enzymes.

$$[100111]I$$
$$\to \quad [100111c]$$
$$\to \quad [10011c0]$$
$$\to \quad [1001c00]$$
$$\to \quad [100c000]$$
$$\to \quad [1010000]$$

The basic notion above, of a symbol filter, is broadly applicable and corresponds to the mechanism of DNA computation. Enzymes move along the DNA performing operations, such as hydration. As the desired computation becomes more complex multiple symbol filters are required, leaving the possibility of one filter operating on another to change its function.

To show string reduction is general-purpose, construct a Turing machine. We could use a symbol for each state of the Turing head (see page 40), but the state is naturally indicated by [xxxx], where the xxxx is a binary sequence, the state number. We take the current tape symbol to the be one to the left of the state, and have substitutions of the form 0[001]→[010]1, to indicate a choice of move to the left and 0[001]0→01[010] for a move to the right.

The lack of respect for bracketing and variable symbols can cause trouble. How to deal with parameterised computation and function calls? How would we design a lambda reduction engine on a string reduction machine? It can be done. The problems can be solved. To solve it once is an excellent programming exercise for honing general programming skills.

But, commonly, a non-trivial level of respect for brackets and variables is assumed in working with reduction machines, largely because it is tedious and otherwise unilluminating to achieve from first principles each time we want to program with strings.

Notion 27: The Face Value of Numerals

A distinction is sometimes stressed by expositors between the abstract concept of *number* and its written form *numeral*. This emphasises that the numeral has an existence in its own right, but obscures the fact that number and numeral can validly be equated. The identification of written form with semantics is natural in computation. If we define the non-negative integers to be *literally* the strings 0, 1, 10, and so on, which are normally taken as a *representation* in binary notation, then we may define increment as an operation on strings by the following axioms:

$inc(0) = 1,$
$inc(1) = 10,$
$inc(X0) = X1,$
$inc(X1) = inc(X)0,$

The symbol X (and any other capital letter) stands for any nonempty string, and string concatenation is represented by juxtaposition of symbols.

$$inc(111) = inc(11)0 = inc(1)00 = 1000$$

Technically we may then say that the abstract non-negative integers are the set of all such systems isomorphic to this. But this leads to logical problems with the term *all*. The approach used here avoids that, and is also similar in spirit to the Von Neumann style encoding into set theory that was used to give pure set theoretical structures for various abstract structure in mathematics.

Extending the identification of syntax and semantics, we interpret *inc*, not as a function, but as a literal string. The entire computation is an expression being reduced by the unification reductions.

```
       inc(X0) → X1
       inc(X1) → inc(X)0
    add(X0,Y0) → add(X,Y)0
    add(X0,Y1) → add(X,Y)1
    add(X1,Y0) → add(X,Y)1
    add(X1,Y1) → add(X,inc(Y))0
     mul(X,Y0) → mul(X,Y)0
     mul(X,Y1) → add(X,mul(X,Y0))
```

Arithmetic is expressed completely by the reductions. The inclusion of the terminal (not involving a variable) cases is left as an exercise.

Given a set of axioms, an irreducible element is one which does not match the left-hand side of any of the axioms. The meaning of a string can be taken as the irreducible element to which it reduces. Of course, for arbitrary axioms there is no certainty that the irreducable element is unique, or even that it exists. However, certain systems (such as lambda calculus) have been shown to have this property, known as confluence. A unique irreducible element is sometimes referred to as a normal form.

If every sequence of reductions ends finitely at an irreducible element, the set of axioms are said to produce a Noetheren reduction system. The property that one string can be modified into another by a sequence of substitutions is sometimes used as a definition of equality within sets described by a language. The pragmatic problem is that determining this equality is not computable in general. One significance of a normal form in a Noetheren reduction system is that its universal existence means that equality is a computable property with a simple algorithm. Just reduce each string to its normal form, and see if they are the same.

An example of this is the expansion of algebraic expressions using only addition, subtraction, and multiplication. By multiplying out all the terms, we obtain pure powers of the variables, which can be listed in a systematic order to determine the equality of two such expressions.

It is significant for our interpretation of strings that we recognise brackets (see page 52). If not, then when we try to compound the expressions, as in $add(10, mul(110, 1010))$, the rule might misfire to set $Y =$"1010)", leading to a syntactically incorrect irreducible. The problem is partially relieved but not solved by insisting that only the whole expression can match. However, if we insist that each variable can only match syntactically correct substrings, then the problem is solved.

But if this approach is too high-level for the reader, rest assured that it is possible, by selecting the reduction rules appropriately, to produce systems that operate correctly, without *any* special interpretation of the syntax. With this in mind a simpler set can be used, $inc(X0) \rightarrow X1$, $inc() \rightarrow 1$, and $inc(X1) \rightarrow inc(X)0$, involving the form $inc()$, which can be thought of as standing in for the increment of an empty string, or just a working string as part of the computation.

Exercise 6: The Face Value of Numerals

This is a non-trivial, but very instructive, exercise in digital algorithmic thinking. It is something (like checking the Jacobi identity for the vector cross product in mathematics is for mathematicians) that every computer scientist should do once in their lives. Thinking of a binary integer is a string of 0's and 1's, develop some arithmetic. Encoding numbers as pairs (see page 215) is useful here.

1. Develop syntactic reductions for equality, increment, addition, integer division, multiplication, modulus, order, and greatest common divisor for unsigned integers.

2. Develop syntactic reductions for equality, increment, addition, subtraction, modulus and order of signed integers.

3. Develop syntactic reductions for division in the rationals

4. Develop complex rational arithmetic.

5. Some people say quantum computers can avoid the limitations (see note 23) of reduction.

   What do you think?

It is recommended that a simple program to reduce expressions given a set of reductions be written in conjunction with this exercise. Brute force search for the substring and copying the whole string during substitution (for example using `sprintf` in C) is probably sufficient, but there are many more-sophisticated algorithms that can be used.

The basic concept of substituting one part of a structure for another is not a side issue in digital computing, but really the central theme.

Macrolanguages (short for *macroscopic substitution*) use essentially the type of approach as above.

Exercise 7: Pure Substitution Computation

Implement binary arithmetic with pure string substitution. The solution is a set of substitutions (see page 56) that inevitably reduce the valid input string to the required output string. It is highly recomended that you write a string reduction engine (in your favorite language) prior to this, so the solutions can be tested and debugged.

Each part introduces a filter symbol, intuitively similar to a Turing cpu, which overwrites the tape as it moves (but can also splice in new cells). The whole computation is a non-deterministic Turing machine. A stationary symbol might generate several filters that move away from it to perform one each of several stages. Binary numbers are represented as [0010110], or [bbabaab] to keep two numbers distinct.

1. Create A, which changes 0s to as and 1s to bs,
   For example, A[01001] becomes [abaab].

2. Create B, which interlaces a 0-1 number with an a-b number
   For example, B[10011aabab] becomes [1a0a0b1a1b].

3. Create S, which adds interlaced 0-1 and a-b numbers
   For example, [1a0a0b1a1b]S becomes [11000].

4. Combine 1,2 and 3 into +, which adds two numbers
   For example, [10011]+[00101] becomes [11000].

5. Create -, which substracts two numbers
   For example, [101]-[10] becomes [11] .

6. Write a multiplication operator *
   For example [1010]*[10] becomes [10100].

7. Write P, which reduces prefix arithmetic expressions with addition, subtraction and multiplication to a single binary number. (Protect each operator from the action of the others).

8. Write B, so that is is similar to part 7, but uses infix arithmetic and recognises parentheses "(" and ")" correctly.

Notion 28: Solving Equations

Technical programming from a formal specification means finding code that is the solution to an equation in unknown code symbols. The specification is the equation the code must satisfy. The concept of solving an equation applies in a very broad context. Computation itself is repeated solution of formal equations. The constraint on the code is an expression in constant and variable symbols.

To solve is to find values that when substituted for the variables produce a true equality. Typically, in $a + b = 12$ the variables are $\{a, b\}$, and constants are $+$ (a known binary function) and 12. The $=$ symbol is metalogical.[9,10,11] To solve $a + b = 12$ is to find values for a and b. The substitution $\{a \rightarrow 4, b \rightarrow 8\}$ acting on $a + b = 12$ yields $4 + 8 = 12$ which is true. So this is a (*not the*) solution to the original equation.

This is the same for an unknown function.

We solve $f(x + y) = f(x)f(y)$ for f as follows:

$f(x) = f(x + 0) = f(x)f(0)$ so either $f(x) = 0$ or $f(0) = 1$.

$f(nx) = f((n - 1)x)f(x) = f((n - 2)x)f(x)f(x) = \cdots = f(x)^n$

$f(m\frac{x}{m}) = f^m(\frac{x}{m})$ so $f(\frac{x}{m}) = f(x)^{\frac{1}{m}}$

That is, $f(ax) = f(x)^a$, and so $f(a) = f(1)^a$ for all rational a. (This extends to complex a if we assume continuity). The formal substitution $\{f(x) \rightarrow b^x\}$ acting on $f(x + y) = f(x)f(y)$ produces $b^{x+y} = b^x b^y$, which is true. The solution is generic. (This equation is definitive of exponentiation).

A *general* solution is a description of all the solutions, often couched in terms of expressions over some free-ranging variables. In the above case, this could be $\{a \rightarrow t, b \rightarrow 12 - t\}$, in which t is a variable taking values from a numerical set, which might be whole, real, or complex numbers.

---

[9]The distinction between proof and truth.

[10]It means, *If you don't already know what I mean then, I cannot explain it.*

[11]It's a Zen thing.

Solving multiple equations, such as $\{a + b = 12, a - b + c = 10\}$ is a similar process, we look for values for all the variables involved that when substituted yield a collection of true equations. In this case, a specific solution is $\{a \rightarrow 3, b \rightarrow 9, c \rightarrow 16\}$, and a general solution is $\{a \rightarrow t, b \rightarrow 12 - t, c \rightarrow 22 - 2t\}$, where t is a free parameter. More generally there might be more than one parameter.

Collecting terms on one side produces $\{a+b-12 = 0, a-b+c-10 = 0\}$. The solution is equivalent to finding values of a and b such that *all* the expressions in $\{a + b - 12, a - b + c - 10, 0\}$ become equal. The substitution is said to *unify* the expressions. Even without arithmetic, any set of equalities can be expressed as unification by forming tuples. For example unify the set, $\{(a+b, a-b+c), (12, 10)\}$ to solve the original equations.

In C, we define a function `int f(int x, int y){...}`. When calling f, in `a=f(23,45)`, the set $\{f(23, 45), f(x, y)\}$ is unified to determine the values x and y take as local variables in the body of f. Commonly the syntactic solution $\{x \rightarrow 23, y \rightarrow 45\}$ is used. But if we know that $f(x, y) = f(y, x)$, a second solution, $\{x = 45, y = 23\}$, is obtained. This is unification with axioms. Unification with axioms is the generic concept of solution of equations.

For commutative f, an optimising compiler might use the second solution for reasons of size or speed. The syntactic (or empty axiom set) solution has the significant property that it works regardless of the nature of f, while other solutions require more information.

Computation is a process of solution of equations. Syntactic solutions, found by unification, exist independent of meaning of the symbols. We determine values for the variables which make the expressions equal. A general solution may exist with free parameters whose value is arbitrary (within the context). The complete solution set depends on the nature of the constants. But, a solution with less axioms is also a solution for the original. Solutions that depend on no axioms work by making the expressions syntactically identical. This is known as a formal solution.

Notion 29: Pure Unification

Definitively, a formal equation is solved without any reference to any semantic domain for the symbols. One solution, for x, y, a, and b, to the formal equation $m(x, y) = m(a, b)$ is the substitution (see page 52) $S = \{x \rightarrow t, y \rightarrow t, a \rightarrow t, b \rightarrow t\}$. Applying S here produces $m(t, t) = m(t, t)$, true regardless[12] of the semantics of m. The substitution unifies (see page 62) the set $\{m(x, y), m(a, b)\}$, making all the expressions identical. More formally, a substitution, S, unifies a set, E, of expressions exactly when $\forall e_1, e_2 \in E : S(e_1) = S(e_2)$.

The input (E, V, C) to unification is a set E of expressions over a set $S = V \cup C$ of symbols, paritioned ($V \cap U = \{\}$) into variables V and constants C. A substitution over V is called an environment. The task is to find an environment that maps E to one single expression. There is typically more than one solution.

An environment S_1 is at least as general as S_2 if there exists S_3 such that $S_2 = S_3 \circ S_1$. Generality is a measure of how little the variables are constrained. The substitution $\{x \rightarrow a, y \rightarrow b, z \rightarrow c\}$ is less constraining than $\{x \rightarrow a, y \rightarrow b, z \rightarrow b\}$, which is less so than $\{x \rightarrow a, y \rightarrow a, z \rightarrow a\}$. A unifier S_1 of E is a *most general unifier* if for any other unifier S_2, S_1 is at least as general as S_2. All the most general unifiers are essentially the same, differing only in the choice of free variable names.

For the example above, $S_1 = \{x \rightarrow p, y \rightarrow q, a \rightarrow p, b \rightarrow q\}$ is a most general unifier, and so is $S_2 = \{x \rightarrow w, y \rightarrow z, a \rightarrow w, b \rightarrow z\}$. The original solution $S = S_3 \circ S_1$, where $S_3 = \{p \rightarrow t, q \rightarrow t\}$.

To unify $M(x, (a, b))$, $M(F(a), (a, z))$ and $M(F(F(b)), (y, b))$, over $\{a, b, x, y, z\}$ we *need* $x = F(a)$, $a = F(b)$, $y = a$ and $z = b$. Lining up the expressions makes this clear.

```
M(x           ,(a,b))
M(F(a     )   ,(a,z))
M(F(F(b))     ,(y,b))
```

By using $a = F(b)$ in other equalities involving a, some reflection should convince that $\{x \rightarrow F(F(b)), a \rightarrow F(b), y \rightarrow F(b), z \rightarrow b\}$ is a most general unifier. But if we included $M(b, (a, b))$, then we would have needed $b = F(F(b))$, for which there is no finite formal solution.

---

[12] Well, not quite (see note 10), but the conclusion is very broadly sound.

Functions might not be constants, so we use s-expressions and denote $f(x)$ by (f, x). To unify $\{(f_1, x_1), (f_2, x_2)\}$ is to simultaneously unify $\{f_1, f_2\}$ and $\{x_1, x_2\}$. The natural problem is to find an environment that simultaneously unifies each set in a collection of sets of expressions, such as $\{\{f_1, f_2\}, \{x_1, x_2\}\}$. One level of computation on each set of expressions produces a collection of sets of expressions. The union of these collections gives an equivalent collection to unify. When a variable symbol occurs in a set of expressions, as in $\{x, f(a), f(f(b))\}$, we may set aside a pair, such as $(x, f(a))$, as giving the definitive restriction on the variable symbol.

Some expression must be of maximal depth, and at each step we break up compound expressions, removing one level. So, eventually all sets contain a primitive symbol. We remove any instance of $x \to x$ and if x has multiple values, we select one, and unify the rest. We eventually have only symbol–value pairs. A dependency exists when x_1 occurs in the value of x_2. If x_1 depends on x_1, or on x_2 that depends on x_1, or there is any longer chain arriving back at x_1, then a loop exists, such as $x \to f(x)$. If there is a loop or a constant is given a compound value, then no finite formal unification is possible. Otherwise, this is an environment that unifies the original expressions. Treating the data as a collection of equalities, the information content is unchanged. The resulting environment is a most general unifier.

We don't have to wait for the complete expansion to detect problems. In actual implementation, the *not-unifiable* result can be returned as soon as a problem is detected.

However, loops are not illogical, and allowing them then the above process does obtain the minimal extra conditions for unification. If we accept these extra conditions we obtain unification. Unification with axioms starts with similar extra equalities. The above algorithm finds the minimal set of axioms required. Unification with axioms does not always admit a most general unifier.

An axiom is a triple (E_1, E_2, V) of two expressions and a set of variables. I stands for all the subexpression reductions $S(E_1) \to S(E_2)$, where S is an environment for V. To compute S, find the most general unifier of E_1 over V with a subexpression of the expression being reduced.

Notion 30: Equality of Expressions

When we look at the two arabic[13] numerals 1,935 and 51,837, we rapidly become aware of whether they represent the same number. This process is often seen as so natural as to not require further explanation. However, if asked about the equality of two roman numerals, such as CCCCC and CCCCLXXXXVIIIII, the situation is not so clear. Nevertheless, by computation, IIIII = V, VV = X, XXXXX = L, LL = C, we can work out in this case that they are equal. Returning to the arabic example, we see that there is a computation. Each symbol of one is checked against the other, to see whether they are all equal.

The form of arabic numerals is canonical. Symbol-by-symbol equality testing of two numerals is a correct test for equality of the numbers. This is because we do insist that arabic numerals are normalised, 'leventy 'leven is 121, but does not normally obtain a high score in an arithmetic exam.

We usually accept non-normalised roman numerals, so we need to do more work. But if we insist that in a roman numeral any symbol that can be replaced by a higher value symbol must be, and that the larger-valued symbols are placed to the left, then we are using a canonical form for the roman numerals, and a symbol-by-symbol check works.

Generically the equality of two tuples is component by component. A set is more troublesome. When we write down a set we give an order, {a,b} is distinct on the page from {b,a} and there is nothing we can do about this. So, we have to learn that the order makes no difference. Proving equality of sets can be quite difficult.

As for rational numbers, when are they equal? Is 4/6 the same as 2/3? The generic test for equality of a/b and c/d is $ad = bc$. But there is a canonical form of rational numbers, no common factors. We can determine it by dividing out any common factors: 4/6 becomes 2/3, which is symbol-by-symbol equal to 2/3.

Strictly, symbol-by-symbol equality is not simple. For you to identify that this x is the same as this x, you have to do a complex vision-

---

[13]Strictly, this is Moroccan Arabs, the rest use the Urdu system.

processing computation, in your head. Further under the right conditions you would say that this x is the same as this x even though they are in different fonts. Writing a program that determines the equality of handwritten symbols on a page is a non-trivial exercise.

What, then, is equality?

By now you should have some doubt that there is such a concept. I hope, at least, I have demonstrated that there is no *singular natural* equality. Rather, our idea of when two things are equal is defined for the given context. For each data type we construct we must decide what equality will mean in that context.

What is equality in computation?

It is a binary relation, a predicate, a Boolean valued function. But it must satisfy some conditions. Firstly, it is clear that $A = A$; nothing that we would call equality could fail in this condition. Then $A = B$ means that $B = A$. This excludes relations such as $A > B$, which behave a little like equality, but are not any type of equality. Also, and very commonly, we reason $A = B = C$ so $A = C$; again this is very deeply fundamental to our concept of equality.

The computer provides us with a definition of byte equality. A memory block is a sequence of bytes, and can be tested for equality as such, using component by component equality. In C, this is automatically available for structs defined by the programmer. Often byte-wise equality of a memory block is sufficient to imply equality of the two abstract data elements. But, as for rational numbers, it is often not necessary. Thus, byte-wise and abstract equality may be different. For this reason,[14] Java does not allow byte-wise equality. You have to define what you mean by equality when you define Java classes, or you cannot test for equality.

It is also logicaly possible (even if inadvisable) for the meaning of a data element to depend on its location in memory, thus making byte-wise equality insufficient for determining abstract equality.

---

[14] And others such as some security reasons.

Notion 31: Equational Reasoning

Equality (see page 66) is well defined by its nature.

$A = A$,
$A = B \Rightarrow B = A$,
$A = B = C \Rightarrow A = C$,

That is, equality is a reflexive, symmetric, transitive binary operation. However, in reasoning with equality it is often assumed without explicit statement that substitution respects equality. But, in C, given x+y=y+x, and substituting z++ for x, we get (z++)+y == y+(z++). The exact status of this equality has varied over the years. Some compilers evaluated ++ as it occurred; others waited until after the expression; others did whatever they pleased at the time. The logical status of this equality is contingent.

We need to include an explicit axiom into our logic system.

$$A = B \Rightarrow m(A) = m(B)$$

If we know $A = B$, then for any(see note 10) expression m we know that $m(A) = m(B)$, even when we do not know what either side of the equality means. A system that satisfied these axioms is said to admit equational reasoning.

Substitution of equals for equals in pure expressions preserves equality because there are no side effects. But in many languages, expressions have side effects. The value of the expression has been taken to be the return value within the language. This is very misleading. For example, given $x + y = y + x$, we might substitute values to obtain $f(1) + y = y + f(2)$, which is not generically true. But, you say, we substituted a different value of the argument to f in each case, this is why the equality is violated. But this is exactly what side effects are about. Hidden parameters and hidden return values.

Systems with side effects do not admit equational reasoning if the side effects are ignored in the equality of the expressions. An expression with side effects can be turned into one without by just listing the variables affected on the side explicitly in the argument lists.

Given, `int f(int x){y=x; return z;}`, the call `a=f(b)` has side effects, but if f is defined by $f(x, z) = (z, y)$, then we have the same effect using $(a, y) = f(b, z)$, and all expressions are pure.

The problem with equational reasoning in languages with side effects is just that it is common to ignore part of the action of the expression. This is essentially a misinterpretation of the notion of equality, rather than a breakdown of equational reasoning.

However, what is true is that certain languages make it very difficult to determine when two expressions are identical. A language like Haskell that admits equational reasoning does so by requiring that all effects be declared.

The equality $x + y = y + x$ is based on the idea that x and y are numbers (for example), but `i++` is not a number, but rather a piece of code. Suppose that `i==2`, can we substitute 2 for `i++`? No, even though this is its value, since `i++` is actually `{t=i; i=i+1; return t;}`, which is not the same as the number 2, or even the variable `i`.

It is difficult to avoid side effects when dealing with interaction. Printing a document is, in itself, a side effect. The essential way around this is to express the program as a whole as a function from a string of input events to a string of output events.

Another complication is that if the hidden parameters of a function are changed it is not required to change the code in which it is used. But if all have to be declared, then the code must be changed every where the function is used . . . resulting in non-modular code. The generic way out of this is to pass records, rather than inline tuple lists; and then the extra fields in the records do not have to be explicitly mentioned in the code. But a full solution still involves more thinking.

The fact remains, however, equational reasoning is often worth the effort due to the increase in robustness of code.

Notion 32: Unification Reduction

Unification reduction is the arithmetic of computation. It is at once a low-level mechanism and a high-level concept. It takes an expression as representing nothing other than itself. It is a casebook of those things you were told not to do in high school (see note 2) like identifying number and numeral (see page 58).

Let E_1 and E_2 be two expressions using variable symbols $x_1..x_n$. To *unify* (see page 64) E_1 and E_2 is to find expressions to subsititute for $x_1..x_n$ so that E_1 and E_2 become the same expression. If we substitute $x = 1$ and $y = 2$ in "$x + 2$" and "$1 + y$", we get in each case "$1 + 2$".

Unification commonly occurs in standard programming languages in the evaluation of function calls. We are told that $f(x) = x^2$. We unify $f(a+b)$ with $f(x)$ to get $x = a+b$, and then substitute into x^2 to obtain $f(a + b) = (a + b)^2$. The sudden appearance of a pair of parentheses is important and their absence is a common novice error, but this is simply the original implicit grouping being made explict.

We may need multiple substitutions going both ways. For example (x, z) is unified with $(1, (1, y))$ by the substitution $\{x = 1, y = 2, z = (1, 2)\}$, or more generally by $\{x = 1, y = a, z = (1, a)\}$, where a is a free parameter.

The process of changing one expression into another by substituting the values for variable symbols is *reduction*. The full process involves three exressions, E_1, E_2, and E_3. We unify E_1 and E_2 to obtain values for variable symbols, and then substitute these values into E_3. Though often mentioned only implicitly, and accepted without comment, unification reduction is deeply fundamental to the concept of both computation and proof.

Languages such as C and Java use limited unification reduction in function calls. In compiling the expression f(x*x,y+2), the identification of expressions to substitute for the formal parameters of f must be made. But this is only unification of flat tuples. In Haskell, we can unify f(x,(a,b),[c,d,e]) or any other compound structure with the original declaration of f. But, no repetition of variable symbols is allowed in the formal parameters. In Haskell, we cannot define equality with the clause $eq(x, x)$. Prolog does allow this. In Prolog, full pure unification (with no axioms) is used for procedure calls. So, a problem of the form $f(x)$ may be changed to $sqr(add(x, 1))$, or $sqr(add(x, 1))$ to $f(x)$.

The complete state of a countable state machine may be described as a string of characters such as "(1,23,a,3.14)" listing the values of all the variables as they would be printed. Syntax respecting subsitutions on such strings provide a mechanism for changing the state of the machine. Any computable process can be expressed in this manner.

An axiom is a logical starting point, the definition of what we may assume. Typically axioms are expressed as unification reductions, even if this point is not formally recognised. The factorial function may be defined by $0! = 1$ and $n! = n \times (n - 1)!$. The 1st axiom states that we may replace the subexpression "0!" by "1", and the 2nd axiom is a non-trivial unification. Repeated application of this unification reduction will change 3! into 3×(3-1)×(3-1-1)×(3-1-1-1)!. With only the given axioms this would continue indefinitely. But, if we have arithmetic defined by unification reduction (see page 58), we can change it into 3×2×1×0!, and thence into 3×2×1×1 and 6.

More general systems of unification with a variety of axioms are studied in universal algebra (see note 3), a study of which is highly recommended for any serious programmer. The semantics of code, including imperative, procedural code, can be expressed as unification reduction. (see page 74)

In a reduction all meaning is erased from the computation. Separation of syntax from semantics is the universal task of the programmer. Meaning is a human-imposed association. A formal system (a program) is a pure syntactic system that is homomorphic to the human system with meaning.

Many bugs arise from the incorrect assumption that the program is imbued with natural meaning. The truth is that the meaning is only in the head of the programmer. Pushing further, we find that the meaning of meaning is emphemeral, and most likely only exists in a single head, and cannot be transfered even from human to human. We transmit only the syntax of written or spoken word.

Exercise 8: Unification Reduction Engine

Write a simple unification-reduction engine.

Of course this exercise is not so simple. But it should be very illuminating for those that attempt it. The basic operation is that the engine matches an expression $E(x, y)$ against a the left-hand side of the substitutions in a database of rules $(A_1(x, y) \rightarrow B_1(x, y), \ldots)$ best thought of as a tuple rather than a set. Finding one that matches, we then substitute the values into the right-hand side to obtain the next expression. For example, with $Add(F(x), y))$, and having the rule $Add(x, y) = Add(y, x)$, reduce the expression to $Add(y, F(x))$. This is repeated until no reductions are possible.

Parsers

Although the target of the exercise is unification and not parsing, attempting to avoid all parsing will mean constant hand built data structures and recompilation. So it is best that your program can parse basic expressions from the keyboard, or from a file. Possibly the easiest expressions to parse are s-expressions. The expression (f a b c) means f applied to (a, b, c). All brackets must be included, so that $f(x + y)$ becomes (f (+ x y)). However, anyone who wishes to build more complex expression parsing is encouraged to do so.

Internally, an expression should be stored and manipulated as a tree. In fact, an s-expression can be seen simply as a notation for a tree. For example, (f a b) means, *the tree with root weighting f, and subtrees a and b.*

Expressions

Trees are fairly easy to implement in C, Java, Prolog or Haskell. In C, a struct node {symbol r; node *child[10]}; will do even though it limits the number of arguments to 10. For the more enthusiastic, a linked list of arguments struct node {symbol r; node *child; node *next}; is more general. In Java, just use analogous classes. You cannot use lists of lists in Haskell to represent an s-expression because the type system will object to the infinite signature. However, it is possible to define an analgous new data structure that does not suffer from this limitation. Prolog comes with unification reduction inbuilt; however, getting at it for the purposes of retrieving the required environment still needs some effort.

Unification

The simplest case treats all symbols as variable, get this running first. Later look at including the list of constants that are not to be given values. The giving of a value to a constant can be checked on the fly or as post-processing on the all-variable case.

We can replace all occurrences of a variable in values at the time that its value becomes apparent. Then it is simple and fast to check for cyclic dependencies. But it is logically neater to eliminate cycles afterwards, and the program could instead give the minimum set of axioms under which the expressions unify.

We need a mechanism to indication non-unification. We cannot use an empty set for this, since two expressions might unify with an empty environment. This suggests adding a special element, not-an-environment. Handling this with an exception in Java is also suitable but does not necessarly constitute improved code.

Substitution

Substitution of values for variable symbols is fairly simple recursively. For example, this is a simple routine to subsitute values into a Prolog List. The arguemnts are the environment (a list of pairs), the original list, and the final list with the variables replaced by their values.

```
subst([],X,X) :- !.
subst(L,[A|B],[X|Y]) :- subst(L,A,X),subst(L,B,Y),!.
subst([(A,B)|_],A,B) :- !.
subst([_|B],X,Z) :- subst(B,X,Z), !.
```

Notion 33: Code Reduction

An expression is a correctly bracketed (see note 13) sequence of symbols that may be written down on a piece of paper or stored in an electronic digital computer memory. Sometimes the bracketing is irrelevant, as in $1 + 2 + 3$, where it is left out because it makes no difference to the value, or implicit, as in $2 + 3 \times 4$, where there is a convention that the terms are bracketed thusly, $2 + (3 \times 4)$. A subexpression is a part of an expression which respects the (possibly implicit) bracketing. So $2 + 3$ is not a subexpression of $2 + 3 \times 4$ because it cuts across the implicit brackets. Given a reduction, $x * y \rightarrow y * x$, where x and y are unification variables, we can apply it to subexpression in situ, for example, as used to produce the reduction $3 + (5 * 6) \rightarrow 3 + (6 * 5)$. This concept is the most primitive in any discussion of digital computation as well as in algebra. Without this or a similar concept we can do no computation, with this we can do all possible computations.

We have a reduction process with suggested inuitive meanings:

(add x 0)	$\rightarrow$	x	$x + 0$	$=$	x
(add x (s y))	$\rightarrow$	(s (add x y))	$x + (y + 1)$	$=$	$(x + y) + 1$
(mul x 0)	$\rightarrow$	0	$x * 0$	$=$	0
(mul x (s y))	$\rightarrow$	(add x (mul x y))	$x * (y + 1)$	$=$	$(x * y) + x$

This defines addition and multiplication of non-negative integers,

for example,

```
          (mul (s(s 0)) (s(s 0)))
  →       (add (s(s 0)) (mul (s(s 0)) (s 0)))
  →       (add (s(s 0)) (add (s(s 0)) (mul (s(s 0)) 0)))
  →       (add (s(s 0)) (add (s(s 0)) 0))
  →       (add (s(s 0)) (s(s 0)))
  →       (s (add (s(s 0)) (s 0)))
  →       (s (s (add (s(s 0)) 0)))
  →       (s (s (s (s 0))))
```

The expression being reduced is an s-expression, and is valid Scheme code. The above is an example of evaluation of Scheme by expression reduction.

When we write a pure function in C code we can think of it in exactly the same way:

```
int f(int x){return x ? x*f(x-1) : 1;}
```

may be read as

```
f(x) → (x ? x*f(x-1) : 1)
```

so

```
        f(4)
    →   4 ? 4*f(3) : 1
    →   4*f(3)
    →   4*(3 ? 3*f(2) : 1)
    →   4*(3*f(2))
    →   4*(3*(2 ? 2*f(1) : 1))
    →   4*(3*(2*f(1)))
    →   4*(3*(2*(1 ? 1*f(0) : 1))))
    →   4*(3*(2*(1*f(0))))
    →   4*(3*(2*(1*(0?0*f(-1):1)))))
    →   4*(3*(2*(1*1))))
    →   4*(3*(2*1)))
    →   4*(3*2)
    →   4*6
    →   24
```

Pure unification string productions of this type can be used to define the semantics of a language precisely at a reasonably high-level. It avoids the complications of trying to explain how the code will be executed on a Von Neumann machine. There are ways to translate this type of definition into a compiler for the language. However, this is a very powerful method, and it is easy to define semantics that can bog down the largest computer. Some restraint is required when using it to define a language.

Notion 34: Programming With Logic

Predicate calculus can be used as a programming language. The principle is straightforward. For simplicity we look only at pure programs that read data in and write out a result.

Take, as an example, the computation of the greatest common divisor, $gcd(x, y)$, which satisfies the axioms on the right using the convention that a variable is universally qualified by default.

$$
\begin{aligned}
gcd(a, a) &= a \\
gcd(x, y) &= gcd(y, x) \\
gcd(x, y) &= gcd(x, y - x)
\end{aligned}
$$

We already have enough information to determine $gcd(50, 15)$,

$$
\begin{aligned}
 & gcd(50, 15) \\
= & gcd(15, 50) \\
= & gcd(15, 35) \\
= & gcd(15, 20) \\
= & gcd(5, 15) \\
= & gcd(5, 10) \\
= & gcd(5, 5) \\
= & 5
\end{aligned}
$$

Each step is a unification reduction (see page 70). By trying all possible rules at each step, and producing a tree of resulting expressions, an automated process can discover a node in which the term gcd does not exist. This is a leaf node on the tree, and is the required answer.

Pure logic programming is an axiom-building exercise. We presume that the computer provides the ability to determine the logical conclusions. This is no different from the requirement that the computer provide the ability to follow through the instructions given to it in C, Java, or Haskell.

Real logic programming is not programming in the sense the term is usually used, it is too powerful. It removes all the basic issues of programming, and replaces them by only the problem of writing specifications, and working out if they satisfy human desires. But real logic programming is not possible, since the problem as posed is non-computable.

Pragmatic logic programming involves a lot of work in determining which of several logically equivalent axiom sets will reduce efficiently under a given unification reduction scheme, as well as including meta-logical information such as advice on which order the unifcations should be tried.

Many aspects of C and Java are logical in nature. A declaration `int x;` is an assertion that `x` is in the `int` set of data elements. A function definition `f(x){int y = x+x; return 2*y;}` asserts an equality between evaluation of $f(x)$ and evaluation of the body of the code.

In Haskell, a logic style program is possible:

```
fact 0 = 1
fact n = n*(fact(n-1)).
```

These Haskell clauses look and act very much like their pure logic interpretation, indeed even the axiom `fact (n+1) = (n+1)*(fact n)` is valid Haskell.

It is trivial to interpret an appropriately written Haskell program as a pure logical scheme. What makes Haskell not a logic programming language is that it does not go in reverse. Logically, the assertion `fact n (fact(n+1))/(n+1)` is just as valid. But working from top to bottom and left to right, Haskell would not finish the computation.

In principle, the notion of *programming in logic* refers not to the construction of a program as a set of predicate calculus axioms, but rather the requirement that the behaviour of the program be unchanged by permuting the axioms in the program, or by reversing the logic of an individual axiom. A logic program is an unordered set of bi-directional equality assertions.

In practice, the art of logic programming is *all about* choosing the order of assertions and the direction of equalities, to make the computations work in practical time. There are no real logic languages, but much progress has been made in the latter part of the 20th century, largely under the guise of optimising compilers and compilers for functional languages.

Notion 35: Negation in Logic Programming

Negation is a complex and subtle concept.

If I say I am lying, then am I lying?

I define the negation of a predicate A, to be the predicate (not A) such that ((not A) xor A) is always true. But it is not axiomatic of all logic systems that such a predicate exists, or that if it exists it will be unique.

The negation of *Fred has a mouse in his pocket* might be *Fred does not have a mouse in his pocket*. But what is the negation of *The present king of France has a mouse in his pocket*. If we say that the present king of France has no mice, we assume that the king exists. There is no problem talking of fictional characters, such as Sherlock Holmes (who has no mice). But, we are talking of a real king of France. The negation is closer to *the king is mouseless, or there is no king.*

Stating the original with more caution, we say *someone is Fred, and something is a mouse, and that something is in the someone's pocket.*

Exists x : Exists y : Fred(x) and mouse(y) and inPocket(x,y)

Negating this

Forall x : Forall y : not Fred(x) or not mouse(y) or not inPocket(x,y)

Either Fred does not exist, or the mouse does not exist, or the mouse is not in Fred's pocket. This very close to *no one called Fred has a mouse in his pocket*. But I did not mean *just anyone* called Fred; I have a specific person in mind. So, I find myself asserting that this specific real individual might not exist.

Is it logically valid to say that Fred (my boss from when I worked as a control systems engineer) does not exist? If not, then from whom did I just receive an email? Is existence a property of an object? I do not claim this conundrum is a logical paradox. There are plausible responses. But our choice affects the method for negating, and whether negation can be done at all.

Negation in logic programming is similarly fraught with difficulty.

We might define negation by automated logical rules for transforming a predicate. But we would have difficulty knowing if these rules are correct, consistent, or complete. It might be better in practice to require the programmer to supply the meaning of negation of each predicate as needed. This is similar to requiring the programmer, as Java does, to supply the definition of equality for a new datatype.

Alternatively, as in Prolog, we may define negation as failure. If a search fails to find a goal, then the negation of the goal is asserted true. Thus, (not g) means run the proof technique, see if it proves g; if not, then take this as a proof of (not g). Mind you, how then are we to list all the solution space of (not g(X))? If g(X) results in an infinite stream of integral instances, then we cannot be sure to compute whether any specific integer satisfies (not g).

Failure to prove and proof of failure are two different things. Given only that X is a real number we would fail to prove that it is positive, and fail to prove it is negative, and thus we have proved that an arbitrary real number is zero.

The logically correct Prolog program

```
positive(1).
negative(-1).
neutral(X) :- not(positive(X)), not(negative(X)).
```

returns the following rather uniluminating results:

```
neutral(2) == yes.
neutral(X) == no.
```

Thus, Prolog has a negation but it should be called *not in the database*. Prolog negation does not have the properties normally required of logical negation, if you want a negation, then you should decide for yourself, and explicitly code, what you had in mind, case by case. The use of the metalogical operators is advised, but great caution is needed to avoid introducing other illogical results.

Notion 36: Impure Lambda Calculus

The phrase *lambda calculus* means different things to different people.[15] The common theme is computation with function-like elements. In this section, we motivate the lambda calculus as a whole by looking at some technical issues of the use of functions.

In orthodox languages we do not need to name an integer to use it. To pass the square of the integer 123 to a function f, we use an expression such as f(123*123). We do not need to define a variable int x = 123*123; and then call f(x). But, if we wish to pass the double application of a function f to a numerical integration routine integrate we need to declare g(x)=f(f(x)) and then pass g as in integrate(a,b,g).

This restriction on function declaration is sometimes conflated with the notion of functions not being first-class datatype. But the notion of first-class datatype is more typically used to mean that the datatype can be stored in arrays, passed as arguments, and returned as values from functions. By this definition, function is a first-class datatype in C, since (implicit) function pointers provided the essentials of this behaviour. But in C we are unable to construct *new* functions without some form of machine-level hacking. It is the ability to construct and operate on arbitrary elements of the datatype that make all the difference in practice between a datatype that is clumsy or one that is deft.

The first thing that lambda calculus gives is a mechanism for in-place function construction and use. For example, $(\lambda x \cdot x^2)$ is the function that squares its argument. More generally $(\lambda x_1..x_n \cdot E(x_1,..,x_n))$ is a function that takes n arguments and returns the value of the indicated expression. In this context, the lambda calculus appears to be a simple syntactic convenience, in which the arguments and code for an anonymous function are packaged into an expression that can be used at the place of the call.

Our earlier example might become integrate(lambda(x){f(f(x)}). Notice that the expression f(f(x)) still occurs because this is our way of expressing the required function. The point is that now we do not

---

[15]This state of affairs is not unprecedented: see, for example, the large variety of approaches to the meaning of the term *differential calculus*.

need to make a declaration, which in particular means that we do not need to know when we write our code what functions we are going to use. Imagine the problems caused if you had to declare all the integers $(1,2,3,45\ldots)$ that were going to appear during the running of a program.

Notice that in the above piece of code a pair of braces {} appears inside parentheses (). In practice, this is often a sign that something unusual is occurring. It occurs in Java when anonymous extension classes are used; anonymous extension classes can be used in a manner very similar to a scheme lambda expression. While at first seeming a small detail, syntactic sugar, it is the ability to use a class anonymously that makes it easily adaptable. In principle, C++ can duplicate this effect by the use of explicit class definitions, but it becomes tedious, and moves the definition of the function away from the place it is used.

Lambda expressions could be used to good effect in other areas of study. For example, in algebra the expression x^2 is often confused with the function $(\lambda x \rightarrow x^2)$. Taking the expression x^2 and producing $(\lambda x \rightarrow x^2)$ is called *lambda abstraction*.

The Newtonian approach to differentiation $f'(x)$ requires us to predefine f, while the Leibnitzian $\frac{d}{dx}x^2$, allows an implicit lambda abstraction. It is interesting to note that Leibnitz was much more strongly into constructive logic and computer science than was Newton. However, beware that $\frac{d}{dx}x^2 = 2x$ uses implicit lambda abstraction. Perhaps we should say, $d(\lambda x.x^2) = (\lambda x.2x)$, just to be careful.

Partial differentiation could be handled by taking an expression, with no λs, and abstracting it. That is ...

$$\frac{\partial}{\partial x}E = (D\ (\lambda x.E))\ x$$

where D is an operator that takes a function of a single variable and returns the derivative. This is a formal, constructive, definition for the intuition that a partial derivative treats all other variables as constants.

Notion 37: Pure Lambda Calculus

Normally unless, and even perhaps if, you are heavily into formal logics, it is best to be introduced to the impure lambda calculus (see page 80) for motivation before tackling the purest form described here. It might also help to review substitution computation (see page 52).

Given an alphabet Σ (intuitively the collection of variable names), not containing "(", ")", "." or "λ", we define the set of lambda expressions $\Lambda(\Sigma)$ over Σ, inductively, as the smallest (see note 18) set that satisfies the following three axioms:

$x \in \Sigma \Rightarrow x \in \Lambda(\Sigma)$ ....we need to start somewhere
$A, B \in \Lambda(\Sigma) \Rightarrow (AB) \in \Lambda(\Sigma)$ ....think *function application*
$x \in \Sigma, E \in \Lambda(\Sigma) \Rightarrow (\lambda x.E) \in \Lambda(\Sigma)$ ....think *function construction*

In $(\lambda p.B)$, p is the *parameter* and B the *body*. The substitution $[x \rightarrow X]$, of the value X for the variable name x, must respect the declaration of parameters in sub expressions that mask the body of the subexpressions from the scope of the variable x.

$$
\begin{aligned}
[x \rightarrow X]x &= X \\
[x \rightarrow X](AB) &= (([x \rightarrow X]A)([x \rightarrow X]B)) \\
[x \rightarrow X](\lambda x.E) &= (\lambda x.E) \\
[x \rightarrow X](\lambda y.E) &= (\lambda y.[x \rightarrow X]E)
\end{aligned}
$$

There are three reductions, alpha, beta and gamma:

Alpha: $(\lambda x.E) \rightarrow (\lambda y.[x \rightarrow y]E)$ ....change of parameter
Beta: $(\lambda x.E)B \rightarrow [x \rightarrow B]E$ ....function application
Gamma: $[x \rightarrow B]E \rightarrow (\lambda x.E)B$ ....reverse application

Alpha reduction as stated above is not always valid. For example, $(\lambda y.[x \rightarrow y]xy)$ is $(\lambda y.yy)$. Alpha reduction $[x \rightarrow y]$ on $(\lambda x.E)$ is valid exactly when y does not occur within the scope of x in E. A free occurrence is not in the scope of any appropriate parameter declaration. There are complete syntactic rules for *free* and *scope*. But, pragmatically, alpha reduction is valid exactly when $[y \rightarrow x][x \rightarrow y]E = E$, that is, when the substitution can be reversed.

We have a collection of expressions equipped with a reduction system. This is a *directed* graph. But each alpha reduction can be reversed by another alpha reduction, and each beta reduction has its inverse in the gamma reductions. Thus, each link can be traversed both ways. Expression A reduces to B exactly when B reduces to A. The reduction graph is undirected. Also, it is clear that if A reduces to B, which reduces to C, A reduces to C, by catenating the reductions from A to B and B to C. We include as a special case the trivial reduction of A to A.

Thus, reduction is reflexive, symmetric, and transitive, and defines a form of equivalence (see page 68) between lambda expressions. Two expressions are equivalent if they are in the same connected component of the reduction graph.

A *normal* lambda expression is one which admits no beta reductions. All normal forms equivalent to a given lambda expression are alpha equivalent. That is, if you can reduce lambda A to two distinct primitives p and q, then p and q are identical except for a change of the names of the parameters. We may think of p as the *value* of A, while A is a compound expression whose value is p.

Each beta reduction is associated with a λ in the expression. If we repeatedly select the outermost (leftmost) λ that can be reduced and reduce it, then if a normal form exists it will be reached after a finite number of reductions. Speaking informally, any lambda for factorial must satisfy $f = (\lambda\ n\ .\ n = 0\ ?\ 1\ :\ (n * (f\ (n-1))))$. So, factorial has no normal form, and neither does factorial of -1, but factorial of 3 does.

The lambda calculus is one of the more successful of a variety of systems for formalising the notion of computation. It has been suggested at times as the basis for physical computational devices, but our desktop computers are based more closely on the Turing and Von Neumann machines. The physical construction of a lambda engine requires large, fast stacks. Possible, but perhaps more complicated than current computers. In its favour, it has been argued that the increased ability to prove lambda systems correct would offset any difficulties. But the commercial reality is that we are less likely to see lambda machines on every desk than electric cars in every garage.

Notion 38: Pure Lambda Arithmetic

Impure lambda calculus (see page 80) is additional syntax for defining functions in terms of operators that we already have. The pure lambda calculus, taken strictly, has no other operators, only lambda expressions. This includes no numbers, no arithmetic, and no conditional statements. The meaning of a pure lambda expression is imposed by its use, outside the context of the calculus itself. Here we discuss a few aspects of how to program in pure lambda calculus. The principle is to construct lambda expressions that *behave like* the structure we are trying to program. This is true of programming in languages such as C, Java or Scheme, but this point is much more explicit in pure lambda calculus.

To construct the positive integers we need a collection of expressions that encode the concept of *that many*. For example, $1 \equiv (\lambda x.x)$, $2 \equiv (\lambda x.(xx))$, $3 \equiv (\lambda x.((xx)x))$ etc. For simplicity we assume left association in the absence of brackets, and obtain $n \equiv (\lambda x.xxxx..x)$ with n occurrences of x.

Although it is then apparent to the programmer what needs to be done to operate on these numbers, pure lambda calculus is heavily flavoured by the point that it is *impossible* for one lambda expression to determine the actual construction of another. Only the external behaviour is available, and that only through explicit test cases.

To justify its meaning as the integers, within lambda calculus we must define increment as a lambda expression. To simplify the expressions, we take the convention of curried expressions in which $(\lambda xy.E) \equiv (\lambda x.(\lambda y.E))$. Like the left associative brackets, this is purely a shorthand, and not the introduction of a different type of expression. It is then possible to define $inc \equiv (\lambda nx.nxx)$.

For a non-trivial implementation of the integers we would want addition. Reviewing the previous construction we might be tempted to try $(\lambda nmx.(nx)(mx))$, certainly this gets the right number of occurrences of x, but they are bracketed in the wrong manner.

The problem is that we need to construct $((((xx)x)x)x)$ from $((xx)x)$ and (xx), this means putting the (xx) in the place of the first x in

$((xx)x)$, which we cannot get at. The way out of this conundrum is to put this facility into the number from the beginning. Redefine n to be $(\lambda yx.yxxx..x)$ with $n-1$ occurences of x. Thus, $inc = (\lambda nyx.nyxx)$, and now $add = (\lambda nmyx.m(nyx)x)$.

Now that we have this bit of inner workings to use, we can look to multiply as repeated addition, except that we need n applications of $+m$, to get $n \times m$. If we reverse the application order so that $n = (\lambda xy.(x(x(x\ldots(xy)\ldots)))$, then inc and add work roughly as above, and $mul = (\lambda nmxy.m(add\ n)(\lambda xy.y))$. This amounts to adding n to 0 a total of m times.

The representation we have developed is reasonably servicable. The definition of the number n as an operator that applies a function n times means that many arithmetic operations are easy to define. Powers, for example could be defined by repeated multiplication. Equality to zero can be tested by a slightly more subtle approach. The function $(\lambda x.\mathsf{false})$ applied zero times to **true** is **true**, any more times, and it is **false**. However, we have not yet discussed how to build conditionals.

We still do not have decrement. One problem with decrement is decrement of 0, which is an error, but we have no mechanism for handling it. By default typically a non-numerical lambda expression will result. But the larger problem is that further operations are not produced in any obvious manner, because the number does not already have the required facility.

An (more efficient) alternative is to represent the number in binary, for example, $(\lambda xy.xyxxyyxy)$. To build the operations, we need conditional structures, which are discussed elsewhere (see page 86).

The reason for the mass of technicalities involved in developing arithmetic in pure lambda calculus is that we are insisting on doing everything from the beginning. This is using pure lambda calculus as a form of assembly language. Once all these pieces are defined, we can proceed at a higher level.

Notion 39: Pure Lambda Flow Control

The conditional can be constructed in pure lambda calculus by an almost trivial mechanism once we realise the manner in which the conditional is used. Refering to the C language, (a ? b : c) returns either b or c depending on whether a is true or false. That is, a is a mechanism for deciding which of b or c to return. Let true and false represent the two options. Now, we can define this directly in lambda. $true = (\lambda xy.x)$ and $false = (\lambda xy.y)$. Then if A is an expression that returns true or false, we have $if = (\lambda abc.abc)$.

This gives the conditional, but how do we make operators that return the appropriate truth value? One idea is to build them into the datatype. So a number n can be $(\lambda t.tab)$, where a is the answer to the question *are you zero*, and b is the number as represented by some other mechanism (see page 84). This makes the process extremely close in style to object programming. We cannot look inside the datatype we have been given, but it will listen to certain requests for information, mediated by methods that it defines, and we can use.

Although the convention of using a name in place of a lambda expression is certainly used heavily, we must recall that this is shorthand for writing out the expression. It is easy to fall into the error of using a name in its own definition. It is an error because if we do then it is no longer pure lambda calculus, but an extension allowing recursive definition.

The Y-combinator, however, is a mechanism which provides the practical power of recursive definition without actually being recursive itself (see page 88). In essence, given a function defined recursively by $f(x) = E(f, x)$, the Y-combinator has the property that $YE = f$; Y manages to find the function that would have been defined by the recursive defintion using E.

Now, we can define (see page 238) the while-loop

```
while t s x = if t x then x else while t s (s x)
```

Exercise 9: Lambda Reduction

It is possible to write a simple lazy lambda reduction engine in Java (see page 262). This or a similar lambda engine can be used to test and debug this exercise. The Java code can get tangled: if you are happy with parsing text files you might want to consider a lambda to Java converter, using lambda calculus syntax such as (L x .   x * x) for lambda expressions.

1. Implement natural numbers with addition.

2. Include subtraction.

3. Include multiplication.

4. Include the ability to test a number for being zero.

5. Include a numeric error value for an invalid subtraction.

6. Include the ability to test any number to see if it is valid.

7. Include a test for equality that subtracts and tests for zero.

8. Include test of relative size that subtracts and tests for validity.

9. Implement factorial using pure lambda all the way.

10. Implement fibonacci using pure lambda all the way.

There are a number of approaches. In the minimumalist approach, with only increment, decrement, and a zero test, we can define the rest by

```
add(n,m) = add(n-1,m+1)
sub(n,m) = sub(n-1,m-1)
mul(n,m) = add(n,mul(n,m-1))
```

But there are more efficient mechanisms. Initially you may find it easier to assume that the subtraction is valid, rather than including the error code up front.

Notion 1: Computing Hyperfactorial Values

We define the Y-combinator (see page 86), also known as the fixed point operator, to be the lambda expression:

$$Y = (\lambda f x.(f(xx)))(\lambda f x.(f(xx)))$$

Clearly, using beta reduction, $Yf = f(Yf)$. So Yf is a fixed point of f, regardless of what f is. Thus, Y finds fixed points. A function may have more than one fixed point. Y finds the simplest fixed point (in a strict technical sense that we will not define here).

A recursive definition such as

```
fact x = if x==0 then 1 else x * (fact(x-1))
```

can be abstracted to

```
hfact fact x = if x==0 then 1 else x * (fact(x-1))
```

The original factorial function is then the minimal fixed point of `hfact`, which is then extracted by the Y-combinator. Detailed understanding, however, is not provided by this definition. But lack of understanding does not prevent the use of the definition to explore its meaning. You do not know what the function $f(x) = x^{96} + 5x^{23} + 45x$ looks like, but you can compute some values, such as $f(2)$. It is similar with lambda expressions.

As $sqr(x) = x * x$ leads us to $sqr(6) = 6 * 6 = 36$, so does

$hf(f) = \lambda x.(x == 0?1 : x * f(x-1))$ lead us to

$hf(\lambda x.0) = \lambda x.(x == 0?1 : x * (\lambda x.0)(x-1))$

noting that $(\lambda x.0)(x-1) = 0$ we have:

$hf(\lambda x.0) = \lambda x.(x == 0?1 : x * 0) = \lambda x.(x == 0?1 : 0)$

As $sqr^2(6) = sqr(sqr(6)) = sqr(36) = 1,295$ we look at $hf^2(\lambda x.0)$.

$$\mathrm{hf}^2(\lambda x.0) = \mathrm{hf}(\mathrm{hf}(\lambda x.0)) = \mathrm{hf}(\lambda x.(x == 0?1:0))$$

By straight substitution we get

$$= \lambda x.(x == 0?1 : x * (\lambda x.(x == 0?1:0))(x-1))$$

Applying $\lambda x.(x == 0?1:0))$ to the argument $x-1$ we get:

$$= \lambda x.(x == 0?1 : x * (x - 1 == 0?1:0))$$

Noting that $x - 1 == 0$ is the same as $x == 1$, we get

$$= \lambda x.(x == 0?1 : x * (x == 1?1:0))$$

Distributing $*$ over ? :, we get

$$= \lambda x.(x == 0?1 : (x == 1?x:0))$$

Finally, the true condition is only evaluated when $x == 1$, so

$$= \lambda x.(x == 0?1 : (x == 1?1:0))$$

Repeating these steps we find that

$$\mathrm{hf}^3(\lambda x.0) = \lambda x.(x == 0?1 : (x == 1?1 : (x == 2?2:0)))$$

Continuing $\mathrm{hf}^n(\lambda x.0)$ expands out the first $n-1$ values of factorial.

In particular, $(hf^{n+1}(\lambda x.0))(n) = n!$

We can now see the mechanism by which the Y-combinator works. Given an expression $E(f)$ in f, which might be used to define f recursively as in $f(x) = E(f)(x)$, the Y-combinator simply applies $E(f)$ to x without ever asking what f actually is. If $f(x) = E(f)(x)$ is a legitimate recursive defition of f, suitable for use in a program, then in the repeated application of $E(f)$ to x eventually it will turn out that the value of f is not required. Thus, the Y combinator manages to return the required value.

Notion 40: S-K Combinators

One fine day longer ago than I care to admit, I noticed on the wall of the corridor of the university I was attending a circular about a talk on programming. *I will show you* it said *how to write a program with no recursion, no iteration, and no variables.* I was fascinated. I had by then realised that recursion and iteration where essentially the same concept. You could build a language with either iteration or recursion playing the central role of allowing repeated application of some piece of code to some data stored in some variable. But to lose both? How could you program anything?

Some reflection on the matter formed in my mind a concept akin to the Y-combinator (see page 86), a constructor for functions using operators that encapsulate the recursion or iteration concept analogous to the summation operator in orthodox mathematics. But, developing this thought I found even more reliance on variable symbols and tricks for modifying stored data. I arrived at the time and place of the talk in a highly dubious frame of mind, expecting a dirty trick.

At this talk I was introduced to S-K combinators, which, unlike pictures of Lilly, did not make my life complete, but certainly did opened my eyes to the point that such an approach was possible. The central issue is really one of how to move the values around.

If I have a number of basic functions available, and operators on those functions, then I can build up more functions. I do not need to have any variables to do this, for example, a summation operator might be defined so that

$$(\texttt{sumOp 0 f}) \ \texttt{n} = \sum_{i=0}^{n} f(i).$$

An example program is (`sumOp 0 sqr`), and contains only constants, no variables at all.

In Haskell, we can use a function such as `sub b a = b - a` in the definition `f x = (sub 5) x`, but since x occurs on the end of the expression on both sides we can instead say `f = sub 5`. The x was an arbitrary place holder. So far so good. But when we try to define `f(x) = x-4`, we get `f x = sub x 4`. Now x is in the middle and cannot be thrown away. How do we avoid using it? We include the operator, `R f x y = f y x` and define `f x = R sub 4 x`. Now, `f = R sub 4`, and we have eliminated x.

A moment's reflection should now convince the reader that what we need is the ability to define arbitrary expression construction where the (unknown) arguments are inserted into an expression being built. At this point it is logically possible that, there being an infinite number of expressions, we might need an infinite number of constructors. However, it has been shown that two are sufficient.

```
K x y = x
S x y z = x z (y z)
```

Defining `I = S K K` so that `I x = x` is worthwhile and we can reduce an SK expression as follows:

```
(S (K S) K) I) f x = f (f x)
(S (S (K S) K) I) f x
S (K S) K f (I f) x
(K S) f (K f) f x
S (K f) f x
(K f) x (f x)
f (f x)
```

The original thought behind SK combinators was that they would make compilation of functional languages efficient, but the size of the expression tends to double each time a variable is eliminated, thus making the expression horribly large.

However, if we abandon minimality, and use other combinators, for example, `C x y z = x (y z)`, then we can reduce the size of some expressions, `(S C I) f x = f (f x)`. The use of a much larger set of rather more complicated "super" combinators, can actually make this approach work. Bu, it is a non-trivial exercise.

Chapter 3

Some Formal Technology

Over roughly the past 3,000 years humans have been building up a store of formal technology. This is a non-material resource that has been an indispensable part of the powerhouse of each great civilisation. While a number of people reject this technology as somehow irrelevant, they typicallly do not realise that they have and rely on large quantities of it. The ability to do arithmetic on integers is an excelent example, previously the preserve of highly trained specialists, the process has been reduced to something that can be taught to school children. The simplicity of this material hides the thousands of years of development of concepts that now seem obvious to we who did not have to create them.

Our society would not run without arithmetic, without algebra. An mechanical engineer designing an aircraft requires a strong background in a variety of formal concepts, the engineer designing the avionics would be expected to have suitable training in electronics, and similarly, the people writing the software need to know the foundations of the understanding of their material. If any of these people do not have a proper foundation, the plane may fail to fly. Or worse, it may fly for a while. An understanding of the streamlined culmination of 3,000 years of human thought is vital to the modern software writer.

Notion 41: The Ellipsis Is Not a Definition

Consider defining a sequence using an ellipsis. For example,

1, 2, 4, 8, 16 ...

What is the next element?

If I now said that the next element is 31, you would likely object.

But, that is exactly what I am going to say.

Let $f(n)$ be the number of regions that a circle is cut into by joining each of n points on the circle to all the others. The points must be in *general position*, this has a more technical meaning but in this context it means that no three lines intersect at one point within the circle. This gives the maximum number of regions into which the circle can be divided by joining n points with lines.

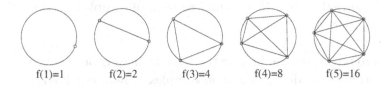

f(1)=1   f(2)=2   f(3)=4   f(4)=8   f(5)=16

This is the sequence under consideration.

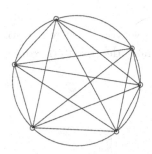

But now the case for $n = 6$.

Counting carefully shows that the number of regions is 31. $f(6) = 31$, not 32. There is a correct closed form for $f(n)$, but it is not 2^{n-1}. Above 6 the correct closed form and the exponential diverge dramatically.

Maybe you had better count the regions again just to be sure.

In fact, for any initial sequence of any finite length, n, we can always find a polynomial of order $n-1$ that will produce the given initial sequence. If we allow higher-order polynomials we can find an infinite number. This shows that the ellipsis, on its own, it quite ambiguous.

The reason that we, as humans, can use the ellipsis with a great deal of success is that we humans use a form of pattern matching. In picking *multiply by two* as the rule for the above sequence, we are matching the pattern to a rule in an idiosyncratic manner. The fact is that humans have a remarkable tendency to agree on what is the *simplest* pattern in the sequence.

To communicate with an ellipsis we need to have this common sense of simplicity. Unfortunately *common sense is neither common nor sense.*[16]

It is common to find in IQ tests sequences of numbers from which we are to deduce the next. However, the problem is not really one of number sequences. The task is to double-guess the compiler of the test. A valid enough exercise, perhaps, requiring a good inteligence, but not the task that it is stated to be. It amounts to a more complex version of scissors-paper-stone.

So, if we wish to be *precise* and be sure there are no bugs in our definition, we need something that depends less on complex human psychology.

In fact this issue leads directly into the problem of inductive knowledge. We believe that the sun will rise tomorrow because it always has before, but deductively this is a fallacy.

Supposing that because you believe something everyone else will also, or at least, should also, is actually one of the most deep-seated causes of social strife around the world today.

---

[16]Attribution uncertain — Voltaire said at least the first half of this.

Notion 42: The Summation Operator

The summation operator $\sum$ from standard mathematics has an alternative computational semantics akin to that of an iterative code loop. It takes an integer function, an upper bound, and a lower bound and returns an integer. (Generalisation to non-integer functions is obvious, but will not be perused here). It is important to understand the basic properties of this operator. Intuitively $\sum_{i=a}^{b} f(i) = f(a) + f(a+1) + f(a+2) + \ldots + f(b)$. But this is not a good definition, it relies on the ellipsis, whose meaning must be intuited, and it suggests at least four terms in the sum.

We could define it iteratively, by stating that

$$\sum_{i=a}^{b} f(i) = \texttt{\{int t=0;for(i=a;i<=b;i++) t+=f(i);return t;\}}$$

where by "abuse of notation" I have used C code to define an inline function. The meaning of this should be apparent. However, this is defining $\sum$ in terms of something even more complicated. How do we know what the C code means?

It is possible to define the summation operator non-circularly in terms of simpler concepts with no hidden meaning. Technically this process requires the ability to parse an expression, but this is lower-level than understanding the C code. To define from first principles, we write axioms. Essential in practice is the use of recursion. We make assertions about the summation operator, assertions which do not contain an ellipsis, and on which we can all agree.

$$\sum_{i=a}^{a} f(i) = f(a) \qquad \text{and} \qquad \sum_{i=a}^{b} f(i) = \sum_{i=a}^{b-1} f(i) + f(b)$$

If you examine these carefully, then it should be clear that whatever the summation operator is, it must satisfy both of these equalities. But these assertions also determine other properties.

Rearranging the second axiom, we obtain

$$\sum_{i=a}^{b} f(i) - f(b) = \sum_{i=a}^{b-1} f(i)$$

Setting $b = a$, and $b = a - 1$, we obtain the following two facts:

$$\sum_{i=a}^{a} f(i) - f(a) = \sum_{i=a}^{a-1} f(i)$$

$$\sum_{i=a}^{a-1} f(i) - f(a - 1) = \sum_{i=a}^{a-2} f(i)$$

From which we can see that

$$\sum_{i=a}^{a-1} f(i) = 0 \qquad \text{and} \qquad \sum_{i=a}^{a-2} f(i) = -f(a - 1)$$

Notice, we learn that as we sum backward we start to subtract elements, rather than adding. This concept will be familiar to those who have done integral calculus, since if you reverse the bounds of an integral you change the sign of the result. A warning though — due to the details of the definition, a zero result is obtained for the upper bound being one less than (rather than equal to) the lower bound.

There is a difference between the above semantics and the semantics of the C code. The C code never terminates if the upper bound is less than the lower bound. However, the recursive definition given has cleaner algebraic properties, and is made from first principles.

This approach can be used to *define* the semantics of C code, for example, by asserting (while noting non-termination if a<b), that

`{t=0;for(i=a;i<=b;i++) t+=f(i);}` $\equiv t = \sum_{i=a}^{b} f(i)$

Notion 43: Propositional Calculus

An utterance that proposes something, such as *the sky is blue* or perhaps *my zebra*[17] *likes tuna in a china bowl*, is a proposition. A proposition might also be written in symbols, encoded in electronic impulses, or distributed on a rag using smelly stains.[18] The important thing is that it is stated in some form of language.

Naturally enough, the propositional calculus is the calculus of propositions. But it deals only with what may be deduced about the truth value of one proposition from the truth value of other propositions. For example, we might reason from *(the cat sat on the mat) and (the dog is large)* to conclude *(the cat sat on the mat)*.

Each proposition is either true or false. If a supposed proposition[19] cannot be given a truth value, then it is not a proposition in the required sense, regardless of whatever else it might be. So the formal aspect of propositional calculus is a calculus of *true* and *false*, of 0 and 1, or anything else that has exactly two cases. This aspect is known as Boolean algebra (see page 99), after George Boole, and from it the structure of most contemporary computational machines is derived.

Some knowledge of Boolean algebra is useful in programming. Many times the author has seen this use:

```
if (x==0) then zero=true else zero=false
```

of a Boolean variable which is tested later by

```
if (zero==false) ...
```

What is the point of declaring a Boolean variable if you do not use it? The above code might as well have used 0 and 1 for true and false, or for that matter 23·5 and 67. There is no actual Boolean algebra here. To reflect the nature of Boolean variables use code such as `zero = x==0`, which is then tested by `if(zero) ...`

---

[17]It would have been a cat, but I wanted an index reference under Z.

[18]With apologies to Red Dwarf.

[19]Such as, *this statement is false.*

Zero is a propositional or Boolean variable, it contains the truth value of some proposition. The purpose of the Boolean type is to encapsulate this logic. As a rule of thumb, if you find yourself using `true` or `false` explicitly, except for initialisation, then it is likely there is something similar happening with the logic in your program.

Not only is it true that many relations between propositions cannot be determined from their truth values, but we are often working without knowledge of truth values. Implication illustrates this point strongly, and is a rapid and deep mechanism to compare different logic systems.

The form of implication used in the propositional calculus is *material implication*. Inspired by the *if this, then that* structure, it is identical by definition to *either that or not this*. But it produces the conclusion that a false statement implies anything.

Some people assert this as an obvious truth, saying once something false is assumed true anything else goes. But in an around-the-coffee-table discussion of the topic, *What if the Americans had built a moon base in 1980*, it it not generally acceptable to suggest that obviously *we would all be eating ice-cream for breakfast*. There is something much deeper than the truth value in our daily discussions. The internal structure of the statements has to be taken into account.

It is inadvisable to try to incorporate deep logic into Boolean variables. Just use them for what they are, two valued variables that store the truth of a proposition, for later checking and combining.

And always remember DeMorgan's law:

$$\text{not (this and that)} == \text{(not this) or (not that)}$$

which can be used to clear nested negations from your programs.

An example, is switching from

```
while(this){that}        to        until(this){that},
```

since in such a transition the sense of the test is inverted.

Notion 44: Boolean Algebra

Boolean algebra is the formal aspect of predicate calculus (see page 97). It is the the algebra of functions on tuples whose elements are drawn from a set of two values. An understanding of this algebra can be built up quickly from the basics.

A function might take any number of arguments 0, 1, 2 ...

If $f : \{0,1\}^0 \to \{0,1\}$, then f is one of two possible functions $f() = 0$ or $f() = 1$. These are the two constants of Boolean algebra.

If $f : \{0,1\}^1 \to \{0,1\}$, then it has, so to speak, two slots in which to put a 0 or 1. This produces 2^2 functions, which are true, $f(x) = 1$, false, $f(x) = 0$, identity, $f(x) = x$ and negation, $f(x) = 1 - x$.

In the binary argument case, we have four slots, leading to $2^4 = 16$ options. In the general case, we have 2^n slots, and the number of functions, 2^2^n, increases rapidly. As a universal algebra, however, Boolean algebra is *primitive*, meaning the set of all Boolean functions is generated from a finite subset of functions. A typical example subset is {and, or, not}, but some singleton subsets such as {nand} or {nor} also suffice.

The whole is just combinatorics of functions on binary sets. To define a binary truth function, there are four slots in the table, and we can fill each of them in with a 0 or a 1. There are exactly 16 possible functions, whatever we may wish to call them.

a	b	0	•	⊅	a	⊄	b	⊕	+	∓	⊕̄	b̄	⊂	ā	⊃	•̄	1
0	0	0	0	0	0	0	0	0	0	1	1	1	1	1	1	1	1
0	1	0	0	0	0	1	1	1	1	0	0	0	0	1	1	1	1
1	0	0	0	1	1	0	0	1	1	0	0	1	1	0	0	1	1
1	1	0	1	0	1	0	1	0	1	0	1	0	1	0	1	0	1

There is a large number of techniques used to manipulate Boolean expressions. Entire books can and have been written discussing the details of this vast technology. Here we have space only for a superficial examination of a couple of techniques.

Truth Tables

a	b	(a	+	(b	•	(a	+	b)))
0	0	0	0	0	0	0	0	0
0	1	0	1	1	1	0	1	1
1	0	1	1	0	0	1	1	0
1	1	1	1	1	1	1	1	1

Under each symbol is placed the truth value it would return. Examining the uppermost operator, and referring to the earlier table, we see that the whole is the operator "+". It is inevitable that each and every expression written using two Boolean variables defines one of the original operators, since there are only 16 and we have listed and named them all. This is very different from arithmetic expression in integer variables.

Boolean algebra

$$a + (b \bullet (a + b))$$
$$= \quad a + (b \bullet a + b \bullet b)$$
$$= \quad a + (b \bullet a + b)$$
$$= \quad a + (b \bullet a + b \bullet 1)$$
$$= \quad a + (b \bullet (a + 1))$$
$$= \quad a + (b \bullet 1)$$
$$= \quad a + b$$

Using rules similar to real algebra: distributivity $a \cdot (b \circ c) = (a \cdot b) \circ (a \cdot c)$, commutativity $a \cdot b = b \cdot a$, neutrality $a \cdot i = a$, and idempotency $a \circ a = a$, we can change the expression into a simpler but equivalent one.

Karnaugh maps

	00	01	11	10
00		1	1	
01				
11				
10		1	1	

There are 16 possible settings for 4 Boolean variables, (w,x,y,z). The top left of the table is (0,0,0,0), the bottom right is (1,0,1,0). The four terms indicated by a 1 form the expression xz. Visual selection of blocks of 1's can be used to minimise expressions.

This list barely scratches the surface of Boolean technology. Other significant issues are logic circuits and binary decision diagrams. Although direct use of these tools is unusual in programming, the occasional facility for simplification is worth the effort in learning at least the basics. The payoff in intuition about digital algorithms is greater.

Notion 45: Predicate Calculus

Unlike propositional calculus, predicate calculus is not typically used within the software itself.[20] But it is deeply significant in software spec-ification and verification.

The predicate calculus is based on predicates and existence. From a computer programming point of view, a predicate is simply a function, with no side effects, which returns a Boolean value. This is the type of code that you would be familiar with from the use `if` and `while`.

We can use the predicate `Boolean animal(thing x)`; to tell us that `animal(cat)` is true. A cat is an animal. And that `animal(telephone)` is false. That is a predicate, a decision process for determining the truth of an assertion with parameters. It extends the propositional calculus from Boolean variables to Boolean functions.

However, the predicate calculus also includes two heavily used operators, existential $\exists$ and universal $\forall$ quantification. The first $\exists x \in S : P(x)$, where P is a predicate (Boolean function), asserts that P does not always return false on the set S. That is, it states that there is some data in S for which P is true. The other $\forall x \in S : P(x)$ asserts that P always returns true. One basic equality of predicate calculus is that $not \forall x \in S : P(x)$ is the same as $\exists x \in S : not P(x)$.

These operators cannot be implemented. Unlike the propositional cal-culus, the predicate calculus is not computable.

A technical point that can be important, and is often missed, is that if S is empty, then $\forall x \in S : P(x)$ is true. Take it whichever way you want, the point is that by definition, $\forall$ states the lack of a counterexample. So if S is empty, there is no counter example, and the statement is said to be vacuously true. Although some people find a psychological objection to this, the fact is that it is a highly simplifying definition in predicate calculus. Use the predicate calculus for a while, and this point should become clear.

---

[20]It is used in the declaration of Haskell types.

Notion 46: Formal Mathematical Models

The construction of formal models in orthodox mathematics is a programming exercise. Construct a set that is appropriately morphic to the desired datatype. Typically we place top-level components into a tuple. The tuple is the same as the record structure, it is a single entity containing the otherwise unrelated entities that we need. The components are often sets of tuples, or sets of sets of tuples. The tuple is the workhorse of orthodox mathematics.

To define a stack datatype, we need a set of stacks S, a set of elements E, and some operations such as *pop*, *top*, and *put*. We require the axioms: `pop(put(s,e))=s` and `top(put(s,e))=e`. Like writing software, there may be many ways to make this concrete. This is one: The stack algebra is a tuple (S, E, pop, top, put), where E is an otherwise undefined set, a type parameter. Also, $\{\} \in S$ and $\forall s \in S, e \in E : (e, s) \in S$. We define $pop(e, s) = s$, $top((e, s)) = e$, $put((e, s)) = (e, s)$.

This trivial construction illustrates the central principles. Begin with sets, from which a multitude of entities emerge via direct and inductive definitions, satisfying non-inductive axioms. We can define a 2-tuple (a,b) as {{a},{a,b}}, a 3-tuple (a,b,c) as (a,(b,c)), and so on. A tree is nested tuples. A function is a set of 2-tuples.

Set theory is a low-level computational model. It is little used directly in programming because it is difficult to build as artifact technology. But, the next level up includes, tuples, sequences, relations, functions, trees, graphs, arrays, integers, bags, strings, and so on. These are used heavily in software and have solid implementations.

Set theory is highly amenable to a large body of existing proof technique. It can be very useful to find a set theory implementation isomorphic to your required datatype.

The distinctive character of non-computational mathematics is the ability to say *the set of all x satisfying condition y* without having to give an algorithm. In programming, this is the specification. A specification does not have to give an algorithm, nor, in principle, even give a method for determining if a program does satisfy the requirements.

Notion 47: The Formal State Machine

The state machine has several natural precise orthodox mathematical descriptions (see page 102). Most structures in computer science do, typically being nested tuples of sets and functions.

A state machine is a 4-tuple (Σ, Q, δ, F), of an alphabet Σ, a set Q of states, a transition function δ, and an output function F.

The alphabet and state space are otherwise undefined parameters of this model, $\delta \in (Q \times \Sigma \rightarrow Q)$, and $F \in (Q \rightarrow \Sigma)$. Intuitively, $\delta(s, q)$ is the next machine state for input s received while in state q, and $F(q)$ is the output associated with state q. Variations of this model include separate input and output alphabets Σ_1 and Σ_2. But we can then use $\Sigma = \Sigma_1 \cup \Sigma_2$. Then Σ_1 contains those symbols in the domain of δ and Σ_2 those in the range of F. Also, there may be a start state $q_0 \in Q$, we handle this by indicating the desired starting state explicitly when used.

When such a machine starts in a given state and a string is input, the machine reaches a definite new state. This extends the transition function $\delta(s, q)$ to the case of s being a string. Explicitly we define

$T \in (\Sigma^* \times Q \rightarrow Q)$,
$T(s, q) = \delta(q, s)$
$T(Ss, q) = \delta(T(S, q), s)$

The set of all $(\lambda q \rightarrow T(s, q))$ generate a monoid, called the transition monoid, homomorphic to the monoid of string catenation.

The external behaviour B is defined

$B \in (Q \times \Sigma^* \rightarrow \Sigma^*)$
$B(q, \epsilon) = F(q)$,
$B(q, sS) = F(q)B(\delta(q, s), S)$.

For each start state q, B_q maps input strings to output strings. This definition is likewise an algorithm. We introduce a null symbol ϵ, such that $\epsilon S = S$ for all $S \in \Sigma^*$

The underlying edge- and node-weighted graph of the machine has links $\{(q, s, \delta(q, s)) | q \in Q, s \in \Sigma\}$ and node weights defined by F. This graph can be used to define the state machine.

Some variations of the state machine indicate a stop state. The machine induces a partial function from strings to strings. Only those strings that cause the machine to terminate on a stop state (having not passed through one earlier) are accepted as input. If the state machine is represented by the underlying weighted graph, there is no reason for each symbol to be accepted by each state, and the natural interpretation is as a partial function.

Since the output depends only on the state, the above machine is a Moore machine. For a Mealy machine we might have $F \in (Q \times Q \times \Sigma \to \Sigma)$, so that given the transition and the input, we determine the output, or $Q \times \Sigma \to \Sigma$ on the presumption that the state and the input determines the transition. Better, perhaps, a representation $(\Sigma, Q, L, s, d, \delta, F)$ in which (L, s, d) is a graph represented by otherwise undefined links, L, and the source $s \in L \to Q$ and destination $d \in L \to Q$ functions.

The concept of a non-deterministic state machine is expressed by having a transition relation, instead of a transition function. The corresponding graph simply has multiple links with the same weight from a given node. A relation can be expressed as a function that returns a set. A non-deterministic machine may be seen to output a collection of sequences for a given input sequence.

In many cases (for example, finite-state machines) we can replace a non-deterministic machine by a deterministic machine whose states are sets of states from the original machine. Thus, non-determinism does not always expand the behavioural repertoire.

Whatever the exact structure of the state machine constructed in this concrete manner, it becomes a datatype that can be used within a computation. Because of the clean mathematical nature we have many options for proving properties, showing that the datatype satisfies the axioms in a specification. Because of the concrete nature of the definition, it is possible to implement this directly on a digital computer.

Notion 48: Several Types of Networks

Many successful datatypes are more points of view than specific structures. A clear case is the graph[21] datatype. There are many different definitions that contradict. One or other of these apply to just about anything. In one incarnation, a graph is a set of ordered pairs, but so is a relation, so is a function, so is a linear transform. In differential calculus, the derivative is a graph, if you want to see it that way.

A graph $G = (N, E)$ is a set N of nodes, and a set E of edges. An edge is an ordered pair of nodes. Thus, $E \subseteq N \times N$ is a relation on the set N. A relation should mention the domain and codomain. So a relation is (D, C, E), where $E \subseteq D \times C$. Now we form $G = (D \cup C, E)$, containing most of the same information. A bipartite graph partitions $N = S \cup D$, so that all edges go from S to D. Thus, $G = (S, D, E)$, is a relation.

All functions have a straightforward existence as a graph. The function $f(x) = x^2$ is a graph with a self-loop on 0 and on 1, an edge from 2 to 4, 3 to 9, and so on. If the domain of f is $\mathbb{R}$, then there is an uncountable infinity of edges, but the structure still conforms to the definition of a graph.

A symmetric graph has edge (b, a) for each (a, b) it has. A symmetric graph is a symmetric relation. One approach to graph theory states that an edge is an unordered pair, $\{a, b\}$. As a datatype this removes the chance of accidentally leaving out (b, a). The unordered pair is more primitive than the ordered in orthodox mathematics. But on a digital computer, a sequence is more primitive than a set.

If we draw a network on paper, with lines and points, then it is easy and natural to have multiple lines between two points. But if we have a *set* of edges, then placing the edge in twice, be it an ordered or unordered pair, is the same as placing it in once. We could use a multi-set of edges, or we could reverse our point of view. A network is a tuple $G = (N, E, s, t)$, where $s, t : E \to N$ are the source and target functions showing where an edge begins and where it ends.

---

[21]Graph nomenclature has no universal standard; learn the concept not the name.

A graph might be $G = (V, n)$, where $n(v)$ is the set of neighbours of v, the nodes that can be reached in one step from v. A large unknown graph can be searched using this model. It is very local in nature.

A graph with a multi-set of edges might also be $G = (N, E, c)$ where $c : E \to$ **N**, showing the number of times each edge occurs. But why stop at **N**? A general edge-weighted graph is $G = (N, E, w, W)$, where $w : E \to W$, and W is the set of weights. If $W = \{0, 1\}$ we have an edge predicate, which tells us if the edge is in the graph, or not. The weight function w is a *decoration*. We can also decorate the nodes of a graph.

Our choice of definition affects the nature of the algorithms available. Two common definitions in digital computing are the connection matrix and the neighbour function.

The connection matrix is good for relatively small, and dense, graphs, possibly with numeric edge weights. m_{ij} is 0 or 1 depending on whether $(i, j) \in E$. From a graph G we can derive the 2-edge graph in which two nodes are connected if there is a path of length 2 connecting them in G. This is taking $f^2(x) = f(f(x))$ if G is a function. Usefully, the connection matrix for the 2-edge graph is m^2. That is, normal matrix multiplication has significance in graph theory. Its significance does not end with this result. A similar matter arises with Markov processes, partly because it can easily be represented as a weighted graph.

But often we do not have global information. Solving the cabbage-goose-wolf puzzle, we expand the graph locally, *discovering* the connections. Where can we go from here? The neighbour function tells us. The two edge graph can be found by compounding this function. The the use of this format is most indicated for sparse or infinite graphs.

There are special cases such as acyclic graphs (at most one way to go from A to B), and trees (exactly one way to go). There is even a theory of *rational graphs* in which an edge may connect three, four or more nodes. The edge-set is a set of subsets of the node-set.

But, we have exhausted ourselves not the graph datatypes.

Notion 49: Informal Petri Nets

The basic petri net is a weighted directed graph, similar to a state machine graph, but with multiple points of activation (called tokens or threads). Each edge represent an action. It is a unified way of looking at a collection of state machines operating in parallel. A special case is two completely separate finite-state machines, in which case the threads are in separate territories.

The activation state of a single state machine is a single node. The activation state of a petri net is a collection of nodes. We can define a graph on collections of nodes. A link exists if the first collection of nodes on the petri net can be followed by the second. Thus, a finite petri net does not invoke behaviour distinct from a finite-state machine, but it does describe it differently, in a manner natural for multi-threaded code.

If two edges are labelled with the same action, then for the edge to be crossed, both must be crossed at the same time. In this way, by bundling together edges that share the same label, each transition can be viewed as having an input set, and an output set. The input and output sets might be different sizes, multiple edges going into the same node. But, the number of threads remains the same. However, if we introduce a single node with an indefinite number of threads, then we can direct links to or out from this node to produce the effect that each transition has an input and output set that can be different sizes.

A bundle of edges with some connections into or out of the extra node can be represented by a bar, with a number of edges coming in, and a possibly different number coming out. The actual edges to the extra node are implicit. In this form, the petri net is a form of rational graph (in which a single edge may connect any number of nodes) using the barred edges as a single edge. The links from the nodes to the transition bar are called input links; the links from the transition bar to the nodes are called output links. The distribution of threads in the nodes is the state of the petri net. A transition with an empty output set is a way of eliminating threads, and a transition with an empty input set is a way of generating threads.

A petri net can be executed by —

1. establishing an initial marking,
2. choosing a set of eligible transitions,
3. firing a transition among the set of eligible ones,
4. going back to step 2 until no more transition is eligible.

A transition is said to be eligible if all its input nodes contain (at least) one thread. If it fires, one thread is removed from each input node and one thread is added to each output node.

Coloured nets are extended petri nets in which threads are differentiated by "Colours". Transition eligibility depends then on the availability of an appropriately coloured thread in all the input places of this transition. Similarly, the output of a transition is not just a thread but a specifically coloured thread. Replacing a node by a collection of nodes, one for each colour, we can represent coloured petri nets as a non-coloured petri net. This effectively makes for as many disjoint petri nets as there are colours; the connection between them is in the bundling of the edges. Coloured petri nets, however, are more concise, and potentially more intuitive than non-coloured petri nets.

The temporal extension to petri nets includes a delay on each transition and node. A thread waits for a while at each node. And when the transfer of threads to the output occurs, it occurs with further delays, assigned to the edges. Extending this again, the stochastic petri net has a random delay. The threads typically move according to a Markov process. The temporal and stochastic petri nets can model time in a multi threaded environment.

Some simple operations require a lot of edges. A thread reaches a specific node, resulting in resetting all the other threads back to a known state. This is what the reset switch does on a desktop machine. Since the thread must return to a known state regardless of which state it is in, there must be a link from every state to the known state. But other transitions must also be prevented. So an extra thread, the non-reset thread, must be required for all other transitions.

Petri nets are strongly related to Minksi neural nets.

Notion 50: Formal Turing Machine

There are many ways to formalise a Turing machine. We have a set of symbols. The cpu is a finite-state machine, equipped with a tape over the symbols. A tape over the symbols admits read, write, left, and right operations. Axiomatically, we need that left is the inverse of right and that read reads what write writes. We do this in Haskell style.

```
read   :: Tape -> Symbol
write  :: Tape -> Symbol -> Tape
left   :: Tape -> Tape
right  :: Tape -> Tape

right (left t)    == left (right t) == t
read (write t s)  == s
```

A Turing tape might be a line or a loop. The exact interaction of read, write, left and right can be complicated. A line of cells is defined by the axiom that (Tape,Symbol,left,read,right$write) is a stack datatype. This is easy if the tape is a pair of an array and an index, the operations should be clear.

The axioms admit unorthodox models; left adds 1 and right subtracts 1 modulo the number of symbols, from every, or just some, of the cells on the tape. By the time you return, the cell contains the right data again.

If the tape is a function,

```
write t s i = if i==0 then s else (T i)
read  t       = T 0
left  t   i = T (i-1)
right t   i = T (i+1)
```

If the tape is a pair of stacks,

```
write (l,r) i s = (put (pop l) s , r)
read  (l,r)     = pop l
left  (l,r)     = (pop l , put r (top l))
right (l,r)     = (put l (top r), pop r)
```

A triple (stack,symbol,stack) is more symmetric.

Notion 51: The Table-Driven State Machine

The formal definition of the state machine (see page 103) involves a number of structures, including tuples and functions. In programming a tuple will typically become a record and a function either a function or an array. In particular, the formal definition revolves around $\delta(s, q)$, which gives the next state given the input symbol and the current state. If we number the symbols and states from 0, then we can simply have a two-dimensional array.

For a Moore machine,

```
char *name[stateCount] = {"a-state","another-state" ... };
char symbol[symbolCount] = "abcdefg ... ";

int delta[stateCount][symbolCount] =
    {
      {1,2,3,4},
      { ...   },
        ...
    };

int f[stateCount] = { ... };
```

So, `delta[s][c]` is the next state if the symbol c is entered when the machine is in state s. And, `f[s]` is the symbol to output from state s.

For a Mealy machine, f is a 2D array indexed by state and symbol.

```
int f[stateCount][symbolCount] = { ... };
```

where `f[s][c]` is the symbol to output if the symbol c is entered when the machine is in state s. The alternative of using (state,state) pairs would mean that the output would be associated with the source and destination states, rather than the actual link being traverse, of which there may be more than one between two states.

Notion 52: Factors of Graphs

We often ignore information. We have integers, we classify them as even or odd, and treat "even" and "odd" as things. Even plus even is even, odd plus even is odd. We justify this by saying that the other information was not required; *any* even integer plus any other even integer is some even integer.

This is *factoring*. A factoring is a partition (classification) whose classes act as individuals. We do not attempt to cover this deep and widely applicable concept directly, but simply illustrates the idea in the context of graph theory.

This undirected graph has the node set $\{1, 2, 3, 4, 5, 6\}$ and edge set $\{\{1,2\}, \{2,4\}, \{2,3\}, \{3,5\}, \{4,5\}, \{5,6\}\}$.

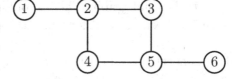

We label the nodes, $1 \rightarrow a$, $2 \rightarrow b$, $3 \rightarrow c$, $4 \rightarrow d$, $5 \rightarrow c$, $6 \rightarrow e$. Now we have two nodes labelled c.

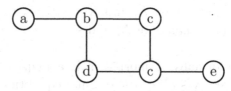

We draw a box around nodes labelled c, being careful not to cross any edges not connected to a c node.

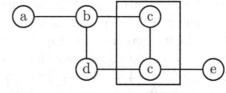

We then erase the information that is inside the box, and write in the label c just once.

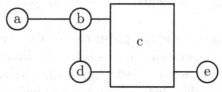

Now we shrink the box down to the size of a node, and we have a graph with edge set $\{a,b,c,d,e\}$ This is one less node than we started with.

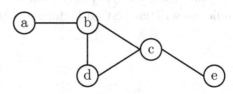

In symbols, the original graph is {{1,2}, {2,3}, {2,4}, {4,5}, {3,5}, {5,6}}. The partition used is {{1}, {2}, {3,5}, {4}, {6}}. Class {1} is linked to {2}, because the edge (1,2) is in the original graph. Class {2} is linked to {3,5} because the edge (2,3) is in the original, and {3,5} is linked to {6} because of the edge (5,6). Taking a deep breath, we express the new graph exactly,

{{{1},{2}},{{2},{3,5}},{{2},{4}},{{4},{3,5}},{{3,5},6}}

Then using the new names a={1}, b={2}, c={3,5}, d={4}, e={6}

{{a,b},{b,c},{b,d},{d,c},{c,e}}

which is the final graph. There should also be a self-loop {c,c} included, which has been ignored for the sake of diagrammatic clarity.

More generally, we partition the nodes N, of a graph $G = (N, E)$ into sets N_1 .. N_k, then treat $\{N_1, .., N_k\}$ as a new node-set. There is an edge between N_i and N_j exactly when there is an edge (in E) between *some element* of N_i and some element of N_k.

Informally, a morphism is a map from one structure to another that preserves all of the original equalities, possibly adding more. The level sets of a morphism factor the original structure. In graph theory, any partition will do, but this is unusual. Positive, negative and neutral factor the integers using multiplication, but not addition. Positive times negative is negative, negative times negative is positive, and so on. The shadow of $3 \times -4 = -12$ is $\square \times -\square = -\square$. But, positive plus positive might be neutral, negative, or positive.

Factors and morphisms apply very broadly. They are implicit in many of the operations in this book. An implementation of an abstract datatype is implicitly a factoring of the virtual machine, generating a morphism into the abstract type. Just like unification reduction, a whole book could be written just on factoring. Many have been.

Notion 53: Products of Graphs

The reverse of finding factors of an integer is finding products of integers. Similarly, the reverse of finding factors of a graph (see page 111) is finding products of graphs. Often, this means constructing a graph whose node-set is the Cartesian product (set of ordered pairs) of the node-sets from the original graphs.

Given two graphs such as {{a,b}} and {{1,2},{2,3}},

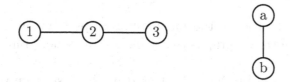

we construct the Cartesian product of the node-sets,

{{1,a},{2,a},{3,a},{1,b},{2,b},{3,b}}

and use it as the node set for a new graph, in which nodes are linked if they are linked in exactly one of the component graphs.

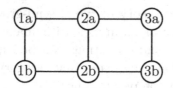

The new nodes are pairs of old nodes, where (a_1, x) is linked to (b_1, x) for all links (a_1, b_1) in the first component graph. And likewise on the second component.

Curiously, factoring using the partition {{1a,1b}, {2a,2b}, {3a,3b}}, we obtain the original graph on {1,2,3}. And factoring using {{1a,2a,3a}, {1b,2b,3b}}, we obtain the original graph on {a,b}. Further, each class in the first partition generates a subgraph that is identical to the graph on {a,b} and vice versa.

This strong record of the structure of the components is not shared by all graph products. Another product is formed by linking nodes when the original graphs agree. The node (a_1, b_1) is linked to (a_2, b_2), if (a_1, a_2) is in the first graph, and (b_1, b_2) is in the second.

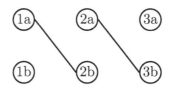

The same partitions produce the same factor graphs, but in this case the classes do not form subgraphs that look like the other graph.

The special property of products illustrated by the first example earns it the title *direct* product. The concept is more broadly applied. There are many ways to form a set of ordered pairs from two given sets. As a set of ordered pairs, any complete onto function has the property that projection back to the original sets is onto. But, only one set of ordered pairs has the property that the inverse image of the elements of one set looks like the other. This is called the direct product of two sets. It is the familiar Cartesian product.

Category theory is the theory of typed semi-groups. In programming terms, it is the theory of datatypes with maps between them. Any collection of datatypes and operations can be expressed as a category. And as a result some have suggested that category theory should be the fundamental model for the programmer.

In category theory, let $G_1 = (N_1, E_1)$ and $G_2 = (N_2, E_2)$ be graphs. Then $G_3 = (N_3, E_3)$ is a direct product of G_1 and G_2 if $N_3 = N_1 \times N_2$ and there are two orthogonal factorings, P_1 and P_2, with classes identical to G_2 and G_1, respectively, and such that $P_1(G_3) = G_1$ and $P_2(G_3) = G_2$. The direct product is unique up to isomorphism. That is, we can change the names on the nodes, but the structure is uniquely determined. In this way, we can refer to *the* direct product, rather than just *a* direct product.

Notion 54: Constructive Numerics

To paraphrase Einstein[22] the difference between the numeric datatypes available on a computer and the classical real numbers is so great as to be grotesque. Classical real numbers are not correct as a model of computer arithmetic. The classical real numbers go one step too far in the simplification of numerical algebra.

To absorb this pragmatic point we must take a deep breath and wade into some of the gory details. Beginning with $\{0\}$, the pure numbers are formed by closure. To close a set is to expand it so that an operation can be applied to all elements. The naturals are not closed under subtraction, but the integers are. Sometimes specific elements are ignored. The rationals are not closed under division by zero.

The closure of $\{0\}$ under increment, is $\mathbb{N}$. Closing $\mathbb{N}$ under subtraction obtains $\mathbb{Z}$ which when closed under non-zero division creates $\mathbb{Q}$. Closing $\mathbb{Q}$ under Cauchy limits obtains $\mathbb{R}$, and $\mathbb{R}$ closed under solution of quadratic equations is $\mathbb{C}$. The construction of $\mathbb{Z}$, $\mathbb{Q}$ and $\mathbb{C}$ is fairly straightforward (see page 223). $\mathbb{N}$ and $\mathbb{R}$ are an act of numerical faith.[23] But $\mathbb{N}$ is an empirically justified axiom of digital technology, $\mathbb{R}$ is not.

$$0 = \{\}$$
$$\mathbb{N} = \{0\} \cup \{n \cup \{n\} | n \in \mathbb{N}\}$$
$$\mathbb{Z} = \{\{(a,b) \in \mathbb{N} \times \mathbb{N} | a + d = b + c\} | (b,c) \in \mathbb{N} \times \mathbb{N}\}$$
$$\mathbb{Q} = \{\{(a,b) \in \mathbb{Z} \times \mathbb{Z} | ad = bc\} | (b,c) \in \mathbb{Z} \times \mathbb{Z}\}$$
$$\mathbb{C} = \mathbb{R} \times \mathbb{R}$$

Informally, $\mathbb{N}$ is $\{\{\}, \{\{\}\}, \{\{\}, \{\{\}\}\}, \cdots\}$. With, $n = \{0, 1, 2, 3, \cdots, n-1\}$, and $n + 1 = n \cup \{n\}$. $\mathbb{N}$ is the result of an infinite loop augmenting it by one integer each time. More formally, the above gives an equation that it satisfied by an infinite number of sets, but $\mathbb{N}$ is defined as the intersection of all these sets. An intersection over any number of sets is well defined.

The real problem is the reals. $\mathbb{R}$ is a partition of the set of rational Cauchy sequences. Informally, Cauchy sequences look as though they

---

[22]Responding to newspaper reports about himself.
[23]The existence of 0 is pure cosmogony.

should have a limit. That is, at any accuracy they eventually stop moving away from where they were.

$$\{f_i \in \mathsf{N} \to \mathbb{Q} | \forall \epsilon \in \mathbb{Q}^+ : \exists j \in \mathsf{N} : \forall i \in \mathsf{N} : i \geq j \Rightarrow |f_i - f_j| \leq \epsilon\}$$

Abstractly, this works, unfortunately, it requires us to construct $\mathsf{N} \to \mathbb{Q}$, the set of all rational valued functions on the natural numbers. It is not possible with a digital computer.

An alternative is the set of Dedekind cuts. A Dedekind cut is a partition of the reals into disjoint U and L, such that any element in U is strictly greater than any element in L. In essence it says that a non-rational real number is a partition of the rationals into all those rationals greater than the value we want, and all those rationals less than the value we want.

We can work with the sequence definition of reals by defining, for example, addition of a and b as the sequence $a_i + b_i$.

We can work with Dedekind cuts in a similar manner,
$$(L_1, U_1) + (L_2, U_2) = (\{x + y | x \in L_1, y \in L_2\}, \{x + y | x \in U_1, y \in U_2\})$$

But the definition of Dedekind cuts does not give any way of building them up inductively and being sure that we have got them all.

Even though Cauchy sequences and Dedekind cuts did not solve the problem, there might be another method that does. But the real problem is that the reals are uncountable. Any digital datatype can be expressed as a finite sequence of bytes, a language. Any implementation of Cauchy sequences would at best result in *Cauchy sequences describable in this language*, which is different from the set of Cauchy sequences, because it is countable. In practice, Dedekind cuts lead us to process algebraic expressions in a digital language, also countable.

While the reals have various nice algebraic properties, they do not exist as an entity within the computing arena. Many sophisticated datatypes and algorithms exist because of attempts to compensate for this. Always we are lead either to massive use of resources, or to software that is certain to fail for some calculations.

Notion 55: Prime Programs

A person computing with pencil and paper will look at the paper and make a decision based on what is there, then take an action with the pencil to change the state of the paper. This will be repeated many times until the required answer is determined. Before *the length of the hypotenuse* is computed, no decision may be made that depends on it. In this way, the collection of decisions available depends on what is written on the paper.

Given the collection of sheets of paper scribbled on in all possible ways, a person computing defines an implicit network. For each piece of paper there are some conditions to test, and the new paper to get when the condition is true. If none of the conditions are true, then the computation terminates. If more than one is true we make a non-deterministic choice.

Similarly, a general program is a network of points of execution linked by guarded commands. Apart from a source and destination point, each guarded command also includes a condition to test and an action to perform.

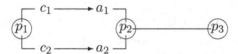

p1:if(C1) {A1; goto p2;} if(C2) {A2; goto p2;} p2:{A3; goto p3;} p3:

Given a specific general program, we label the nodes. Using the labels as the destination for gotos, we can systematically produce a standard linear text-based program that directly implements the flow of control in the general program. Each link is transliterated to code of the form `p: if(c){a; goto q;}`, the order of which is unimportant.

Without gotos, a piece of code has two links, to the code above and below. Extra control blocks, such as a while loop, must be included in the language. Each has exactly two terminals and so can replace a single link in the network. This control building mechanism conforms to the natural structure of a text program.

The replacement of one link by a compound network with two terminals corresponds to filling in the blanks in a control block syntax such as while A do B. Given a finite collection of block primitive, writing a block equivalent to a network is an exercise in network decomposition. This can be difficult, or impossible.

Some blocks cannot be composed from other blocks. Without a conditional statement in the language, it is impossible to write one exactly. These programs are called *prime programs*. They cannot be built up from others and are obvious candidates for inclusion in a language as inbuilt control blocks. With all the prime programs available as inbuilt control structures, sequential code with no labels could produce any network of code.

The primality of a program is not assigned, it is a derived property. It is a fundamental characteristic of the program, it either is, or is not prime. There is a non-trivial result that there are an infinite number of prime programs. So no finite set of blocks can be used to build up all program control structures. That is, no block-structured programming language can generate all control flows.

Code duplication means a lack of robustness in software. There is no mechanism to ensure that intentionally duplicate parts remain identical. The two might be modified differently. This duplication can be avoided by the use of control flow variables, but these make the code more obscure, producing lack of reasonableness. However, in practice, either code duplication or flow variables must be used in software written in block structured languages.

A classic example of a limitation is made clear when we need to output terms with commas between then as in $(1, 2, 3, 4)$. We need one more number than comma.

```
for(i=0,i<n;i++) {print(a[i]);put(',');} print(a[n]);
```

```
for(i=0,i<n;i++) {print(a[i]);if(i+1<n) put(',');}
```

Notion 56: Showing that Factorial Works

The Haskell program

```
f n = if n==0 then 1 else n * (f (n-1))
```

is a transliteration of the definition $0!=1$, $n!=n*(n-1)!$ of factorial. So, the axioms $(f\ 0)=1$ and $(f\ n)=n*(f(n-1))$ hold. It is clear that any value returned from $(f\ n)$ must be the correct value of $n!$. We seem to have shown that the code is correct.

But this Haskell program

```
f n = if n==0 then 1 else (f(n+1))/(n+1)
```

also satisfies the axioms. And this program is clearly not going to terminate for positive n.

Logical adherence to the definitive axioms is *partial correctness*. To show that a program is a correct implementation of a function defined by axioms, partial correctness is necessary, but not sufficient. We also need to show that any execution of the code on valid input will eventually halt. A partially correct program that is also sure to terminate on valid input is *fully correct*, or simply, *correct*. Correctness is usually proved by showing that the correct value is returned *if the code halts*, and separately showing that the code will halt.

A useful technique for showing that code will halt is finding a positive integer characteristic of the digital data that is sure to reduce.

For a non-negative initial value, the arguments to the first program proceed as n, n-1, n-2, eventually reaching 0, where the program will halt. More cautiously, if $n > 0$, then n will strictly reduce to $n - 1$ at each call, but $n - 1 \geq 0$, so n is never negative. Any strictly reducing integer is eventually not positive, thus n is eventually 0. By inspection, the code terminates on 0. Therefore the code eventually halts for any non-negative input. A quick check shows that it will not halt for negative input.

In the second program we get n, n+1 ..., which clearly does not reach
0. Notice, for n>36, 36-n will reduce to 0. But, since 36-n=0 is not a
termination condition, this is not a correctness proof.

Another Haskell program is

```
f x n = if n==0 then x else f (n*x) (n-1)
```

By looking at the value of n we know the code will halt. But how do we
know the code is correct? Logical invariants. An invariant is an assertion
that is true after each step, if it is true before. In this case, x*(n!)=m!.
We apply the f to positive n. The next call will be f (n*x) (n-1), and
if x*(n!)=m! is true for this call, then (n*x)*(n-1)!=x*n!=m! is true
for the next. Initially we call f 1 m, and so initially 1*(m!)=m!. The
invariant is true for the first call, and if it is true for any call it is true
for the next. Thus, it is true when the code eventually halts with n==0,
at which point x = x*1 = x*(n!) = m!.

Proving a program is a form of testing and vice versa. Substituting 3
for n and doing a manual code walk is a proof that $f(3)$ is correct. But,
it is completely impossible to check all valid values for n. Our increased
confidence from spot checks can only come from have at least a little
knowledge of the code logic. Finding an assertion that substituted into
the code proves to be invariant, is a generic extension of testing $f(3)$.
Substituting the code itself into an inductive proof technique is like a
code walk, but more powerful. A code walk is often done with n *is some
positive number*. The inductive proof just covers more cases.

Trying 99, 100 and 101 in *for i=1 to about 100* is a legitimate proof *if
you know the basic code structure is correct*. A couple of test cases legiti-
mately show correctness, when coupled with some code logic. Informally
you probably have invariants and reducing elements in mind when you
convince yourself that a loop will work. If not, you are writing random
code, not programming.

Although code walking can be useful for non-technical code, such as
various business applications, it can be completely misleading when it
comes to technical code. Some proving is always required. It is more
important that this proof be rigorous than greatly detailed or complete.

Notion 2: Proving Bubble-Sort

However it is cast, the code for factorial (see page 119) is really a for-loop. We know beforehand exactly how long the loop will run because the counter counts down to 0, one each iteration. So it is very clear that the code will terminate.

Consider the following code in C:

```
going = 1;
while(going)
{
  going=0;
  for(i=0;i<n-1;i++)
    if(a[i]>a[i+1]){going=1; t=a[i+1]; a[i+1]=a[i]; a[i]=t;}
}
```

How many times does the loop run? We do not know. It depends on the nature of the data a[i]. It is unclear when or even if it will terminate.

The termination condition is obtained from the code logic. The flag going is cleared and only reset if the inner loop conditional body is run. So the flag remains 0 exactly when $a[i] \leq a[i+1]$ for all i in $[0..n-2]$.

Informally stated, $a[0] \leq a[1] \leq a[2] \leq \cdots \leq a[n-1]$

From this clearly $i \leq j \Rightarrow a[i] \leq a[j]$, which is a formal statement that the list is sorted. Thus, *if the loop terminates*, then the list is sorted. But, to show that this is a correct sorting routine, we still need to show that the code will terminate, and that when it does the collection of numbers in a[ ] is the same as the ones we started with.[24]

Let $\epsilon(x) = \begin{cases} 1 & : & 0 < x \\ 0 & : & x \leq 0 \end{cases}$ and $c = \sum_{j=0}^{n-1}\sum_{i=0}^{n-1} \epsilon(i-j)\epsilon(a[j] - a[i])$

So, c is the number of (i, j) for which $(a[i], a[j])$ is in the wrong order: that is, the number of violations of the formal sortedness condition.

---

[24]Otherwise `"for(i=0;i<n;i++) a[i]=i;"` would be a linear sorting routine.

In C notation,

```
c=0; for(j=0;j<n;j++) for(i=0;i<n;i++) c+=a[j]>a[i];
```

Obviously, c is a non-negative integer. The body of the inner loop of the sorting routine is `if(a[i]>a[i+1]) {swap(a[i],a[i+1])}`, thus $[\cdots, w, x, y, z, \cdots]$ becomes $[\cdots, w, y, x, z, \cdots]$ exactly when the pair (x,y) was out of order.

The relative order of all other terms with respect to x and y is unchanged. We could indulge in some fancy footwork with the indices, but the conclusion is clearly that the count of violations has reduced by exactly 1. The count was initially positive, always non-negative and if there are any violations then the body of the conditional will run at least once. This code will eventually halt.

The number $c' = \sum_{i=0}^{n} \epsilon(a[i] - a[i+1])$ of local violations is not so useful. In the list [3,4,1,3], swapping the middle elements to get [3,1,4,3] actually increases the number of local violations. But the number of local variations must *eventually* go to 0, even though it may go up and down before reaching that point.

Intuitively, since we are swapping the entries, it is apparent that the number of occurrences of each value in the array is unaffected.

More technically, define
$$m(x) = \sum_{i=0}^{n} \epsilon(a[i] - x)$$

Examination of the body of the conditional shows that it can never affect the value of $m(x)$.

Can we *systematically* determine correctness of every program? No. No more than we can solve all of life's problems. But, in practice, while writing repetitive code reasonably the proof of correctness can be achieved.

The selection of an invariant should be an automatic part of program design, and included in the annotation for any loop that is not entirely trivial.

Notion 57: Reasoning About Code

Naive code reasoning means trying to intuit code semantics by inspection. It is no more sensible than trying to grab the solution to $x^3 + 4x^2 + 3 = 0$ out of thin air. Instead, we should recognise that code equations can be solved for code semantics, using manipulations analogous to solving polynomial equations. The semantics of code is the mapping it induces from the initial machine state to final machine state.

We solve integer equations, $x + 3x = 8$, collect terms, $4x = 8$, divide by 4 on both sides, $x = 4$. Solved.

We can solve the *functional* equation $f(x+y) = f(x)f(y)$. The function f is the variable whose value is to be determined. Now, $f(1x) = f(x)^1$ and $f((n+1)x) = f(nx+x) = f(nx)f(x)$. From this $f(nx) = f(x)^n$ or equivalently $f(x/m) = f(x)^{1/m}$. So, for rational $\frac{n}{m}$, $f(\frac{n}{m}) = f(1)^{\frac{n}{m}}$. From this, and assuming continuity, we have $f(x) = b^x$ is a solution for an arbitrary choice of b.

An equation is a logical constraint. We could use others, such as $x^2 > 3$. A specification is a set of axioms for the requested code. We wish to find at least one code fragment realising these axioms. Finding the entire set of solutions might help optimise speed, space, or understanding. Writing good code is a cross between doing algebra and word puzzles and has much in common with poetry.

The semantics of a code fragment S is a transformation $F_S(X)$ on the machine state. A specification is an equation to solve for S. For example, given $F_S(a, b) \rightarrow (b, a)$, solve for S. Experience tells us that {t=x; x=y; y=t} is a solution. However, we introduced a new variable t, so this fragment actually has $F_S(a, b, c) \rightarrow (b, a, a)$. Does it matter? Typically not, it is usual to allow auxiliary variables in code fragments (although occasionally not in embedded code). But this is not *strictly* a solution. The original equation *is* solvable, for example, by the code fragment: {a=a-b; b=a+b; a=b-a}. However, to allow auxiliary variables we can specify $F_S(a, b, c) = (b, a, x)$.

We may state this as a relationship between logical conditions on the variables before and after the code. Subject to a=x and b=y being true immediately before, we require a=y and b=x to be true immediately after. A specification states the desired post-condition, given that certain pre-conditions may be assumed.

For example, let x be a byte, taking on values from 0 to 255. We want to check whether x is 2 less than the value stored in a multibyte variable y. We try x+2<y, but if x was 255 and y was 257, this computes the wrong result, since $x + 2$ would be 1. But the above code works perfectly well if we have reason to know that $x < 254$.

For example in a loop: `for(i=1;i+2<max%255;i++) body;`

So under the pre-condition $x < 254$ the code fragment `t=(x+2<y)` sets `t` to the truth value of the assertion that $x + 2 < y$. But without this pre-condition we might change the test to be `for(i=1;i<max-2;i++) body;` which works as long as $max \geq 2$.

In some design methodologies this is called the *contract* approach. But the present author, having been involved in the use of a number of legal contracts, does not feel that this term invokes the level of rigour required. And the use of the idea predates the use of this terminology. So I will not mention it again.

All code has some pre-condition for the desired post-condition, even if it is a statement such as *the compiler is working*. In practice, when debugging, keep in mind that the compiler might be wrong, but remember that the programmer being wrong is a hundred times more likely. We typically assume machine functionality and just state that a piece of code that produces the post-condition no matter what the (legal) state of the variables is, has a pre-condition *true* for the desired post-condition.

The same code fragment may establish different post-conditions given different pre-conditions. It is not the post-condition that the code fragment establishes, but the connection between the pre-condition and the post condition. This is the equation that we solve (implicitly or explicitly) when we write a program.

Notion 3: Deriving Some Code

A Boolean-valued function is a predicate.
In C code, an integer-valued function.

Given a specific predicate,

$$P(n) = \left(\sum_{i=1}^{n} i = \frac{n(n+1)}{2} \right)$$

how we can write a C code implementation?

We could write a summation routine, and compute directly,

```
int P(int n){return sum(1,n)==(n*(n+1)/2);}
```

Instead, look for a property that to use to simplify the code.

Suppose we know the value of `P(n)`, can we we deduce `P(n+1)`?

Looking at the predicate body we see that

```
      P(n+1)
  =   {sum(1,n+1)   ==  (n+1)(n+2)/2        }
  =   {sum(1,n) + (n+1) ==  (n+1)(n+2)/2 }
  =   {sum(1,n)  ==  (n+1)(n+2)/2 - (n+1) }
  =   {sum(1,n)  ==  (n+1)(n+2)/2-2(n+1)/2}
  =   {sum(1,n)  ==  [(n+1)(n+2)-2(n+1)]/2}
  =   {sum(1,n)  ==  [(n+1)(n+2-2)]/2      }
  =   {sum(1,n)  ==  [(n+1)n]/2            }
  =   {sum(1,n)  ==  n(n+1)/2              }
  =   P(n)
```

We have shown that `P(n+1)=P(n)` for any integer n, which means that P is a constant function. By inspection, $P(1) = 1$ so $P(n) = 1$ for all integer n.

Thus, the C code is   `int P(int n){ return 1; }`

Translating this into a mathematical theorem we have shown that

$$\forall n \in \mathbf{Z} : \sum_{i=0}^{n} i = \frac{n(n+1)}{2}$$

To illustrate, try this out on a specific case:

```
     sum(i= 1 to -3) i
==  sum(i= 1 to -2) i - (-2)
==  sum(i= 1 to -1) i - (-2) - (-1)
==  sum(i= 1 to  0) i - (-2) - (-1) - 0
==  sum(i= 1 to  1) i - (-2) - (-1) - 0 - 1
==  1 + 2 + 1 - 1
==  3
==  (-3)((-3)+1)/2
```

While deriving this code (or proving the theorem, it's the same thing) we made implicit use of a property of integer functions. If P is an integer function and for each integer n, P(n+1)=P(n) then P is a constant function.

Like Euclid's parallel postulate (at least in Playfair's restatement), this feels obviously true, and surely should be provable. But, it is an axiom, not a theorem, in studies of integer functions.

It is *the Principle of Mathematical Induction.*

Often it is stated differently.

If P is an integer function, and for each integer $n \geq m$, $P(n+1) = P(n)$, then for each integer $n \geq m$, $P(n) = P(m)$.

If P is a property (Boolean function) of integers, and P(0) is true, and $P(n) \Rightarrow P(n+1)$, then $P(n)$ is true for all non-negative integers n.

If P(0) is true, and given $P(0)$, $P(1)$, ... $P(n)$, we can prove $P(n+1)$, then $P(n)$ is true for all non-negative integers n.

This simple idea forms the core of large quantities of rigorous work in mathematics and computing.

Notion 58: Logical Conditions

Stronger and weaker conditions: A condition C1 is stronger than a condition C2 if C1 being true forces C2 to also be true, but, C2 does not force C1 to be true. For example, $x > 0$ is stronger than $x > -1$ since if $x > 0$ then x must be > -1 as well. But if $x > -1$ it is still possible that x is not > 0, for example, if $x = -1$. If C1 is stronger than C2, then we say that C2 is weaker than C1.

Pre- and post- conditions: A pre-condition is a condition that is true just before the execution of a command. A post-condition, given the pre-condition, is a condition that is true just after the command has executed. For an integer variable x, a post-condition of $x = x * x$ is $x \geq 0$, since this requires no further pre-conditions, we say that it is a post-condition with pre-condition **True**. But to establish $x > 4$, we need beforehand $x! = -2, -1, 0 ,1$ or 2. So, $|x| > 2$ is a pre-condition for the post-condition $x > 4$ of $x = x * x$. We say that $|x| > 2$ is a pre-condition for $x > 4$, the command being determined by context.

Sufficient pre-condition: In symbols we can say: $P \overset{S}{\Longrightarrow} Q$ and in words, P is a sufficient pre-condition for Q given the code fragment S. Defining a swapping routine $F_S(a, b, c) = (b, a, x)$, we could make the pre-condition $a = a_0, b = b_0, c = 23$. This is a pre-condition that allows S to establish the desired post-condition. It is *sufficient*, but it is more restrictive than we need.

Weakest pre-condition: The least restrictive pre condition required to establish a post-condition Q is called the *weakest pre-condition* for Q. It has the definitive property that it is implied by any other pre-condition for Q. For example, $x > 10$ is a pre-condition for $x > 1$, but it is rather strong, $x > 2$ is a weaker condition and is also a pre condition, for $x > 1$. If we look at all the pre-conditions for $x > 1$, we find that $|x| > 1$ is the weakest pre condition for $x > 1$. The concept of the weakest pre-condition is very important. It is the least condition that needs to be proved (or established by initialising code) in order for Q to be established after the command has executed.

Strongest post-condition: Look again at $x = x * x$. $x > -10$ is a post-condition, but it does not tell the full story. $x > -10$ is weaker than the post-condition $x > -5$, which is still not as strong as $x \geq 0$, which is the strongest post-condition for this command. The strongest post-condition we can establish depends on the pre-conditions we know. Given the strongest thing known to be true before the command, we can work out (in principle) the strongest thing true after the command. The strongest post-condition of the previous command must imply the weakest pre-condition for the current command. In correct code we have a chain: weakest pre-condition implies strongest-post condition, implies weakest pre-condition, and so on.

$$P \Rightarrow P_1 \overset{C_1}{\Longrightarrow} Q_1 \Rightarrow P_2 \overset{C_2}{\Longrightarrow} Q_2 \Rightarrow Q$$

For example,

```
[true]        if( x<-9 or x>9 ) x=0;     [|x|<10]
[|x|<11]      x = x*x+1;                  [0<x<102]
```

The first command has a post-condition $|x|<10$ whose weakest pre-condition is "true" (no extra conditions are needed). The pre-condition $|x|<10$ is sufficient (given $x = x * x$) to establish the post-condition $0<x<102$. The first command has a strongest post-condition that is stronger than the weakest pre condition for the post-condition of the second command.

A software specification S, implicitly or explicitly, gives pre P_s and post Q_s conditions for a code fragment C. The pre conditions are things the specification allows the programmer to assume. The post conditions are things the code must establish. To satisfy the specification demonstrably, the proven pre-condition P_c of the code must be weaker than P_s, and the post-condition Q_c must be stronger than Q_s.

$$P_s \Rightarrow P_c \overset{C}{\Longrightarrow} Q_c \Rightarrow Q_s$$

Notion 4: Random Program Proving

We have a bag containing some black marbles and some white marbles. And no other marbles. We randomly remove a pair of marbles. If they are the same colour then we place a black marble in the bag. If they are different colour then we place a white marble in the bag. This process can be expressed symbolically as follows:

$$[\text{ BB } \rightarrow \text{ B } ; \quad \text{ BW } \rightarrow \text{ W } ; \quad \text{ WW } \rightarrow \text{ B }]$$

Let w be the number of white marbles and b the number of black marbles. If w is even before one of these commands, then it will be even afterwards. The condition $even(w)$ is both a pre- and post-condition of all the commands. So it is an invariant of the body of the program. Similarly $odd(w)$. Thus, the parity of w is unchanged throughout the execution of the program. Each completed operation reduces the number of marbles by exactly one. The program halts when there are less than two marbles in the bag. So the program will eventually halt with one marble in the bag, and the parity of the white marbles unchanged. Thus, the bag will contain precisely one marble, which will be black or white, showing even or odd parity of the original number of white marbles.

Although rigorous enough for most purposes, this argument can be completed with more precise logic. In the case at hand, this is not required. But going through a simple example in detail can illustrate the process that is definitely required for more complicated cases in which the result is not intuitively clear. If at all possible, the more detailed logic should reflect an intuitive argument.

The command BB->B means $(w, b) \rightarrow (w, b-1)$ and has the guard $b>1$. A guard is a blocking pre-condition. That is, we are assured by the machine that the command will only run if the guard is true. Similarly, BW->W is $(w, b) \rightarrow (w, b-1)$ with the guard that $b>0, w>0$, and WW->B is $(w, b) \rightarrow (w-2, b+1)$, with the guard $w>1$.

Although physically distinct, BB->B and BW->W are just $(w, b) \rightarrow (w, b-1)$ with different guards $b>1$ and $b>0, w>0$. So, we could have replaced them with a single command with the disjunction of the guards.

The program obtained is

```
[
b>1       -> (w,b)=(w,b-1)    |
b>0,w>0 -> (w,b)=(w,b-1)    |
w>1       -> (w,b)=(w-2,b+1)
]
```

Inspection shows that the change in $w+b$ is always -1. However, all the guards require $w+b \geq 2$. Thus, as long as $w+b \geq 1$ is true before, it must be true after; it is an invariant of the program body, and thus an invariant of the entire program. Similarly, for $b \geq 0$ and $w \geq 0$. Now, if $w = 2m+p$ where $p = 0, 1$ beforehand, then the possible values after are $2m + p$ and $2(m-1) + p$ afterwards. Thus, the statements $\exists m : w = 2m + 0$ and $\exists m : w = 2m + 1$ are both invariants of the program. The termination condition is the negation of the conjunction of the guards. That is, $b \leq 1$ or $b \leq 0$ or $w \leq 0$ or $w \leq 1$, which reduces to $b \leq 0$ or $w \leq 0$. The post condition is the conjunction of the termination condition and the invariants. $w + b > 1$, $w > 0$, $b > 0$, $w = 2m + p$, ($b \leq 0$ or $w \leq 0$). With $w \geq 0$, $b \geq 0$, ($b \leq 0$ or $w \leq 0$), it is apparent that $(b, w) = (1, 0), (0, 1)$, and since $w = 2m+p = 0, 1$, we have $m = 0$, and $(b, w) = (1 - p, p)$. From which we conclude, the one remaining marble will be black if the parity of white is even, and white if odd.

The reasoning illustrated above can be used to give insight into the operation of a program, to find out what is going wrong and how to fix it. It can also be used to start with the required transformation from pre-condition to post-condition, the specification for a piece of code yet to be written, and determine what that code might be. But, just like baking a carrot-cake, you have to practice the technique, or you might not be able to eat the result.

You do not have to have a strong grasp of formal logics to be able to follow the style of reasoning. If you have a determination to think things through clearly you should be able to analyse your own code and code you get from others, according to this type of reasoning. In practice, checking pre- and post-conditions can save a lot of time and catch obscure bugs that are very hard to test for. This is a method for creating robust code quickly.

Chapter 4

Limitations on Exact Knowledge

In which we find that not every problem is solvable. And realise that one of the great advances during the twentieth century was the recognition of this fact in a formal setting, and various proofs that specific well-posed problems where not solvable.

Despite knowing that we would like to take these proved limitations on computers as an indication that a human is not like a computer, due to not suffering these limitations. We realise that the proofs are sufficiently general that they apply to any exact and provable method of determining answers. If we accept that the computer program might make errors, then we can produce approximations to the solution of these problems. This does not contradict the proof that knowledge is limited. And this acceptance of errors in reasoning is the way that human beings have evolved.

Any finite problem domain is computable, no matter how big. The limitations come when the domain involves the infinite. But keep in mind that counting 1,2,3 ... involves the infinite.

So errors or incompleteness in computation are inevitable, just as an aircraft must suffer drag, and a machine that does work must waste energy. But we must avoid the opposite error of accepting the level of bugs in commercial software as inevitable, we can do a lot better than we are currently doing.

Notion 59: Finite-State Limitations

Finite machines can solve a variety of useful problems (see page 22).
But there are some simple things that no finite machine can do.

Consider checking for correct bracketing on an expression that has only
brackets. "(()()(()))" is correct; "(()" is incorrect. Limit this to the
special case "(((...()))...)" of many "(" followed by many ")". The
future behaviour of the finite state machine is fully determined by its
current state. After feeding in n "(" we want the machine to recognise
balance after n ")". But since n is unlimited, this is an infinite number
of different behaviours. We eventually run out of states. As we feed
more "(" into the machine it will circumnavigate periodically a single
loop of states. No finite-state machine can solve this part of the correct
bracket problem, and so no finite state machine can solve the correct
bracket problem itself.

Generalising this, we have the pumping lemma.

Suppose we have a machine that classifies some set of strings. If that
class contains any string S, whose length is greater than the number
of states in the machine, then at some point in the processing of S a
state, x, must have been visited for the second time. Thus, there was
a substring B of S=ABC that drove the machine from state x around
a loop back to state x. Thus, if we repeated that substring, ABBBC,
the extra B's would not affect the state from which the string C was
processed. And so the category of ABC and ABBBBC would be the
same.

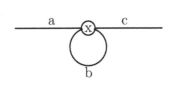

That is, for any string with length greater
than the number of states of the machine,
there is a substring that can be repeated
indefinitely without affecting the classification. This gives us a large class of problems
unsolvable on finite-state machines — anything in which a behaviour may be repeated
indefinitely, but not forever.

Finite-state machines can't count.

Notion 60: N log N sorting

It is clear that, on any given computer there is a non-trivial lower limit, as function of n, to the time taken to sort an array of n elements. But, just exactly what is the fastest way to sort a list on a given machine, and exactly how many machine cycles does it take? The problem looks daunting, but there must be an answer. It is possible to gain some insight by examining the problem rather than the computer.

A comparison-based sort is one in which the only material available for handling the data is a routine that answers the question of whether or not element x is less than element y. This is enough information to sort with, and is a common in practice.

Each comparison gives one of two answers, greater than, or not. The sorted list is one of the $n!$ possible permutations of the input list. It could be any of them. Thus, the program is making a decision between $n!$ items, using experiments with binary outcomes. It must make a number of experiments d, such that $2^d \geq n!$. That is $d \geq \log n + \log(n-1) \ldots$ The right-hand side is greater than $\log n + .. + \log n/2$ and so it is greater than $n/2 \log n/2$, which is order $n \log n$.

No algorithm sorts a list in the worst case under the order of $n \log n$ steps. With any fewer steps the program has too little information to select the answer, whatever other processing it might be doing.

This holds for comparison sort. Interpolation sort works in time proportional to n. But it not only looks at whether x is bigger than y, but also at how much bigger. There is some chance of sorting the elements by placing them on a number line. If the initial list is reasonably dense on the line, then it only takes about time n to do this.

A matrix multiplication algorithm must take at least n^2 steps. That is how many elements it has to read and write. But this is a very primitive test, applying it to sorting only states that it takes at least time n. The $n \log n$ limit for comparison sort is a very solid limit obtained from something other than counting i/o operations. It strongly reflects the nature of the processing required.

Notion 61: Russell's Paradox

Although not usually expressed that way, Russell's paradox is arguably one of the first recognitions of computational limits. Other work, such as that on the solvability of polynomials in terms of radicals, deserves to be seen in this light, and came earlier, and is much more complex and extensive, but Russell's paradox appears in the setting of the start of the modern and probably the only seriously capable attempt to grasp mathematics entire, and give the whole substructure a firm constructive foundation.

Goethe had just finished his work on set theory and logic, with the intention of basing all of mathematics on construction with sets. Out of this background we get the idea of equating 0 with the empty set {}, 1 with the set {{}}, 2 with {{},{{}}}, and in general, n with the set of natural numbers less than n. This idea was taken to the limit by Conway, who invented the surreal numbers, in which all the number systems are constructed in a completely regular manner from a few basic completion rules. Thus, if set theory could be shown to be logically rigorous then so could all the number systems, and in its turn the entire structure of mathematics.

In 1900, Hilbert set forth his famous 23 problems, in which he included the completion of a system for mechanically verifying all truths in Mathematics. It should be noted that Hilbert was not a believer in the mechanical approach to mathematics, but rather saw it as a way of, in principle, removing all troubles with the *definition* of what is truth, replacing it with a notion of mechanical proof. But, in practice he wanted to continue doing mathematics in the classical manner.

Although the recognition of Russell's paradox predates Hilbert's 23 problems, nonetheless it contains the core of the thought that Gödel used in his proof that Hilbert's request could not be filled. Curiously, Gödel also was a strong believer in absolute truth, while his reaction to Hilbert's request has left the definition of Truth problematic.

This is the context for Russell's result in a modern light.

We may in principle define a set by a logical condition to be satisfied by its members. If the condition is contradictory, then we simply have no members in the set. The set is empty, but we still have a set.

Now, consider the logical condition, *is a member of itself.* That is, we have a condition on sets $S \in S$. The idea of such a set is plausible. We have the set of all sets with less than two elements, but since there are more than two of these the set of such sets is not an element of itself. Alternatively, the set of all sets with more than one element has more than one element, and so is an element of itself.

Now, consider the set of all sets that are not members of themselves. Call it R, then $S \in R \equiv S \notin S$. The question of whether $R \in R$ is resolved by looking at $R \in R \equiv R \notin R$, which is a contradiction. Whether we put the set of all sets that are not members of themselves in itself, or not, we still have a logical contradiction. Thus, states Russell, set theory is logically flawed.

Speaking for myself, the way out is simple. There is no set that satisfies the definition of being the set of all sets that are not members of themselves. There is, in principle, a set for *the set of all sets that are not members of themselves, except for itself,* but not for Russell's condition. All this means is that not all logical assertions define an entity. Just like $x \in \mathbb{R}, x^2 = -1$ does not. If we go up a level and ask what is the set of all x that satisfy this condition, the answer is the empty set, and likewise, what is the set of all sets that satisfy Russell's condition, also the empty set.

However, the work related to this led to the general hesitation that is still felt today in the definition of sets that contain themselves.

The reason that Russell's paradox is important in computer science is that it contains essence of the proof of all the non-computability results, such as the Gödel theorem. What happens when you apply a definition to itself?

Notion 62: Pure Lambda Paradoxes

We know something of the mechanics of lambda calculus. We can reduce expressions, and model computation. But, what is the *meaning* of a lambda expression?

Some writers insist that there must be a meaning underlying the lambda expression, similar to the meaning of numeral 2 being the number 2, possibly made concrete by the coding to 2={0,1}={{}{{}}}. However, there is no need for any expression to have any meaning at all in the sense of being mapped to a semantic domain. What matters is that it is an expression reduction system that can be used to construct any computable structure up to isomorphism.[25]

A typical approach is to say a lambda expression L represents a function F. A function (in pure set theory) is a set of ordered pairs. But L may be applied to itself, so the first element of one of the ordered pairs in F would be F itself. This leads to an infinite descent not acceptable within orthodox set theory.[26]

We are left with the task of finding some domain of functions in which self-application is possible, in a finite depth.

Joseph Stoy in particular [11] goes to some length to produce such a domain. However, careful reading shows that he eventually replaces the function by a number that represents the function. Thus, the argument to the function is not the function itself, but effectively the code for the function. His mechanism for determining the value of a lambda expression amounts to an interpreter, expressed in arithmetic terms instead of text-strings.

The notion that an executing program may take its own source as input (for example a compiler) is no contradiction. It is a familiar situation in computer science.

The Y-combinator is a mechanism for constructing a fixed point of any given lambda expression. But if we construct, using a c-like syntax, the

---

[25] Actually injective homomorphism is sufficient.
[26] Strictly this is not actually a *logical* contradiction.

expression $P = (\lambda x \cdot (x == 0) \; ? \; 1 \; : \; 0)$, then $P \; 1 = 0$ and $P \; 0 = 1$. No matter what x is (an elephant for example), $Px \neq x$. Thus, P has no fixed point. It is possible to construct numbers and conditionals within pure lambda, so surely our shorthand has done no damage to the concepts. What is going on here?

Although some sources make heavy weather of this, the answer is very simple. There is no generic equality testing available in pure lambda calculus. The point becomes intuitively reasonable when we realise that lambda expression equality means equivalence under the reduction system, but this is non-computable. What a lambda expression computes is always computable, so equality is not available as a lambda expression. Equality over specified domains is available, so this is not a problem with the use of lambda expressions to model computation.

What, however, happens if you extend lambda calculus with an oracle that can answer equality questions? Do we then have an unresolvable logical paradox?

The use of lambda expressions to answer questions about lambda expressions is like asking a Turing machine to answer questions about Turing machines. We quickly reach the computational limit.

In fact, H.G. Rice's theorem states that the only computable predicates defined on the *behaviour* of a Turing machine are empty and full. That is, the predicate that admits every thing, and the predicate that admits nothing. Thus, we can expect that there are no non-trivial properties of the behaviour of a lambda expression that can be computed within lambda calculus via a lambda expression.

A technicality here is that the normal way in which a Turing machine is fed into another Turing machine is as a representation in its memory. So, at least a Turing machine can answer questions such as *does this Turing machine have three states*. This sometimes enables it to answer the question, *does this Turing machine do that*, but not, of course in generality. But, with lambda expressions, since the manner of feeding one lambda expression into another is by allowing it some form of access to the output, we cannot answer such questions at all, except where we can ask the expression (and trust it is telling the truth).

Notion 63: Godel's Theorem

The liar's paradox is a classic.

This statement is false.

Is that statement true or false? If it is true then since it states it is false, it must be false: a contradiction. If it is false then since it states it is false, it must be true: another contradiction. We cannot consistently assert this statement to be either true or false. Godel obtained a significant twist on this by replacing truth with proof.

It would be possible to write a book on the nature of Godel's theorem. Several people have in fact. One of the best for the recreational (but determined) reader is *What is the Name of this Book?* by Raymond Smullyan [20], who has written several books related to this aspect of logic.

Godel's theorem has three aspects. The first, sometimes said to be deeply important and ingenious, is actually trivial in the modern computing environment. The set of all finite-length assertions written in a finite alphabet can be mapped one-to-one onto the non-negative integers. Consider a string to be a number in a base the size of the alphabet (256, for example). Letting space be encoded, for convenience, by 0, it is clear that any string is a number. This idea is central to theoretical computer science. (We can knock badly formed assertions out of the picture if we need to). Godel's system involved taking powers of the primes to encode the symbols. This enables the use of an alphabet of indefinite size within the same system, although there are other ways to achieve this effect.

The second point, which is much deeper, is that in any sufficiently general logic system every computation has a fixed point. This idea also appears in lambda calculus (see page 260) and leads directly to the proof of a number of limitations on exact computation. If every computation has a fixed point, then what about the computation that checks if $x = 1$ and returns something else?

The concept that is on the front page of the paper in which Godel introduced his proof is as follows:

Suppose we have a logic system in which we can formulate the assertion, *this statement is unprovable in this system.* Now, if this assertion is provable within the system, then it must be false, and the system has proved a false assertion, and logically is an incorrect system. Alternatively, if the assertion is indeed unprovable, then the system is unable to prove a true assertion, and so it is incomplete.

The rest of the paper is dedicated to a construction of this assertion within the context of ordinary arithmetic, thereby showing that any system sufficiently general to be able to formulate fairly typical questions about arithmetic must be either logically incorrect, or logically incomplete.

This removes the possibility that mathematical truth, as we understand it, can be defined in terms of a proof procedure. Programs and proofs are closely related, this basic issue is behind the halting problem, proof of non-computability.

Godel showed that if number theory is consistent, then there is no proof of this using predicate calculus.

The story does not end here. In particular, Gerhard Gentzen showed that arithmetic can be proved complete and consistent if we may use transfinite induction. This is a form of mathematical induction, the basic statement of which is

If $p(0)$ is true and
from knowing that $p(m)$ is true for all $m < n$ we can prove $p(n)$,
then $p(n)$ is true for all n.

Applied to integers, this is finite induction, applied to all transfinites, this is transfinite induction. However, this does not resolve all the problems of proof, and the principle has to be posited as an axiom. It is a bit controversial, like the axiom of choice.

Notion 64: Non-Computability

There are many simple, precise, clear, understandable and desirable specifications that cannot be implemented. And one of them is the key to understanding the reason none of them are possible.

On a digital computer a program is stored in a file. This file is a stream of bytes. If we have only keyboard input and screen output, then the input and output are also streams of bytes. We may feed the output of one program into another program, or into a file. Likewise, the input may come from a program or a file. The file may contain a program. In this manner, we may feed the source for a program into its executing self as input. There is not even a whiff of any paradox here. A compiler takes programs as input as a matter of routine. A compiler may compile itself.

Programs that take programs as input include compilers, debuggers, interpreters, pretty-printers, translators, dynamic web pages, and text-editors. While most programmers spend little of their time actually writing such programs, the concept should be familiar.

A great concern in the computer environment is debugging and testing. Some programs exist to help: debuggers, tracers, syntax checkers and proof systems. But their assistance is irregular. We would like a tool that tells us that our program is fine. To narrow the problem down, consider infinite loops. A request to a program (terminating or interactive) should eventually produce a response. To fail to halt and provide this response is a bug. Testing can be very lengthy. And it is hard to know if all cases have been considered. Response times might be large, and if the question is whether it will *eventually* respond, then we can never be sure from a test that we have waited long enough. Wouldn't it be good if we could have a program that would tell us this up-front, and quickly?

Let us call this program Halts(P,A), telling us whether program P halts if given argument A. Now, because I am contrary, I write some new code that calls Halts ...

```
Prob(A) = if Halts(A,A) then loop else halt
```

Informally, `Prob` checks to see whether the given program halts if given itself as argument, and then behaves oppositely.

Substituting `A=Prob`, we find that

`Prob(Prob) = if Halts(Prob,Prob) then loop else halt`

And, wondering if this will halt we find that

`Halts(Prob,Prob) = not Halts(Prob,Prob)`

Whatever answer `Halts` produces it will be wrong. So either it produces a wrong answer, or it never halts when tackling this case. It is not alone in having problems. You try answering the following question correctly:

Will you answer this question in the negative?

So any implementation of the halting question is either incorrect or incomplete. This is a specific, reasonable desirable program that can't be written, and the first to be proved so. There is no program that satisfies the axiom `P(A,B)` ≡ `A halts on input B`.

This still leaves open the possibility that a partial halting solution exists that works for all programs except this case. But further work has shown that answering other, seemingly harmless and unrelated questions amounts to the ability to solve the halting problem.

Many programs have been shown to be impossible. But, curiously all of them have been proved through this one special case. The halting problem is the only thing that has been proved directly to be non-computable. If you can embed this (only semi-practical) problem inside another problem, then the other problem is non-computable. That is all problems proved non-computable have a proof that goes through a sequence of embeddings down to the halting problem.

We cannot be certain to solve integer multi-variate polynomial equations [14]. We cannot be certain to determine whether or not an axiom system implies the equivalence of two expressions. We cannot be certain to compute geometric properties of a solid.

Notion 65: Solving Polynomials

Much of modern mathematics revolves around questions of computation. The problem of computing the exact roots of a polynomial from the coefficients in its power series has been particularly fruitful in generating new mathematics, as has the problem of exact solution of differential equations. Since the solution desired was a finite expression in some given language, the concept is particularly suitable for discussion in computer science. Taken as a purely symbolic exercise, the problem is essentially one of finding an algorithm to reverse the effect of a relatively simple symbolic manipulation. The problem can be difficult or insoluble.

One classic result in this area is commonly expressed by asserting that you can't solve polynomials above degree 4. This is misleading. For example, we can solve the equation $x^5 - a = 0$. The process is easy to understand using complex numbers. Further, there is a theorem that any 5th-order polynomial has 5 (possibly repeated) zeros. More correctly, we construct the set of expressions involving "+", "−", "×", "÷" and "$\sqrt[n]{}$: $n \in \mathbf{Z}^+$", and call these radicals. Then the theorem is that the general 5th-order polynomial has no solution in the radicals formed from its coefficients. However, as Felix Klein showed, it is possible to find solutions to all polynomials in the set of expressions using trigonometric functions.

So no algorithm constructing radical expressions can correctly determine the roots of all polynomials, simply because for some polynomials those solutions do not exist. However, Matiyasevich [14] developed the following non-computable problem. *Given a multi-variate polynomial over the integers, determine whether it has any roots over the integers.* He showed how to use a solution to this problem to solve the halting problem (see page 140). The solution exists, but we cannot be certain to find it.

Gröbner bases can be used to reduce simultaneous multi-variate polynomial equations down to a minimum of equations in a minimum of variables. The larger part of the technique involves a form of book-keeping to assure that the sequence of reductions will eliminate lower and lower powers of the other variables. But, we might not be able to compute the solution to the resulting equation.

Notion 66: Churche's Thesis

Alonzo Churche said,

All models of effective computation are equivalent.

This sounds like a mathematical theorem but is actually more a part of physics. We do not know exactly what the set of such models are; rather, we have found that no matter how we try to build a computer, eventually, as its capacity is increased, the set of problems it solves expands out to a computable limit. Beyond this capacity added components at best only increase the speed, not which problems can be solved.

Like the speed of light in relativity, we can approach the limit, but reaching it requires infinite resources and exceeding it is impossible.

The technical content of Churche's thesis is the demonstration of the equivalence of all the most general models of computation so far designed. This is normally done by writing simulators.

A register machine can simulate a stack machine, because an integer is effectively a stack of digits, pop(123)=12, top(123)=3, push(3,12)=123. A stack machine, with at least two stacks, can simulate a Turing Machine, by treating one stack as the tape to the left, and the other stack as the tape to the right. To move left, push(top(left),right), pop(left). If we squint a bit, the distinction between a register, stack and Turing machine disappears. Likewise, a Von Neumann machine is largely just a multi-tape Turing machine. It can simulate a Turing machine by ignoring all but one of its memory pointers.

An n-stack stack machine, or n-register register machine, can be simulated by an n-pointer Von Neumann machine by using one pointer per stack, and interlacing them by shifting each pointer by a multiple of n each time. We have a loop of simulation; stack simulates register simulates tape simulates pointer simulates stack. Thus, all are equivalent in what they can compute, although they may vary in the speed at which they compute it.

All these simulations are worthwhile exercises to try in detail.

Notion 67: Algorithmic Complexity

The cpu of a desktop machine is a finite-state machine. Each time the cpu is clocked it takes a single step. During the execution of a program, a specific, though typically very large, number of steps are taken. A cpu running at 10^20 steps per second would go through 10^21 steps during a 10-second run of a program. These numbers are not ephemeral, they are specific, calculable numbers. We can write code-testing software that will provide these number for us. To be truly exact we normally need operating system or hardware assistance, but it can be done.

Our program takes input. To be concrete, it is an integer factoring program that takes a string of digits as input. We can measure the size of the input in a variety of ways, for this discussion, by the length of the string of digits. There are many numbers with the same number of digits. Each specific number fed in takes a specific number of steps. If we plot the number of steps taken against the length of the string we might get a plot a bit like the following:

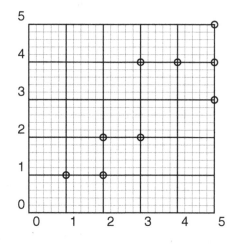

In binary the two numbers of length 1 are "0" and "1", and they each take a specific number of steps. At least one of them must take a minimal number of steps. Likewise for the four strings of 2 digits, and 8 strings of 3 digits and so on. For each length n, with have minSteps(n), the minimum number of steps taken. Likewise we have maxSteps(n), and avgSteps(n), the latter giving the average number of steps for the length n input strings.

Although technical difficulties arise, in particular interaction with other threads, interrupt service routines, components of the operating system, and so on, it is possible in practice to determine these numbers fairly accurately for a typical program running on a typical machine and get a worthwhile plot of the complexity of the program.

The minStep(n) function is the best-case complexity, and maxStep(n) the worst-case complexity, and avgStep(n) the average-case complexity. Comparing these functions gives a mechanism for comparing the behaviour of different programs that compute the same thing.

Each program we run on the machine can be stored in a file, and a file is a sequence of bytes, which naturally make digits in a base 256 number. Thus, each program has a unique identity number. Selecting only those programs that correctly solve indefinitely large factoring problems, we can subclassify them according to which algorithm they implement.

We can determine the worst-case complexity for a specific program. We can also define the worst-case complexity of an algorithm to be the best worst-case performance over all the programs that implement it. Likewise, the worst-case complexity of a problem is the best worst-case complexity over all algorithms that solve it.

Over all the programs that factor integers as string of digits, one is best, we refer to this performance as the complexity of the factoring problem. Of all the programs that implement a specific algorithm for factoring integers, one is best. This performance is the complexity of that specific algorithm.

This is only one concept of complexity. There are others such as space complexity or the number of times a specific subroutine is called and there are other ways to measure the size of the instance of the problem. But the basic principle and the central point is the same. For a given computer, there is a limit to how fast a problem can be solved. There is a limit beyond which further acceleration is no longer possible. In many cases (see page 133), but by no means all, these limits can be determined, and achieved.

However, this discussion has avoided some complications. Firstly, taken strictly, complexity functions are not always comparable. Simply put, one algorithm might be good for one type of integer, and another algorithm good for a different type. Secondly, for pragmatic reasons (it is difficult to get the exact answer) most of the work in this area uses the *order of complexity* approximation which takes a limit to infinity, and has controversial relevance to the finite behaviour of practical programs.

Notion 68: P and NP

The class P of computational problems on a given computer is the class of problems for which there exists an algorithm that runs in polynomial steps. More specifically, the worst-case number of steps is bounded above in order by some polynomial.

Although similar classes exist for functions other than polynomials, the polynomials are particularly significant. The slow-down simulating one machine on another is typically of polynomial order. So, polynomials form the smallest order class for which *if it can be done that fast on one machine it can be done that fast on another.* The class P means, by default, polynomial time problems on Turing, register, stack, or Von Neumann machines.

Tractable is often used to mean, *of polynomial order of complexity in the worst case.* Tractability is not specific to a specific computer but is generic of our computational technology.[27] Whether this usage is pragmatically justified is another matter. For typical problems we are interested in, a degree 96 polynomial complexity could easily be worse than an exponential. This has been the case for the simplex algorithm for solving linear programming problems, which is exponential, but until recently the only alternatives where intractable (in practice) polynomial algorithms.

Determining the complexity of a problem has some subtle traps. For example, it was shown that comparison sorting is $(n \log n)$, but this assumed that a single comparison is constant time. However, to compare two indefinitely large numbers in practice we have to scan down a list of digits. If the numbers are constrained in size, then there is a cap on the time taken. But, more generally, the comparison could take up to order of the logarithm of the length of the list, suggesting a complexity of $(n(\log n)^2)$.

For theoretical studies, decision problems are usually used. This means a problem to which the answer is yes or no, such as, *is this number prime.* This makes the proofs easier, and there are a variety of theorems showing how to convert various decision problems into more general

---

[27]Quantum computing and other possible future developments being ignored.

cases. Further, the decision problem cannot take more than the same order of time than the full problem, (such as, find the factors), and so an intractable decision problem means an intractable problem.

The N in NP stands for non-deterministic. NP is the class of problems for which there exists a polynomial time algorithm on a non-deterministic machine. A non-deterministic version of any of the standard machines can be described validly, but informaly, as a machine that can duplicate itself and run in parallel as many times as required. Or, alternatively, as a machine that magically guesses right each time but is constrained to prove afterwards that its guess was right. Most practical problems are NP, since if it is intractable to check the solution, it is hard for the solution to be of any more use than a random guess.

The ability to go non-deterministic is beyond our technology, and it sounds like a major advantage. In fact, it sounds like so much of an advantage that it must have given the game away. Certainly it can be very easy to write very fast solutions on such a machine. For example, find the solution to a Diophantine equation: guess the solution and substitute it into the equation to show that it works. Finished.

But no one has been able to prove (at the time of writing) that there are any problems that the non-deterministic machine can do in polynomial time that can't be done likewise on the deterministic version. This is despite a great effort being put into the question by a great many greatly competent people. The area is full of subtle trips and traps. A minor change to the specification can make a major change to the complexity.

An irksome complication is that the performance of the deterministic machine can often be improved if it is given a (true) random number generator. That is, not a magic guessing device, but simply a guessing device.

The set P is all those problems that can be solved in polynomial steps. The set NP is all those that can be checked in polynomial steps. If a problem can be solved in polynomial time, then it can be checked in polynomial time, simply by solving it and checking the solution.

P is a subset of NP. It is unknown whether NP is a subset of P.

Notion 69: NP completeness

There is a special class of NP problems that may be the key to determining whether P=NP (see page 146). Some of the NP problems are sufficiently general that it is possible to reduce any other NP problem to a special case of these general problems. These special problems are termed *NP complete*.

The *satisfiability* problem is, *given a Boolean expression in n variables, determine whether any truth assignment to the n variables will make the expression true*. The proof of completeness of satisfiability amounts to demonstrating a collection of Boolean expressions that simulates a Turing machine. For example, a two state machine would need a variable for *the machine is in state 1* and for *the machine is in state 2*, and then the exclusive disjunction would be included in the Boolean expression. Similarly for each of the tape states.

A Turing machine has an infinite tape, and infinite time available, which suggests an infinite number of variables are required. But we are assuming up front that the problem to be simulated is bounded by polynomial steps, and thus does not use more than polynomial time or polynomial space. So we can use only a polynomial collection of variables to express the entire run of the Turing machine.

A decision problem is one that just answers yes or no. We extract the answer to any decision problem from the Boolean expressions for the Turing machine by simply asking if there are values for all the variables defining the Turing machine states that involve the required cell being a 1.

The proof that satisfiability is NP complete does not mean that it is intractable. But, if anything in NP is intractable, then satisfiability is. Thus, we have the strongest statement we can make about the intractability of this and similar problems.

Like the halting problem is used to show things non-computable, all the proofs for intractability amount to showing that the problem can be reduced to a special case of satisfiability.

Notion 70: Turing Test

Can a machine think?

Perhaps this is not a programming issue. Perhaps you will never have to think about it. I hope so. But, for me, this conundrum arises naturally out of computer technology. The response typically tells you more about the respondent than about machines. What do we mean by *think?* What is intelligence and consciousness? Does a computer have a soul?

Edsger Dijkstra said, *the question of whether a computer can think is no more interesting than that of whether a submarine can swim.* A fish and a submarine both move through the water. All the rest is the semantics of the word *swim.* But many people see a moral slant on this leading to deep discussion or emotive argument.

Turing's test is simple; it might not be right, but it gives a fairly clear response. If the machine can pretend to be a human in the context of a textual conversation (think "mailbots"), then it is intelligent. This is hard to do. Strong attempts such as SCHRDLU and Eliza exist, but none have really worked. To an alert (and antagonistic) human the machine eventually produces gibberish.

One major criticism of Turing relates to the principle of a machine with a very very large memory, containing every likely question, and an appropriate response. This would require peta-bytes of storage, but it might be within our technological capacity, if the whole world was determined enough. Surely this is not intelligence.

Turing was avoiding metaphysics, pragmatically he has a point. Pathological cases such as a look-up conversationalist are going to be pretty rare in the world. But, philosophically, there is a problem. Two entities might get exactly the same result, and yet one is doing it with intelligence, and the other without. The lookup table and brute force search, with enough cpu cycles behind them, are examples of fairly unintelligent methods that do solve problems.

Intelligence means ability but also optimisation: i.e., solving a problem, yes, but also to do it with the least processing.

Notion 71: Natural Language Processing

Computer language and natural language tend to be very distinct. In computer language the syntax tends to be separate from the semantics. In natural language you may need to understand the sentence in order to be able to parse it.

Time flies like an arrow.

Fruit flies like an orange.

The parsing is different only because we think there is no such thing as a *time fly*. But, perhaps they make the arrow disintegrate eventually.

Time (flies (like (an arrow))).

(Fruit flies) like (an orange)

First, *like* is part of an adverbial phrase, and then a verb, while *flies* is verb and then a noun.

In testing a computer program for natural language understanding one thing to keep in mind is that humans make mistakes, so it is unfair to begin with the idea of error-less natural language processing.

That that is is that that that that is not is not.

Further, and this is partly why humans make errors, the problem is not precisely defined. Each human at each moment has a slightly different interpretation of language. The suggested "right" answers are just aspects of language that are fairly consistent from time to time and person to person.

But in practice this can be a very interesting programming exercise. Write a program that can read a mathematical word-problem, and produce the right answer.

Joe goes to the shop and buys two bananas at three dollars each. He started out with ten dollars, how many dollars does he have left?

Notion 72: The Computable Reals

As a digital datatype, the real numbers do not exist (see page 115). However, some related types do (see page 223). These include naturals, integers, and rationals. We can also represent a number by an algebraic equation such as $x^2 = 2$, deducing that $(2x)^2 = 8$. We have computed that $4\sqrt{2} = \sqrt{8}$. These are algebraic numbers. We could extend them by including symbols for π, and the axioms of the algebra of the trigonometric functions.

How far can we go?

Instead of a specific expression language, expand to a general purpose language. This is as general it gets. Each real number is a program that outputs digits. A real number is an infinite sequence of digits.

$$\pi = (3; 1, 4, 1, 5, 9, 2, \dots)$$

We can add element by element, and then normalise. Since the sum of two numbers between 0 and 1 is between 0 and 2, it is often possible that there will be no further carries modifying the leftmost digits, and thus we can produce some digits of the required number.

But we can define a number by selecting a Turing machine and simulating it. The n-th digit is 0 if the Turing machine has not halted by step n, and 1 if it has. We do not have to solve the non-computable halting problem, we just simulate the steps of the machine.

But computing the sign of such a number does mean solving the halting problem. So this is non-computable. And since $a > b$ is the same as $a - b > 0$, order is not computable. And since neither is $a = 0$, we cannot check $a = b$. When adding $0.999\cdots$ and $0.000\cdots$ we do not know if the result is greater than 1. We are not even sure of the first digit.

It is true that, finitely in many cases, and in the limit to infinite time in all cases, the computation will produce an answer. But we have no way of knowing how long we have to wait. Such a datatype leaves us uncertain about how many resources we will need, and how much of the answer we can trust.

Notion 73: The Diagonal Argument

We count, 1, 2, 3, 4, ..., ∞. What comes next? Why does it matter?

A basic understanding of the lower transfinite numbers helps a programmer to understand datatypes. In some significant cases, transfinite arithmetic can determine the impossibility of an implementation and suggest which subtypes could be implemented instead. At the very least, what it means for a datatype to be countable needs to be understood. The *diagonal argument* suggested by Cantor is pragmatic.

Although in actual execution the bytes representing an instance of a datatype might be scattered throughout memory, in principle, and in practice, each instance of each digital datatype can be expressed as a finite sequence of contiguous bytes in memory. By including an extra start bit of value 1 on the left of the sequence (to avoid the sequence starting with a string of 0s), we can code any instance of a digital datatype as a single binary integer. Not all integers must represent an instance of the type, and an instance might occur twice as an integer. But this does not affect our next conclusion.

By generating each integer in turn, 1, 10, 11, ..., and ignoring those that do not represent our datatype, we produce a sequence of instances that will eventually produce any specific instance we like to think of. We have an infinite list that contains all the instances. This list-ability is what is meant by the term *countable*. We have shown that all digital datatypes are countable. It was once supposed that all datatypes where countable. But Cantor discovered otherwise.

1	0.	0	1	0	1	...
2	0.	1	1	1	1	...
3	0.	1	1	0	0	...
4	0.	0	0	1	0	...
5	0.	0	1	0	1	...
:	:	:	:	:	:	

We imagine that we have a datatype representing all real numbers from 0 to 1. Every real number is expressed as an infinite binary expansion to the right of the fractional point. Some real numbers are represented in two ways, with trailing 0's, or trailing 1's. But each pair differs by more than one bit. Now, we list all these numbers. A number (0.0100...) can be read from the main diagonal. It is between 0 and 1, and should be on the list.

But generate a new number whose digits are obtained by complimenting the digits on the diagonal and we are in trouble. That is, digit n of this new number is the complement of digit n of the n-th number on the list. So the binary expansion produced is not one of those on the list since it differs from the n-th expansion at the n-th bit, for each n. This number is not on the list. Our imagined datatype is a fiction. No datatype can represent all binary expansions. And no datatype can represent all the reals between 0 and 1, and so no datatype can represent all the reals.

This is a generic argument, a general strategy for showing that a datatype is uncountable, and thus cannot be represented on a digital computer. Any attempt to do so will leave out more instances than it includes. In a very precise sense, any implementation of the reals leaves out so much more than it includes that the ones that are included are insignificant.

This is an important argument that should be understood by any programmer. A countable datatype is one that can be put into an indexed list as above. An uncountable datatype is one that cannot. On the desktop computer, *all* datatypes are countable. But, reals are not countable, and so no desktop datatype can represent them.

Similarly, integer or symbol sequences, integer functions, relations on the integers, subsets of the integers, paths on a square grid, and integer-weighted trees do not exist on a desktop digital computer.

When given a datatype that is asserted to represent *all* elements out of one of these or any other uncountable type, the programmer is advised to look carefully to find out where that assertion breaks down. In practice, at best, some other sub-datatype is being represented. Sometimes, as in the case of floating-point numbers, this datatype is not even a proper subtype, as it is not homomorphic, and it will produce incorrect answers if used without caution.

Finite sequences, finite subsets of the integers, finite paths, functions on a finite domain, and finite trees as well as integers, rationals, and algebraic numbers (most of which have a non-periodic expansion) are all possible, as is anything else for which an explicit language of finite expressions can be developed.

Chapter 5

Some Orthodox Languages

In which we learn a few things about specific contingencies.

Regardless of what should or could be, a choice is made as to what is. In the programming context, certain languages are available in practice, and others are not. Certain languages run quickly in practice, and others do not. In order to program in practice we must have some awareness of these properties.

Compiler and machine technology can overturn the relative merits of languages, but most likely the next language will come out of the group of currently existing ones, with some modification.

Notion 5: The Nature of C Code

C is one of the most common languages of the past quarter century. An industry common denominator, it has inspired the syntax and semantics of many languages (sometimes by people reacting against it). A superficial familiarity with C is useful for the contemporary programmer (like a familiarity with Latin). The origins of C are entwined with those of the UNIX operating system [17]. C is a low-level language, good for embedded code, with strong machine control and consequently machine dependencies. There are many dialects. The C here is not always ANSI standard. It is closer to the loosely defined *classic* C which long-term C programmers grew up with.

A C program is a soup of function and data definitions. C is block structured with delimiters "{" and "}". Each block may have local data, but function definitions are all global. Any name exported from any file becomes global to the entire program. It is best to give functions unique names. Important normally hidden system utilities begin with an underscore character to avoid accidental conflict.

The basic arithmetic operations "+", "−", "*", "/", and "%" work on a few fixed-size signed and unsigned n-bit integer types, int, long, short, char. Despite its name char is really a short int. Bit-wise binary operations include and &, or |, exclusive or ^, shift <<. Floating point types are float and double.

Labels and gotos are available in C, although they are not often used. A label definition ends in a colon, "aLabel:". No interaction is defined in C, but standard libraries include formated file interaction routines.

C has a tuple datatype struct, and the ability to name new types. The name spaces for struct and typedef are independent. Variable declarations in C are rich in algebraic structure and have their own idiosyncrasies (see page 157).

There are no Boolean, string, or array types in C. The facilities of these types are provided by integer and pointer operations. There is a strong assumption that the machine is a Von Neumann machine and that various items are stored in contiguous memory. C was designed to be easy to compile. The earlier compilers made it very easy to know *exactly* what assembly language would be produced and had simple interfaces for explicit inclusion of assembler in the C program. It is often important in dealing with C to think explicitly about events in the underlying Von Neumann machine.

A significant feature of C is the pointer type. `int *p = &x;` sets up p as indicating the address of x, so that `y=*p` has the same effect as `y=x;`.

```
int x; ......................................... variable declaration
x = 6; ..................................... assigns 6 to the variable x
x = 2*y+35/23; ................................... general expression
int inc(int x){return x+1;} .................. Function definition
x += 6 ......................................... means x = x + 6
```

Control structures such as `if(x){..}`, `while(x){..}` have controversial arithmetic conditional semantics. The numerical value given is tested. If it is zero the body is skipped, otherwise it is run.

Expressions such as `x>y` have a numeric value (0 or 1) and `x+=x>y` is legal, incrementing x if it is bigger than y. There is a conditional value expression, `x ? y : z`, which continues the use of arithmetic in place of Boolean logic (see page 99).

There have been various attempts over the years to claim that C has, or should have, a Boolean. To interpret 0=false and 1=true leads to the conclusion that the C conditionals are broken and need cautious handling. These thoughts inspired some of the design of Java. However, the problem is only in the conflict between C and other languages. C itself is still best understood by admitting that the loops operate on arithmetic values, not Boolean.

Strings are ASCIIZ, null-terminated arrays of character codes. `a[i]` means `*(a+i)`. C is probably the language that is most happy with the use of pointers, providing a very flexible and powerful (and some would say dangerous) ability to obtain, modify, and de-reference them.

C is full of features that most people either love or hate (see page 157).

Notion 6: Reading C type-declarations

A type declaration associates a structure with a symbol. Commonly, this is a description of how to compose the structure, showing how the data might look in memory. Thus, it can be a distinct jolt for the unwarned to find that a C type-declaration is a description of how to decompose the structure, showing how the symbol might look in the code. Confusion over this point has led to an unwarranted lack of appreciation of the benefits of the C approach. Here, we demonstrate the notion that C type-declaration style is simply the natural dual of the construction style.

A declaration of a compound type indicates the way in which the symbol can be used in code, for example, array reference [ ] is the inverse of the array type-construction. So if x = array of thing, then x[i] = thing and x[a]=b is a valid use. Function type-construction is the inverse of function call ( ). Thus, if x = function:thing->thing, then x(thing)=thing and x(a) is a valid expression. Similarly, the C pointer de-reference is the inverse of the pointer declaration. Thus, if x = pointer to thing then *x = integer. This point is illustrated in the compound example below.

The last line contains the components of a C declaration of a pointer to an array of pointers to functions that take int and return int, which is int (*((*x)[ ]))(int).

```
if   x = pointer to array of pointer to function:int->int
then
              *x = array of pointer to function:int->int
          (*x)[i] = pointer to function : int -> int
      (*((*x)[i])) = function : int -> int
(*((*x)[i]))(int) = int
```

This declaration may be read as a construction by reading from the inside out. (1) Look at the innermost symbol x; (2) look at the first operator applied to x, it is *, and the inverse of * is a pointer to; (3) the next operator out, the one applied to *x is an array reference [ ] its inverse is an array of; (4) next we have * applied to (*x)[ ] the inverse is as before; (5) following this pattern, the next operator is applied to *((*x)[]) and it is a function call its inverse is is a function that takes int, (6) finally the primitive (non-composite) type of the whole is declared to be is an `int`.

```
       1           2            3             4
x is a| pointer to| an array of| pointers to|
       1           2            3             4
```

```
            4                 5                    6
            | functions that take int| and return int|
            4                 5                    6
```

With a bit of practice you can read C declarations in their inverse form, as above, or just look at it as a description (as given) of the syntax of the use of the symbol. A C declaration, as above, does not just declare the type of x, but also the type of *x, (*x)[] and so on. Valid uses of x include y = (*((*x)[5]))(6) if int y, or y = (*((*x)[5])) if int (*y)(int), this makes it possible to check mechanically if the use of x in the code is correct; just check to see that it looks like a subexpression of the type declaration.

Some texts unwisely suggest staging the declaration. But the supposed "brain strain" of C declarations comes from trying to view them in inverse form.

No strain arises if they are recog-   `typedef int type1;`
nised as decomposition declara-   `typedef type1 type2(type1);`
tions. Personally, I find the staged   `typedef type2 *type3;`
type-declarations to be harder to   `typedef type3 type4[];`
use, but it is an individual choice.   `typedef type4 *type5;`

The central thing to remember is that you can convert between the syntax and type-declarations (C to Pascal for example) using a step-by-step process. It is quite easy, as long as you do not try to invert it all at once implicitly in your head. Remember to take an explicit step-by-step approach to derive the relation between the two styles of declaration. It is best if you learn to think of type declarations equally as composition or decomposition instructions.

Notion 74: C Pointers to Functions

Pointers in C are a much richer datatype than pointers in most other languages, such as Pascal or Java. (Technically, this rich structure also exists in C++, but there is a conscious effort to try to ignore it). Except for floating-point data and records, all C type-declarations declare some variant of an integer or a pointer.

A C function header: `int f(int);` is sometime equated with a Pascal forward function definition. But the syntax is identical to a C type declaration, except for the mild complication that `int f(int)` and `int (*f)(int)` are the same declaration. C implicitly de-references a function pointer in a call, if no explicit de-reference is made. The distinction is that `int f(int)` declares a constant pointer to an integer function, which is set to point to a block of known machine code, but `int (*f)(int)` declares a variable pointer to an integer function. In this declaration, the pointer might not be initialised to anything in particular.

Array declarations are similar. The first example below is analogous to a function forward declaration. It states that `a` points to a block of ints, but says nothing about what those ints are. The second declares what the ints are. Both the first and the second declare `a` as a constant. The third declares `a` to be similar, but to be a variable and not to be initialised to point to any particular block of integers.

```
int a[10];         // const pointer to uninitialised memory
int b[2]={1,2};    // const pointer to initialised memory
int *c;            // uninitialised variable pointer
int c[];           // alternative syntax for above
int *d=a;          // variable pointer pts to same thing as a
char *s="fred";    // variable ptr pts to {'f','r','e','d',0}
```

Strings are just null-terminated arrays of character codes, the syntax `'a'` means, literally, the numeric character code for the character a. If you memorise the character codes you never *need* to use this syntax. The brackets are an operator, $a[i] \equiv *(a+i)$. This is reflected in the ability of the C++ programmer to overload them, showing that they are not just syntax. It is a level of abstraction. The indexing method for a new pseudo-array datatype can be declared, shading its memory print from view.

The following code uses a constant function pointer declared by a function declaration in a context in which it is not called. This is not a "special convention" in which the name of a function used on its own is converted silently to a pointer to that function. Rather, parentheses ( ) are an operator on pointers, analogous to the brackets [ ] for arrays. They construct a call with the given arguments. In classic C this meant pushing the arguments onto the stack in reverse order. The caller then cleared the arguments. These semantics rely heavily on the presumption of an underlying Von Neumann machine for their definition.

```
#include <stdio.h>

typedef int (*int2int)(int);

int twice(int2int f, int x){return f(f(x));}

int fn1(int x){return x+1;}
int fn2(int x){return x*1;}

main()
{
printf("twice(fn1,3) = %d\n",twice(fn1,3));
printf("twice(fn2,3) = %d\n",twice(fn2,3));
}
```

The rule that *whoever put it on the stack takes it off*, in classic C, lead to a lower incidence of stack crashes. In certain classic C compilers, expressions such as 0x0FFF(6) were valid, and would call the indicated absolute location in memory. The command 0() was one of the fastest ways to crash a computer that had improper memory protection. Classic C is definitely "shoot first and ask questions later", but that is part of its charm, and most of its power.

Notice that the function pointer f as an argument to twice is used as a function name, since that is what it is, while in main, the function name is used directly as a function pointer, since that is what it is. The typedef is needed to make this example work neatly because it allows us to define a function *reference*, an implicitly de-referenced pointer.

Notion 75: Taking C on Face Value

Ignoring all mythos, C is high-level assembler, which is both a strength and a weakness. It has no array, Boolean, string or character types. The expression 'a' *means* the numerical character code corresponding to the lowercase of the first letter of the Latin alphabet. Typically, but not universally, this will be 97 (using ASCII encoding). Thus, 'a'+3==100. There is nothing even faintly illegal or illogical about using 'a' in an arithmetic expression; 'a' is a numerical value. The ASCII system is specifically designed to have arithmetic performed on it. To capitalise a lowercase letter, subtract 32; so, 'a'-32=='A'. That the default char type is *signed* not *unsigned* shows that it is not a character, but a numerical type. There is no concept of the sign of a character.

Typically memory is divided into 8-bit bytes, each of which is given a numerical index, called its *address*. If a numerical variable p contains the address of a data element in memory, then p is said to be a pointer. Pointer operations such as x=*p; may need to know how many bytes of memory to process. In C, each pointer variable has a size associated with it. If p has a size of n bytes, then p+1 means the address of the byte n bytes further in along memory. Thus, p+i gives the address of the byte i*n bytes further on. Since this is a simple way to implement arrays (as used in assembler) it was incorporated into C with the notation p[i] == *(p+i) == *(i+p) == i[p]. Linear array references in C are shorthand for pointer arithmetic.

A string is an ASCIIZ memory block, a list of character codes in memory, terminated by a 0 byte. The expression "The cat sat on the mat", means a pointer to a block of memory that has been initialised to contain the appropriate character codes, and the terminal 0 byte. As such it is also an array.

Taking this on face value,

```
"the cat sat on the mat"[3] == 'e'
3["the cat sat on the mat"] == 'e'
```

C is designed to be easy to compile. One dimensional arrays are implemented as contiguous elements in the linear memory of a Von Neumann machine. The distinction between a pointer and a one dimensional array is syntax not semantics.

There is no Boolean type. Expressions such as `x==2` in C are arithmetic. `c=0;for(i=0;i<=n;i++)c+=a[i]==0` is a method for counting the number of zero elements in an array. There is strong precedence for this from classical mathematics, where it is written $c = \sum_{i=0}^{n} \delta_{a_i,0}$. Specifically, (`x==y`) is the same as the Krönecker delta δ_{xy}.

The operator `!`, pronounced *not*, is not a Boolean operator, but an arithmetic one. For example `x-=!!p;` subtracts 1 from x as long as p is not NULL. Actually, NULL is traditionally just `#define NULL (0)`. `!x` is 0 when x is positive or negative, and is 1 when `x=0`. That is, (`!x`) is the same as $\delta_{x,0}$.

Conditionals in C code are *arithmetic* conditionals not *logical* conditionals. The control structure `if(x){...}` executes the code in braces exactly when $x \neq 0$, where x might be an int, a float or a pointer. The expression `if(!p){...}` in C, where p is a pointer, is completely valid, syntactically and semantically, and does not involve an implicit `==NULL`.

On recognising that these operators are arithmetic, there is no confusion using "logical" operators in arithmetic expressions. Confusion arises only when the mythos that a conditional must take a Boolean meets the reality of the semantics of C. Boolean type is an abstraction, but not a requirement. Boolean types are often used in logic, but rarely used in mathematics. A typical assembly language has no Boolean, rather it has instructions such as *decrement and skip on zero*. Its actions are controlled by the value of numerical terms.

The exact semantics of C has been strongly coloured by reinterpretation of various structures according to the prevailing politically correct theory of the day. However, the pragmatics is that C was designed to be easy to compile, and to give access to the underlying machine in order to facilitate the writing of system software. Many of its operators are posited on the assumption of a simple linear memory arrangement in a typical Von Neumann architecture.

Notion 76: Functions and Other Data in C

What distinguishes `int p[3]` from `int p[ ]`? In the first we define a constant pointer pointing to a compiler allocated memory block of 3 ints. In the second we declare a pointer that might point anywhere. De-referencing it is likely to produce a memory fault. We can point it to valid memory using `p=malloc(3)` and change our minds later, pointing it elsewhere. When we initialise using `int p[3]={1,2,3}`, we specify the values to be placed in the memory where `p` is pointing. The record `{1,2,3}` is written into memory. Likewise, `int p[ ]={1,2,3}`.

A function is a piece of memory like an array. The distinction between `int p(int x)` and `int (*p)(int x)` is that the first declares `p` to be a constant pointer into memory and the second declares `p` to be a variable pointer. We can initialise the memory to which `p` is pointing by `int p(int x){return x*x;}`. The machine code for `{return x*x;}` is written into that location. (Often the data size associated with a function pointer is one byte. But it would be more reasonable to make it the size of the compiled machine code block.)

Normally, a record in C is the contiguous placement of the elements in the order specified in the declaration, possibly with padding for byte alignment. The initialisation `p=6` stores the value 6 in memory at the location `*p`. `p[3]={1,2,3}` means place the values 1, 2, and 3 contiguously in memory. Record initialisation is the same except that the types may be different, `p={1,2.5,"cat"}`. An array can be naturally indefinitely extended. A record has no natural extension (except perhaps extending the last element into an array). The initialisation `int p(int x){return x*x;}`, is yet another variant on the setting of the bytes in memory to which a pointer points.

A function is data, similar to an array or a record. We use the array as `p[2]`, the record as `p.two`, and the function as `p(2)`. Externally, little is different, except that a function represents (in C) a value you can't change. `p[2]=2` is ok, `p.two=3` is ok, `p(2)=3` is not. But this is a datatype technicality, not a conceptual error. We could build a function datatype whose individual values could be assigned. An extension of C might admit the axiom `(f(2)=3)(2)==3`.

The machine code-block nature of a function in C is demonstrated by copying the contents of a function into an array.

```
typedef unsigned char byte;
byte a[100];
int f(int x){return x*x;}
void init(){int i; for(i=0;i<100;i++) a[i]=((byte*)f)[i];}
```

Some compiler and machine-specific modifications may be required to avoid type and memory faults, but this can normally be made to work. The array pointer can be called by using a( ) instead of the usual a[ ].

The declaration int p[10] does not declare an array in any abstract sense. char *p="the cat" declares a pointer, and points it to a block containing "the cat". Likewise int p[10]; declares p to be a pointer to a block of 10 ints (without specifying the value of the ints). The usage q=p is not a *special convention* in which p is quietly converted to a pointer to its first element; rather p is already a pointer, and p[2] a compound expression using the operator [ ].

Less regular are multi-dimensional arrays. Unfortunately, there has been strong philosophical conflict on this matter. If, in line with assembler, we take p[i] to be shorthand for *(p+i), then p[i][j] is *(*(p+i)+j). So int p[10][20] declares a block of 10 pointers to blocks of 20 ints. Some compiler writers took this approach. Others took it upon themselves to recast to inconsistent semantics.

If int p[10] defines p as an array, then sizeof(p) is 10*sizeof(int), and q=p copies the entire array. int p[10][20] declares a block of 10 blocks of 20 ints. In classic C compilers, sizeof(p) was the size of a pointer, and q=p copies the pointer. However, in one recent compiler, sizeof(p) was large, but p=p gave an *incompatible types in assignment* error. This is logical spaghetti, p has been made fundamentally different as an l-value and an r-value.

The motivation is that multi-dimensional arrays were traditionally $x+n*y$ indexing into a memory block. Pointer blocks are more complex. The C compiler writers could have admitted true multi-dimensional declarations such as int a[10,n], so that p[2,3] becomes *(p+2+3*n). Unfortunately the notation p[1][2] was miss-appropriated instead.

Exercise 10: Face-Value C Exercises

In C code the "logical" operators are actually arithmetic operators that return integer values, typically 0 or 1. If they are *thought* of as arithmetic operators, no confusion should arise.

The expression `y=(x>0)*5+6` will set y to either 6 or 11, depending on whether `(x>0)==0` or `(x>0)==1`, one or the other of which must be true. The conditional expression `a ? b : c` tests its first argument a, if `a!=0`, then it returns b, otherwise it returns c. This is an arithmetic function in the same sense that a unit step function returns a value that in C is written `x>0`.

1. Rewrite `if(x>0) y=y*y; else y=6;` using only arithmetic operators, do not even use the `a?b:c` construct.

2. What does this code compute:

   ```
   unsigned int f(unsigned int x, unsigned int y)
                   {while((x%=y)&&(y%=x));return a+b;}
   ```

3. The C modulus `x%y` is typically equivalent to `x-(x/y)*y`, which may be negative or positive. Classically, $0 \le (x \bmod y) < |y|$ This difference breaks some algorithms.

   Write an expression in C for the classical modulus.

4. One generic problem is a loop of the form `"A;while(T){B;A}"`.

   For example, `print(i);while(i<10) {i=f(i);print(i);}`

   Rewrite this generically without code duplication.

5. Given that only that 'a'..'z', 'A'..'Z', and '0'..'9' are each contiguous, write an arithmetic expression in C code that will convert a single hex digit to its equivalent as an integer.

Notion 77: The C Preprocessor

The C preprocessor is a much maligned textual substitution system. Over the years much has been said, and many spleens have been vented. Today the C preprocessor is attenuated. It does not re-read its input, so indefinite loops are prevented. This is a pity; classically it was possible to write some very interesting things in the C preprocessor.

```
#define sqr(x) x * x
```

Caution, (sqr(5+6))==41 because the substitution is *uninterpreted* textual. sqr(5+6) is changed to 5+6*5+6, the value is 41, not 121. We can use brackets to avoid this; #define sqr(x) (x)*(x) or sqr((5+6)).

x=5;y=sqr(x++); sets x==7 and y==25, on the compiler I have here. The macro expands to y=x++*x++;, C does not specify exactly what to do — when are the increments performed? In this compiler, the choice is that all the post increments are done after the evaluation of the expression. But no matter the choice, x is incremented twice. This is treated in many texts as a bug waiting to happen. But, it is a matter of how it is approached.

The problem is psychological not logical. sqr(x++) is not a C function call. Exactly when and in what environment is the argument evaluated? The macro is call by name. The expression x++ is handed over and evaluated as required, in the local environment. It is related to passing a function pointer, int sqr(int f()){return f()*f();}.

When you hand an argument to a macro you are effectively creating an on the spot function. This is logically valid. But if you hand over functions with side effects you can get into trouble. The problem is not with macros, it is with the side effects, and the (wrong) presumption that a macro call is the same as a function call. This motivates some to use all capitals in a macro call, SQR(x++).

The bad press the C preprocessor has received is undeserved, especially in the light of the multitude of similar engines hidden within contemporary dynamic web-page systems. It should not be overused, but text processing is a vital generic pragmatic utility.

Notion 78: C Functions are Data Again

This code is a solution to the problem of how to return one of a parameterised family of C functions from pure C code.

One naive approach is simply to return a pointer to a function. But this means that the code for each individual function, one for each parameter value, needs to be included in the program. For an int parameter, this would be a prohibitively large amount of code.

The value returned must be a *real* C function. It is possible to encapsulate a generic function, with extra parameters in a struct, creating a new abstract function type. But some non-standard method is needed to access the values of the function.

This example is an extension of another one (see page 191).

In a broader context, this is dangerous code that may suffer from many portability problems. However, it is intended to illustrate the nature of C code, and a few things about functions. This code compiled and ran using the gcc compiler on a variety of common platforms.

The concept is to copy the actual code of a prototype function into an array, where it becomes just bytes. Using a special integer value as a flag we hunt for it in memory, and then replace it with the required value. The actual memory for the code has been allocated from the heap.

The power of a C program to modify itself, and other code (think about a sort routine in C in which you hand over a pointer to code in your own program) is one of the reasons that the designers of Java paid some attention to restricting recasting, and especially recasting to a block of bytes. But there are ways to attack other code with Java as well.

Both Haskell and Scheme have inbuilt lambda constructors that specifically allow the construction of new functions as a datatype that can be returned. Java, with its anonymous extension classes can do something surprisingly similar. Some traditional assembler was written as self-modifying code, although that it often frowned on today.

```
#include <stdlib.h>
#include <stdio.h>
#include <stream.h>

typedef int fn(int);

int f(int x){int g=0x1234; return g*x; }

int hex(int a){return a<10 ? a+'0' : a-9+'A';}

fn *mulfn(int m)
{
int i;
int p=200;
char *a = (char *)(malloc(100));

for(i=0;i<100;i++) a[i]=((char *)f)[i];
for(i=0;i<100;i++) if((a[i]==0x34) && (a[i+1]==0x12)) p=i;

*((int *)(a+p)) = m;

return (fn *)a;
}

main()
{
printf("%d\n",sizeof(*f));
printf("%d\n",(mulfn(234))(10));
printf("%d\n",(mulfn(1253))(10));
}
```

Notion 79: Java Code

Java is one of a family of languages with pseudo-C syntax and semantics. But, the Java philosophy is very different from the C philosophy, and the analogy between rapidly breaks down beyond the superficial.

Java is a dedicated objected-oriented language.[28] But to suggest that Java is distinct from C simply in supporting object programming is at best misleading. Java has eliminated the ability to attack the detail of the underlying machine; added automated formal memory handling via garbage collection, included a strong typing philosophy, added true Boolean, character, array, and string types; eliminated pointer arithmetic; ignored macro processing; and incorporated a nested hierarchical library system. The Java virtual machine, however, is a technicality, and does not indicate a significant distinction. Java, like C, is designed to compile easily to Von Neumann machine code.

Despite the differences, the mnemonic value of C for the Java programmer is strong. The entry point is "main". Block structure is denoted by "{" and "}"; and the basic definition, expression, and command syntax is almost identical. Except for changes incurred by the inclusion of a true Boolean type, control structures (`for`, `while`, `do` and `switch`) have the same syntax and semantics. Likewise (? :). Types `int`, `char`, `float`, etc., exist in Java with a formalised C semantics. Operators, such as compound assignment, `+=`, and all the arithmetic and logical operators exist with the same syntax. In overall appearance, a block of Java code may appear to be C code. At the detailed level, neither the syntax nor the overt semantics is certain to distinguish a Java code fragment from a C code fragment. The syntax of array referencing and function activation is also similar but this is true over a much broader range of languages.

Some parts of Java have different syntax, but similar pragmatics. The use of import directives in Java, such as `import java.io.*`, is the same as the typical use in C of `#include <stdio.h>`, except that in Java the importation is at the link level, rather than the level of textual substitution. (The * is a wild card and means importation of all elements of that pattern).

---

[28] Except for arithmetic, since objects are bad for some things.

Other parts have the same syntax, but different semantics. Array references in Java look identical to those in C, but the semantics are strongly different. In C, linear arrays and pointers are are largely identical. In Java, the array type is an abstract type and all explicit use of pointers has been removed, allowing only *references* (implicit pointers without arithmetic).

In exchange for this fairly major loss from C, there is a garbage collector. This could not exist in the unfettered pointer environment of C, and means that there is no explicit deallocation required. Thus, (assuming the garbage collector is functioning correctly) you will get no memory leaks in Java. This is a significant reduction in things that a programmer has to worry about when debugging a program.

```
class Hello
{
public static void main(String args[])
        {System.out.println("Hello Java World");}
}
```

The only top level structure allowed in Java is a class, all other data definitions, including functions, must occur within the context of a class definition. The simplest Java program requires one class, the syntax of which is almost the same as C++, and closely tied to the C struct definitions. Java (the JDK) is annoyingly determined about the names of files — they must have the extension java — it is not optional, and if the file contains a package entry point, it must be (called main) inside a class of the same name (including capitalisation) as the file.

Java inheritance is singular, a class can only *extend* one parent class. However, a virtual inheritance is available using interfaces. An interface is a declaration of a collection of functions to be provided. When a class *implements* an interface it is a compile-time error not to include all the required functions. It is a limited form of abstract datatype axiom declaration. Some complaints have been levelled at Java for the lack of variable types in this context.

Notion 80: Pointer Casting

For a typical language designed to compile easily to Von Neumann machine code, each inbuilt datatype instance has an existence as a block of bytes in memory. Contrary-wise, each block of bytes in memory *could* be interpreted as an instance of a datatype. If a block of one type is written into memory, and then read out as a block of another type, then a form of type conversion has occurred. In C, this conversion is performed by expressions such as `x=*((int*)&y))`. This is very different from `x=y` which may involve implicit operations on the stored data.

Changing the type of a pointer does not affect the bytes that it points to. Only sometimes will this have a high-level meaning. A language specification does not typically define the result of a pointer-type cast. But, pointer type casting is a mechanism for machine-specific type manipulation, such as switching byte order in a multi-byte integer. In Java, generic pointer casting is disallowed. This is a philosophical decision, the Java semantics are defined in terms of a specific Von Neumann machine, and so pointer casting would have had a well-defined meaning.

Generically, a pointer is an index into the memory of the machine, analogous to an integer index into an array. In C, `&x` means the index of the location were we will find `x`, and `*p` means the contents of the memory at the location indicated by `p`. Thus, `*(p+2)` has an analogous meaning to `A[2]`. In classic C there is no distinction.

The term *pointer* has been used fairly consistently over the last few decades of the twentieth century to denote variables that contain the address of a data structure in memory, or abstractions of this (such as indirect addresses through tables). In assembler and C, there is a natural inclination to do arithmetic on pointers. The sum of a pointer and an integer is a pointer to another location. The type of a pointer in C includes the size of what it points to, and `p+1` is interpreted as `p + sizeof(*p)`. Pointer typecasting changes the size used implicitly in pointer arithmetic.

The term *reference* has become popular in certain circles. A reference is a cut-down pointer, with implicit de-reference and the ability to be copied, but with no operations that return any pointers other than ones you started with. Promoters of the use of references often claim that references are not pointers. Some Java proponents are bothered by the suggestion that Java has pointers, and write at length in refutation. This is a political bun fight. I will try to avoid it. In Java, a declaration of a variable as an object does not result in an object being created. Each Java object variable is really a variable storing a reference to an object. This does affect the semantics, and can be a trap for the unwary.

In C, if we have two pointers we can equate the items they point to by explicit de-reference: `*p = *q;`. But, in Java, there is no explicit de-reference, so we need another method. Java uses `p = q.clone()`, where `q.clone()` returns a reference to a new (identical) object. The method `clone` is part of the Clonable interface. But, the details of the copy have to be provided by the programmer. There is no default method for obtaining a new copy of an object. In Java, you can only get a copy of something, if that something cooperates. Obtaining a new copy is a memory based concept. Cloning has no meaning in Haskell.

Similarly, $*p == *q$ is used to test for (literal byte-wise) equality of entities in C. But, in Java, apart from not having the de-reference required ($p == q$ is treated as pointer equality) there is no default test for equality. Java does provide an interface that includes `equals()`, but this has to be deliberately provided by the programmer. This constraint is strongly in line with abstract datatypes, for which equality is often different from structural equivalence. Also, the ability to test for equality enables us, by constructing an object of the same class, some facility to determine the contents of an instance of the object. Apart from being non-modular, it also has severe security implications.

If appreciated correctly, the Java constraints on copying and comparing can be used to promote clean abstract datatypes, but only if the programmer is already willing. The axiom `q.clone().equals(q)` should be true, but there is no certainty that any given object will satisfy it. Haskell has a culture of specifying more complex axioms than the Java interfaces and desiring that the programmer prove the properties for new instances of a class. But this is not enforced within the language.

Notion 7: Reference Typecasting in Java

In Java, the declaration

```
myclass myobject = new myclass();
```

defines `myobject` as a *reference* to an instance of `myclass`.

De-referencing in Java is all implicit; so most of the time the pointer nature of objects is hidden. But it does exist.

```
myclass obj1 = new myclass();
myclass obj2;
obj1.x = 6;
obj2 = obj1;
obj2.x = 7;
System.out.println(obj1.x);
```

Since `obj2=obj1` copies the reference this program prints out 7.

In C any pointer typecast is allowed; the semantics depend strongly on the nature of the machine. In Java, a reference may only be cast to a class to which it is actually referring, that is, to a super-class, or to a sub-class that the instance actually is at run time. Any attempt to cast to a reference to something else is a run-time fault. Java keeps type information at run time to achieve these checks.

However, since a type can always be passed to a function that requires the super-type, there is no reason to cast to a super-type unless the super-type has some vital material that is not included in the class. This suggests that refactoring the class hierarchy is called for.

Alternatively, to cast to a subclass, and be certain to avoid a run time fault, either there is reason to know that the instance is really an element of the subclass when it is passed, in which case why not call a less generic function, or the behaviour of the code will vary depending on whether the instance is in the subclass or not. This is ad hoc polymorphism.

Casts in Java are logically a polymorphism mechanism.

Notion 8: Java Field Modifiers

Each variable or function in Java occurs within a class or object. An object is an instance of a class. A field declaration declares its type. A field definition states exactly what it is. A method is conceptually the same, but syntactically different. It is a function valued field. Methods and fields both take up space.

Each class has space to store *Class Fields*. Each object has space to store *Instance Fields*. The modifier `static` indicates a class field. Otherwise a field is an instance field. This is pragmatically similar but not semantically the same as the term static in C. In C, static means *defined outside the invocation of a function*, in Java static means *defined outside the instance of the class*. With co-routines the concept is the same. Class variables are values in the scope of a collection of co-routines.

A non-static field is not usable from a static context. If there are no instances then there is no field, if there are multiple instances, then there is ambiguity.

In C++ the definitions in a class are set off by `public:` and private designators, in Java, the `public` modifier is used individually on each field.

```
default    .................................. instance field
default    ......................... seen only in its package
public     ............. seen anywhere its class can be seen
private    ........................... seen only in its class
protected  ................. in its package and subclasses
abstract   ......................... not implemented here
final      ........................... may not be over-ridden
static     ...................................... class field
```

Notion 9: Abstract Methods in Java

A method designated *abstract*, in Java, is a method for which no code is being supplied. The actual code resides in an extension class. To designate a class abstract is simply to disallow the creation of instances of that class. Since a method does need code, any class that contains abstract methods must itself be designated abstract. But a class may be designated abstract even if it has no abstract methods. One motivation for doing so is to emphasise that a given class is acting as an archetype for a number of conceptually related extension classes.

An example follows:

```
abstract class myclass
{
abstract int fn1(int x, int y);
int fn2(int x){return x*x;}
int a;
int b=0;
}
```

To state that a method is abstract is to state that you will not supply the code for it right now. But this is conceptually impure. In the above example, we have two int variables. One of these is given a value and the other is not. To create an instance of this class correctly you should supply the missing value. But Java does not require any special warning of this fact. To be more regular, we should have had to specify that the uninitialised variable was abstract. Contrary-wise, if there is a default value for an int variable, such as 0, then the obvious default value for a method that returns int is a constant method that returns 0. Likewise the default for an object is a null reference, and so the default for an abstract method returning any class is apparent. This is a design decision, Java could have had these defaults.

Since Java insists that every method in every object *must* have code associated with it, it is not valid in Java to create an instance of a class that has a function designated as abstract. However, it is perfectly valid to create an extension class. Such extension classes may be implicit. This enables a style that is very close to the initialisation of a function-valued field.

For example:

```
myclass my = new myclass()
                {
                int fn1(int x, int y){return x*y;};
                int a=6;
                }
```

In this example, not only the code for **fn1**, but also the value of the uninitialised variable is given. Technically this is creating an instance of an extension class of **myclass**, which is why the instance creation is legal. If the code was not given for **fn1** the Java compiler would complain that the extension class should be designated as abstract since it does not implement **fn1**.

This error message is slightly opaque, unless you understand that the constructor is creating implicit extension classes. Further, there is no way that such a designation can be given for the implicit class. However, other than for this error message you can ignore the implicit extension for programming purposes.

The error message **java.lang.NullPointerException** is also rather opaque, you get it if you refer to an object that has not been initialised with **new**. This is particularly curious when you take into account some people's insistence that Java has no pointers.

Because an implicit extension class may be immediately passed as an argument to a function, Java has the curious distinction of admitting to its syntax the nesting of braces { } inside parentheses ( ).

These implicit extension classes may be called *anonymous* extension classes. If you look in the directory where the Java code is compiled to byte code, you will find that these actually occur explicitly as class files. Thus, this mechanism never does anything that could not have been duplicated by creating explicit classes. But the syntactic convenience can make a major contribution to clear code, if used correctly. On the other hand, some authors, including Sun, feel that its use should be kept to a minimum.

Notion 81: The Object Data Type

There is a lack of pragmatic consensus on the exact meaning of the term *object* in software. Different languages provide different implementations. Generically an isolated object is a tuple (like a C struct) whose fields may be functions whose local environment implicitly includes the tuple. An invocation `x=thing.method(a,b,c)` is another way of saying `(x,thing)=thing[method](thing,a,b,c)`. That is, the method may return a value, but it also modifies the object through which it was invoked.

However, objects are also linked together into a network. If a field is not defined in a specific tuple, then the network is searched for a tuple that does define that field. This approach has been used in CODASYL data bases (see page 183), and was quite popular prior to around 1980, when it was replaced by the relational database concept.

Various search strategies have been tried. The general trend is toward a simple tree structure which is searched upward to the root (for example in Java), however, C++ has a directed acyclic graph searched in a similar manner. If no searching is required, then classes and objects become identical to orthodox records with function valued fields (in C, function pointers).

Typically declaration of the object network is done by specifying *classes*. A class is an object which can be inherited from. They are linked together into a network. They also include a type definition for *instances* of the class. Instances are simply objects which are designated as not being inheritable from, and when created are linked by the network directly to the corresponding class. An instance is a leaf in the network. Generally it is only the leaves that are referred to as being objects.

Alternatively objects may be said to be grouped together into classes. A class is a collection of tuples with the same type signature. This is the approach used in Haskell, and is sometimes given as the generic concept for objects. But this is misleading. In Java, a class exists in its own right and has variables and methods that can be used even if no instances exist. A Java class does have a tuple associated with it, just like an instance. With each class definition there is the definition of the class tuple and the definition of the instance tuple, the class tuple being designated by the keyword "static". Without the use of static, the definition could be seen as the pure class definition as a collection of objects.

Classes themselves are not first-class objects and cannot be passed around to functions. They remain always accessed as variables global in the context in which they were defined.

In Java,

```
class <name> extends <parent> {
int x;             // .... instance variable
static int y;      // .... class variable
int f(){...}       // .... instance function
static int g(){...} // .... class function
}
```

The **extends** keyword designates the parent of the class and is the only means of constructing the inheritance network. The idea in C++ is similar, but it uses a colon instead of a keyword. In Java, methods must be declared and defined within the syntactic context of the class definition. In C++, this is optional, a method may be indicated as belonging to a class by the use of ::.

Java gives the option to add or overwrite fields when declaring a new instance of a class. The methods so defined have access to the variables active in the context of the definition. An implicit extension class is created to handle this situation. Although it may at first appear to be syntactic sugar, overwriting methods can be used to great effect to simplify complex code. In C++, extra class names must be created, and fields initialised to cover the required local variables.

Inheritance in C++ differs from that in Java (see page 181).

Notion 82: Manual Objects

Sophisticated constructs in languages may assist but are never indispensable. By the regular use of compound code fragments, and some bookkeeping, it is possible to incorporate new constructs in an old language. Indeed, this is the core task of the programmer. If all constructs already existed, then the programmer would not (exist).

Often this is easier than it looks. A large part of the idea of an object datatype is syntactic sugar. The following demonstrates how to incorporate aspects of objects in C code manually. We begin by encapsulating a collection of functions in a record by using pointers.

```
struct counter
{
char name[10]; int value; void (*addto)(); void (*print)();
}
```

The following gives an example of its initialisation and use.

The setup function:

The mainline:

```
void setup
(struct counter *this,
int n, char *s)
{
this->value=n;
strcpy(this->name,s);
this->addto = counter_addto;
this->print = counter_print;
}
```

```
main()
{
struct counter g;

setup(&g,1,"fred");
g.addto(&g,2);
g.print(&g);
}
```

At the simplest level, an object is a record that includes data and functions. To make it possible for each function to access the other fields of the same record, we use the discipline (see note 1) that the first argument is always a pointer to the record. We can hide this in a macro (or function call) such as #define call(g,m,x) g.m(&g,x) if we desire. The record field constructor (the "" ".") is actually a function. And we could define dot(g,m) to return the appropriate material from the record. We are replacing compiler operation with program code.

C++ lets a method access other fields via the predefined `this` variable. C++ also has compound function names such as `counter::print`, and allows function code to be included syntactically inside the record definition. However, these changes are syntactic sugar, reducing the programmer discipline required, but not changing the essential semantics.

```
struct counter       // C++ would call this a class
{
char name[10];
int value;
void addto(int n, struct counter *x) {x->value+=n;}
void print(struct counter *x)
      {printf("value of %s is %d\n", x->name,x->value);}
}
```

We have not discussed in-line functions, operator overloading, polymorphism and inheritance. Only the last relates to objects. The other three could be included in C without making it an object-oriented language. Dependence of operations on the type is produced by including a standard **type** field in each record. Inheritance can be produced by incorporating pointers to the parent and default fields that refer to the parent. However, this bookkeeping is much less local syntax and sugar. It would be possible, through the special syntax for record lookup, to incorporate inheritance, but the code required is non-trivial.

The method used here, of incorporating disparate parts into a record structure, is very general. The record structure, mathematically a tuple, is a fundamental tool in formal construction. Both in constructive mathematics, and in computer science (which are almost the same thing) the essential approach is to define the underlying structure in terms of compounded tuples and then to define algorithms that operate on them. The concept of a higher level-structure, or abstract datatype, is simply the notion of respecting the intended structure by operating on these ultimately through the definitive algorithms.

Notion 83: Inheritance and Dynamic Type

Object field inheritance interacts with dynamic type. The dynamic type is the type of the datum; the static type is the type of the variable. Object inheritance structures are essentially CODASYL databases. The objects and classes are records in this structure. An object is distinguished as a record that cannot be the target of an inheritance link. Typically the graph will be acyclic. The problem is to decide from which type to determine the field.

Java and C++ offer opposite default solutions. In C++, the field is taken from the static type, unless the declaration of inheritance is tagged with the **virtual** keyword. Overwriting of fields can be prevented in C++ by the =0 indicator, or in Java by the **final** keyword. A distinction being that C++ silently calls the old method, while Java compilers flag an error if an attempt is made to overwrite a final method.

```
abstract class small{int a=1; int f(){return 10;};}

public class big
{
 public static void main(String args[])
 {
  small my = new small(){int a=2; int f(){return 20+a;}};
  System.out.println(""+my.a+" "+my.f());
 }
}
```

The program above demonstrates that in Java, overwriting methods means that the method of the dynamic type is referred to, but overwriting variables does not entirely work. Effectively, the variable as declared in the superclass still exists, and if you refer to it from general code, you will get that variable. But if you refer to the overwritten variable in an overwritten method, then you will get the field in the extension class. This is almost as if there were a public and private field of sharing the name.

The output is **1 22**, demonstrating that external access to the field accesses the old variable, which still exists, while internal accesses find the new variable. It is possible to access the new variable externally by using a method to return its value. So, if all non-method fields were private this type of behaviour would not be apparent.

I can't think of any circumstances where this makes good sense.

The default behaviour in C++ is to take the method from the static type. This is dangerous. An example given of when you might want this is an initialisation function. There is an initialise in the super-class that handles all the generic initialisation, and this can be called by the sub-class initialisation method by the same name.

I argue that if you have overwritten a method in a subclass, and still want to refer to the method in the super-class, then you have not validly over-written the method. The method in the super-class is doing something different from the method in the subclass. In the example above, we should have an init() function in the superclass, and a superinit(), where init() can call superinit(). Then in the subclass we have subinit(), and the overwritten method init() in the subclass can call both superinit() and subinit().

Notion 84: CODASYL and Objects

The concept of type as a set of data elements is pure. But most languages do not implement types this way. Rather than type being deducible from the explicit structure of an object, type is indicated by an implicit tag. Each class instance has an extra field, the type number. This is a *because I told you so* type system. Often operators check this tag to determine which piece of code to call internally. This is called polymorphism, but it essentially just a way of providing an implicit integer switch. Such a process is logically non-modular. Parametric polymorphism, code in which the tag is never referred to, is just code in which the polymorphism of the operators used handles all the polymorphism.

In the pure sense, a child class is an instance of the parent class. All the fields of the parent exist in the child. All the methods of the parent work in the child. For example, the `area()` method of a polygon class works on the square class, even though there is a more efficient method for this special case. Extra fields and methods may be available in the child.

But, pragmatically, it may be desired to implement the child very differently: to store the side length and centre of an axis aligned square, instead of the vertices, for example. The methods of the parent class no longer apply to the child. But we should still be able to answer all the parent questions within the child. A square still has a collection of vertices, even though they may be computed rather than stored in an array. We insist that either the old method still works, or that a new externally equivalent method is provided under the same name. We only overwrite a method when the old one will not work as well or at all. Thus, once we have overwritten a method, we *never* want to call the old method again.

When a method is called on a specific instance of a type, there is the static type of the variable in which the instance is stored, and the dynamic type indicated by the tag in the instance. The search for the method actually to call should begin with the instance, and not the variable it happens to be stored in.

In C++ the default mechanism for choosing the field is to choose the static type. If you specify virtual inheritance then you get inheritance from dynamic type. It is possible to prevent a method being overwritten in java by giving it the `final` attribute. C++ will not stop you trying to overwrite a `const` method, but may just silently call the old one. A Java compiler indicates a fault if you attempt to overwrite a final method. In Java, the default mechanism is to inherit from the dynamic type for methods, and the static type for fields.

In practice there is a strong lack of consensus about what an object is. But all the definitions that I am aware of are instances of the CODASYL database concept. This idea was marginalised by the relational database concept after the 1970's, possibly partially due to support from academia. The relational database concept has a clean theoretical foundation called *relational algebra*. Whether this is sufficient reason to prefer the relational database is moot. The situation is similar to the case of linear versus non-linear control systems in engineering. The former is more understandable, the latter is more adaptable.

A CODASYL database is a collection of records with fields. A field in a record may contain data or a pointer to another record. The user has a pointer to a record, and makes a request for a field from that record. If the field contains data, then the data is returned, as though the database was relational. If the field contains a pointer, then a graph search is performed, starting at that record, until a record is found whose corresponding field contains data. The nature of the search algorithm and the structure of the graph of connections gives the detailed semantics of the database.

It may be that the notion of inheritance is getting mixed up with problems of security. If you can make a subclass of an object, and then hand it over to something that expects that sort of object, but this new one overwrites some central important security methods, then security might be compromised. True, this is a problem, but it is inherent in the idea of letting general users make new subclasses of system objects.

It is clear that standard-language object-systems allow the contradiction of the basic axioms expressed here, so that a child may behave in no manner like the parent. And it is not clear that education counters this with programmer discipline.

Notion 85: Typecasting

Generically, a type is a set of potential data. Any set will do, types are logically arbitrary. A type could be all the integers, $\sqrt{2}$, π and the string The cat sat on the mat. There is no unique *true* type for a given datum. Most languages introduce a type system, a method of ascribing types to each variable and datum. A type ascribed to a variable is called its static type, and the type of a datum it refers to is called its dynamic type. Exactly which types are allowed depends on the language. In practice, types are selected either for conceptual or implementational unity. Unfortunately, many type systems have conceptual faults. For example, while the integers are a proper subtype of the reals, the integer type is not typically a subtype of the floating-point type; in fact they are almost completely unrelated. And yet the myth persists that they model pure arithmetic.

A fundamental operation in C, C++ and Java is typecasting. Each data element comes with a designated type. If the type of an element is a subtype of another type, then we may change the designation to the other type, without invalidating the state of the program. This is a *true* typecast. Logically, we are free to cast the type of a datum to any type to which the datum *actually* belongs.

But, sometimes there are (subjectively) natural partial maps from one type to another. For example, (float)5.0 may be seen as equivalent to (long)5. Thus, long x=5.0 is often thought of as a non-operation. If the map loses no information (an injective isomorphism) then this position *might* be justified. However, for typical floating-point and integer types the operation is non-trivial and lossy. Not all floats can be correctly converted to long, nor all longs to float. Also, the map $x \rightarrow \exp x$ maps reals without loss onto positive reals. Is it a type cast from reals to reals? Sometimes there is known and accepted loss of information, int x=5.6 is often seen as *valid*.

The static type of a variable indicates the set of data to which it may refer. Type declarations serve the dual purpose of enabling automated optimisation of code and providing logical cross-checking. Static type checking is the same as *unit analysis* in physics. If two physical quantities are equated, and one of them is an area, then the other should also be an area. Equating an area and a length is seen as a non-sequitur. The philosophical status of this approach is debatable. The ancient Greeks felt that all numbers had units, and avoided equating non-compatible numbers, but it has been seen as an advance that modern numbers have no units. At the same time, the logical bookkeeping does tend to increase the hamming distance between valid programs and can be a good discipline to keep the thinking clean. Unfortunately, a lack of type faults does not even begin to suggest a lack of bugs. Speaking personally, it is very rare that type-checking finds any program bugs.

This introduces a more general notion of typecasting. In truth, any typecast that is not just a bookkeeping exercise should be viewed as a map between types, not as a typecast. In this direction, (newtype)x is an expression, in C, C++ and Java, whose value is the *natural* equivalent of variable x, as an element of the type newtype. So the value of (int)5.6 is 5. Often, there are quibbles about exactly what should be returned. But the idea is to return something plausible, rather than disallowing the operation.

The Java typecasts are like C++ type-safe down-casts. There is no equivalent in Java of the C style no-questions-asked pointer typecast. Numerical constants such as (2.6) are double by default, and should be cast explicitly to float to put them in a float variable. Trying to put (2.6) in an int will result in a *possible loss of precision* error. However, the (int) cast *will* do the conversion. This is a kludge.

Haskell, however, has a very different approach, and no typecasts. It does have a variety of maps between types, but they are specifically functions, and not a special case syntax or semantics. The Haskell type of a symbol does not (typically) have to be declared because the Haskell system deduces the type from its usage. This is a vast improvement. The type system is checking that the usage of the symbol is logically consistent, rather than that arbitrary tags have been assigned in a regular manner.

Notion 86: The Concept of Type

What is a type? There are two approaches. A type is a collection of data elements, or an arbitrary tag. A data element is admitted to a type because of who it is, or because of who it knows.

If we declare

```
typedef atype thing;
thing fred;
atype club(atype x){return x*x;}
```

then will **fred** be acceptable in the **club()** and should he be?

In C and Java this type of code declares a trivial subtype that can be used in the same places, and do the same things as the original.

Originally in C, a field name was an offset, so $r.f=*(\&r+f)$, analogous to array semantics. This was easy to compile, and consistent with classic C. But the field names were global constants. No struct declarations could reuse a field name. Also, any field name could be used on any record. Something similar is true in Haskell, each field name is a global function, and can't be reused.

Any set of (int,string) tuples is interchangeable; this is an accidental equivalence, contingent on a particular choice of implementation. One tuple might be student numbers with student names, and the other tuple a new string type that includes the length of the string. Sometimes structural equivalence is the right thing, sometimes it is not.

To avoid this, we can concentrate on the name of the type, it was named for who it knows, not who it is. In this case, declaring a new type with a new name means starting from scratch with something that behaves the same, but is not interchangeable. But if we do base a new type on the old, we most likely wanted at least some of the characteristics of the old. This leads to a desire selectively to inherit from the original, on creation of the new.

In practice, type is what we say it is.

Notion 87: Type-Checking

Type is often confounded with type-checking.

Clarity of thinking about the type of data can improve design. Being clear about exactly what your data is may provide a hint to the required algorithm. But the usual type-checking system does not provide the required generality, and may be a hindrance.

In C and Java a logic error might generate a type fault, a long range syntax error. But such errors are very coarse. Language familiarity should reduce this fault rate to that of typos.

My number must be between 10 and 99. But neither C nor Java allows me to define a type that is a subrange of the integers. I must use my own type-checking code. Only a very few, arbitrary errors of no logical depth are type faults. Logically, any data error is a type fault, the data is not in the correct set. But mostly we must roll our own type-check.

The type-checking system is a simplistic collection of inbuilt assertions that the programmer can't turn off. The use of void pointer and pointer type casting in C, and streaming objects in Java are examples of subverting the type system. The type system got in the way.

Haskell is much better. It is strongly typed, but type declarations are not required. Haskell derives the natural type of a variable from its usage. But, like waking up before the alarm goes off, it is the mental discipline of the type system that is significant, rather than the type-checker itself.

But Haskell has limits. A direct implementation of the Y-combinator is not possible: $(\lambda f.(\lambda .fxx)(\lambda .fxx))$ generates a type fault. A tokeniser cannot use nested lists for parse trees. Haskell is preventing something perfectly logical, although, in this case because of the difficulty of implementing the required extensions. In Haskell discussions, I have heard the suggestion of coding a data type as a string to avoid a type fault. This is the Haskell version of subverting the type system.

Notion 88: Subtypes and Programming

The ability to declare a subtype, to use

```
{1..5} x;
```

to mean x might be 1, 2, 3, 4, or 5, but nothing else, is not often provided in languages, and even less so is 0, 2, 4, or 6. Logically we could use set builder notation, {a*a : a in [1..100]} x;. And in Haskell, list comprehension provides this power, but not for defining types. The mythos of type systems is that they help the programmer. But the reality is compiler and hardware design. Not simply that a fantasy type system is harder to implement, but that a restricted language is easier to implement.

To truly be for the programmer a type declaration should simply be the declarative assertion that the variable x will only ever be an element of a particular set. If at compile time it can be determined that the condition is violated, then a warning or an error should be generated, or, if not, then at run time a log message or an exception.

The use of assert commands in C is a partial realisation. If the compiler can tell that the assertion is statically violated, then it should generate a compile time error. Otherwise, the problem is left to run time.

```
try{ x = 1/x; } catch(ArithmeticException e){ ... }
```

If the exceptional condition occurs while the loop is running, then a jump outside to an error handling code should occur. Divide-by-zero is a type fault, the second argument to divide should be a non-zero value.

A type restriction is a particular case of an assertion *this must be so* in the program. Assertion checking should be in three phases: proof, compile, and run. The lint system for C programs was a utility that checked for problems with the code, at several levels as required, from no checking to rigidly strict checking. But, like a grammar checker, the existence of difficulties should not actually *physically prevent* the programmer from generating the code.

Notion 89: New Datatypes

A large part of program design is datatype design. Clearly marking out the datatypes and their axioms can be a very robust manner of coding. Done correctly, the completion of the datatypes is the completion of the entire program.

It automatically leads to logical modularisation, in which proving, testing and debugging can be performed piece by piece instead of worrying about the whole program at once.

Although object orientation can be of assistance, the true assistance to abstract datatype design is more likely the record structure, of which the isolated object is an instance. A well-defined and well-proved abstract datatype can be easily reused, both literally as source code and also in variations of code fragments in a program.

If we know the concept we do not need all the details.

```
struct stack {int n; datum d[100];};
typedef struct stack stack;
typedef int datum;
stack pop(stack s){s.n--; return s;}
datum top(stack s){return s.d[s.n-1];}
stack put(stack s, datum d){s.d[s.n++]=d; return s;}
```

The above is one of the quickest ways to get a basic stack in C. It is limited in size, but often this is an acceptable restriction. As it stands there is very little error handling. This type of code should be second nature to any programmer. It is not typically required to use a more heavy-duty, and proprietary, stack from a library.

```
stack newStack(){stack s={0};return s;}
int empty(Stack){return !s.n;}
int full(Stack){return s.n>=100;}
```

If the concept is clear, then the code will be.

Notion 10: Functions Are Data

This code illustrates the idea that functions are data in a very literal sense. The code for the function is copied into an array and then passed around and called. This idea can be extended to the modification of the code in situ (see page 167).

```
include <stdio.h>

#define byte unsigned char

int f(int x)
{
if(x==0) return 5;
if(x==1) return 2;
if(x==2) return 6;
if(x==3) return 1;
if(x==4) return 3;
}

byte a[200];
```

```
main()
{
int (*p1)(int x);
int (*p2)(int x);
int i;

p1 = f;
printf("f(3) is %d\n",p1(3));

for(i=0;i<200;i++)
{a[i] = ((byte *)f)[i];}

p2 = a;
printf("a(3) is %d\n",p2(2));
}
```

On a Von Neumann machine the code that actually runs is machine code. Machine code is essentially just a list of integers, typically bytes from 0 to 255. Sometimes the code is separated out into data and code sections, but the principle is to concatenate all the code into one list of small integers.

Under these conditions it is possible to just pick the code up as an array of bytes, and copy it to another location. Since C allows the recasting of pointers, it is possible to reinterpret the pointer to a function to be a pointer to bytes in memory, and thus gain the required access.

In practice various system characteristics can get in the way of this naive approach. For example, on more recent systems, for security reasons, the code that has been copied into a data area might not be allowed to be executed as code. On older, or embedded, systems there might be absolute references into the code that are broken by shifting it.

Notion 11: Java Threads

In Java, a thread is an instance of a class that extends the inbuilt class
java.lang.Thread. The following example illustrates the basics.

```
import java.lang.Thread.*;

class myThread extends Thread implements Runnable
{
String whoami; int sleep_time; int counter = 0;

public myThread(String w, int t){whoami=w; sleep_time = t;}

public void run()
{
while(true)
 {
 System.out.println("thread"+whoami+"["+counter+"]");
 counter++;
 try{Thread.sleep(sleep_time);}
 catch(InterruptedException e){}
 }
}
}

class multi
{
public static void main(String [] args)
throws InterruptedException
{
myThread thing1  = new myThread("cat",500);
myThread thing2  = new myThread("dog",637);
int counter = 0;

thing1.start();
thing2.start();

while(true)
 {
 Thread.sleep(800);
 System.out.println("main["+counter+"]"); counter++;
 }
}
}
```

Notion 90: Scheme Code

The motivation for Scheme is a form of list unification reduction. Expressions are nested tuples. So f(x) is represented as (f x). We then express operations as reductions, (* 1 1) → 1, (if true a b) → a, and so forth. Programming means to add a new reductions such as (fact x) → (if (= x 0) 1 (* x (fact (- x 1)))). Programs are executed by reducing the data to an irreducible term.

The Scheme syntax for this is
(define (fact x) (if (= x 0) 1 (* x (fact (- x 1)))))

Compound data, otherwise known as records, or tuples, exist in scheme as lists, written directly as '(1 2 3 4). (The quote is required to prevent scheme from attempting to execute it). Technically a list is a compound ordered pair. The ordered pair in scheme is (a . b), written with a full stop instead of a comma. A list is then a pair of the head and tail of the list. That is, (1 2 3 4) = (1 . (2 . (3 . (4 . ())))). The left hand side just is a shorthand for the right, not different internally. Under this assumption we can write the definitive list operations:

```
(car (a . b))  →  a
(cdr (a . b))  →  b                (car (1 2 3 4)) → 1
(cons a b)     →  (a . b)          (cdr (1 2 3 4)) → (2 3 4)
```

The reduction symbol → is an active equals sign. When confronted by the expression on the left, the computer replaces it with the expression on the right. Any state that fits the pattern on the left is changed to the corresponding pattern on the right.

The program below illustrates some typical features of scheme code.

```
(define
    (sum a)
    (if (= a '()) 0 (+ (car a) (sum (cdr a)))))
)
```

To get the most out of Scheme, recognise that functions are data. This is important in general programming, but in Scheme in particular the function and the data are structured the same way. Functions, or at

least their definitions (which amounts to the same thing) may be manipulated like any other list, using car and cdr. Functions really are
first class, moreso than the usual, passing as values, and storing in compound structures (which happen in C as well). The function in Scheme
can be manipulated, transformed, combined, or just created out of the
raw material at hand.

```
(define
  (map f a)
  (if (= a '()) '() (cons (f (car a)) (map f (cdr a)))))
)
```

In scheme, an on-the-fly function can be defined using the lambda expression: `(lambda (x) (* x x))` evaluates to a function that takes an
argument and squares it. The action of the lambda expression may be
expressed by the reduction

`((lambda (x) (f x)) a) → (f a)`

Thus, we can write `(define (addn n) (lambda (x) (+ x n)))`

Which defines the reduction `((add n) m) → (+ n m)`

The semantics of a program with no side effects may be expressed as
string productions, often making it fairly straightforward to verify the
program as correct. A lack of side effects means that the action of the
code depends only on what you see at that point in the code. Scheme
does, however, have operators with side effects.

A minor peculiarity of Scheme, which can be quite useful, is the generalisation of the head and tail operations; caar is the first element of the
first element.

`(caar '((1 2) 3) == 1`, and `(cadr x)==(car (cdr x))` and so on.

Scheme also has an excellent big-numbers package. An indefinite precision integer type is built in, and a typical installation can compute
factorial 5,000 in a short time, from a user-supplied definition.

Notion 91: Declarative and Imperative

Technically, imperative programming is when you tell the computer to do this and to do that; declarative programming is when you tell it what is true. All *programming* languages have aspects of both. A language that was *purely* declarative would produce no output; it would be merely a logical assertion. At the very least it must say the equivalent of *I want such and such to happen*, which while technically declarative is imperative in intent, like a parent saying to a child *I want you to clean your room*. At the other end of the spectrum, it is hard to envisage a language that has *absolutely* no declarative content. Keep in mind that a variable *declaration* is a declarative part of a program.

Looked at too closely, the distinction between declarative and imperative is a point of view. The C code assignment `int x=6;` of the initial value to a variable seems imperative, but can be restated as a declaration that initially there should be a logical equality `x==6`. This is not just wordplay, in Haskell, a declarative language, assertions such as `x=6` are used in exactly this manner.

In many respects the distinction between imperative and declarative is a matter of outlook. Expanding on this, we can show that the entire action of an imperative program can instead be expressed as logical declarations about a temporal sequence of values. In the code `for(i=1;i<6;i++) t=t+a[i]` we can treat each variable as a function of clock-tick time. We add a new subscript to indicate the clock-tick number. Thus, we have i_n, t_n and $a_n[i]$. For exposition we take one clock-tick per line. So, `t = t + a[i]` means that $t_{n+1} = t_n + a_n[i_n]$ where n is the clock-tick on which the instruction was begun. This turns an imperative program essentially into a declarative one.

In Haskell we may view `fact 0 = 1 ; fact x = x * (fact (x - 1))` as a pure declaration. We are simply stating things about the factorial function. It is up to the computer to figure out how to answer questions like *what is* `fact(6)`. Alternatively we may see this code as an imperative command.

```
fact(x)
{
if x==0 then return 1
else if x==x then return x * (fact(x-1))
else error
}
```

In fact since Haskell (a supposedly declarative language) does actually search for expressions from the top of the file to the bottom of the file, it can always be rewritten in this mode. A similar comment applies to many implementations of Prolog.

This shows how to rethink C code as simply being a declaration about the property of the factorial function.

That is, `f(x){ if t(x) then return A else return B}` as an imperative, is just a way of saying `if t(x) then f(x)==A else f(x)==B` which is more declarative.

Like the idea that functions can encode any computation, the notion of declaration can be used to express the semantics of anything. In particular, `x=6` is simply the assertion that the machine state after this command has executed will include `x==6`. That is, `command(i) == x=6` implies `state(i+1) => x==6`

Any statement in a declarative language may be seen as effecting a transfer function that takes the machine state before the execution to the machine state after the execution.

Abstractly, any collection of indivisible commands can be seen as single compound command with semantics that assert if such and such element is executing, then when the next command that is not in the set is executing, such and such will be true.

Notion 92: Sorting with Pure Substitution

Sorting in procedural languages is often done, or at least taught, in the context of mutable arrays. In pure substitution we do not have mutable arrays. If we define a pure array type naively as a list, it is linear time to look up.

An easy sort to define with pure expressions is insertion sort. The program has a definition of insert that runs in linear time. Likewise it has a definition of sort given insert.

```
insert a [] = [a]
insert a (x:xt) | a > x = (a:x:xt)
insert a (x:xt) = x : (insert a xt)

isort [] = []
isort (a:xt) = insert a (isort xt)
```

An optimal comparison sort takes order $(n \log(n))$ steps. The above code does n insertions each taking about $n/2$ steps for a total of order n^2 steps.

Can we improve the performance?

Sorting algorithms with $(n \log(n))$ performance abound in procedural programming. But, direct copying of the concept into pure substitutional language can produce (n^2) performance.

Actually this distinction is less between procedural and functional languages and more between accessing an array, over accessing a list. The speed in procedural languages is often derived from constant time lookup arrays. This can be added to pure substitution languages and indeed exists in languages such as Haskell. If, in C, we had lists rather than arrays of elements, we would run into similar problems. In C we might get around this by using pointers, again a potentially random-access system.

Heap-sort is a fairly good array-based sort that works apparently because of the fast array accesses, giving fast access into an array, or at least a pointer to the last element of the heap. But neither a doubly linked list nor a tree with a pointer to the last element, is easy to construct from lists. Haskell is pure reduction. With some conceptual changes it is possible to write a fast heap sort in Haskell, but, naive merge sort in Haskell is fast (see page 199).

If we count the number of reductions required, as a generic measure of efficiency in this context, then we see that pure reduction can be unexpectedly inefficient if we just do things the same old way. Stack is easy, queue is hard, deque is harder. Adding capacity to pure reduction can be unexpectedly difficult. However, good fast substitutes and distinctly non-procedural methods do exist. The difficulties are from expectations, the way in which programmers are trained to program. This code needs a different outlook.

Quicksort is a classic fast sort in procedural code. We define it as follows, using all the paraphernalia of Haskell.

```
qsort [ ]     = [ ]

qsort (x:xs) =    qsort [y | y<-xs,y<x]
              ++ [x]
              ++ qsort [y | y<-xs,y>=x]
```

The logic of quick-sort is that we split the list into those elements greater, and those smaller than a selected list element. Then we sort the sublists and catenate the result. The difficulty with this is the choice of the pivot element. Even procedurally, this will be bad if a bad pivot is chosen. For pathological data the list will split into distinctly unfair sublists, resulting in the longer list being of order n in length. This produces order n^2 performance. A random choice of a pivot, constant procedural time, makes this very unlikely. The trick is to split the list roughly in half, but to do this in pure functions for arbitrary data we need to scan through and find an appropriate element, analysis of the distribution of data is going to take as long as a sort, and one that looks quickly down the list each time adds a linear scan which means order n^2 performance.

The above implementation of quick-sort, for example, works fine on the list [1..500], but runs out of memory on [500,499..1]. It does not even do well against insertion sort.

Notion 93: Fast Sorting in Haskell

Although quicksort is not what you[29] might like it to be (see page 197), and heap-sort requires a bit of thought to implement in pure substitution code, merge sort can work fairly well naively.

In an array, split the data in the middle, and then run in-place. Here it is more natural to split the list into every second item.

```
split [] = ([],[])
split [a] = ([a],[])
split (a:b:c) = (a:at, b:bt) where (at,bt) = split c
```

The merge takes the smallest item off either list, and continues building.

```
merge ([],x)=x
merge (x,[])=x
merge (a:at,b:bt) | a<=b = a : (merge (at,b:bt))
merge (a:at,b:bt) | b<=a = b : (merge (a:at,bt))
```

To sort: split, sort, merge.

```
sort [] = []
sort [a] = [a]
sort x = merge (sort a, sort b) where (a,b) = (split x)
```

Use each function name above for the order of its complexity. Substituting directly from the code[30], $split(1) = 1$ and $split(n+1) = split(n)+1$, so $split(n) = n$. Likewise for $merge$.

```
sort x = merge (map sort (split x))
```

Starting with $sort(n) = 1 + 2n + 2sort(n/2)$, and using the substitution $n = 2^m$, we look at the solution to $f(m+1) = \alpha + \beta 2^m + 2f(m)$, this is $f(m) = a2^m + bm2^m + c$, (check by substitution), where a is a free parameter, $b = \beta/2$ and $c = -\alpha$. so $split(n) = an + bn\log(n) + c$. Split affects β, which affects the speed, but not the order of the sort

---

[29] Actually I never liked quicksort, heap-sort is more conceptually robust.
[30] Normal technique, squint at the code to get the complexity recurrence relation.

Notion 12: Named Code Blocks

In C and Java, blocks are generic. Each block is opened by "{" and closed by "}". When there are deeply nested blocks it can be difficult to tell which block is being closed. Programmer discipline is often used, with strong control over indenting (often leading to bitter conflict). One approach to improving on this is different key words to terminate different types of block. There could be `endWhile` and `endFunction` etc. The type of each block termination is clear. Often this is enough to make it obvious precisely which block is being closed.

Like many rigid type-based languages fixes, it can indirectly reduce the difficulty but is not a general solution. We have to always include the type, while in the majority of cases it is not needed. And if the nested blocks are of the same type, it is of no use at all.

We need a system for closing blocks in which we can be completely sure, if required, that we are closing the correct block. A method that we do not have to use if we do not want to.

For example: each block has an optional name tag:

```
while(test) begin: blah blah blah end:
```

— or —

```
while(test) begin myblock: blah blah blah end myblock:
```

True, there is still a chance of picking the same local name for a block, but the chance of a problem is much less. You can choose which blocks to give names to. Used sparingly, as it should be, this gives a very solid solution to the block-marker matching problem.

Sometimes this is a programmer discipline, block names placed in a comment at the close brace. Unfortunately, the comment might be incorrect, or misleading, and should usually be ignored.

This is a type system, but the programmer has complete control. It is a type system that is an actual aid to the programmer.

Notion 94: Logic in Prolog

Prolog is so named as a contraction of *Programming with Logic*. This is misleading, and in order to program successfully in Prolog the prospective logic programmer must understand a few home truths.

Prolog cannot make the assertions (A or B) or (not A). Prolog can only assert a conjunction of Horn clauses. Horn clauses are clauses of the form C or not (P1 and .. and Pn), giving a mandatory conclusion as a consequence of the optional premises. Because the horn clauses are conjoined, we might have C or not P1 and C or not P2, which is identical to C or not (P1 or P2), but this disjunction is behind negation, and does not contradict the original assertion of impossibility.

Prolog is not monotonic. That is, if you add material to the database, something that was true before might become false. Also different lists of answers might occur, different orderings, and answers that are still true might be never be generated.

Prolog has no existential quantifier. However, it is possible to remove statements of the form $\exists X : p(X)$ by defining a constant x and stating that $p(x)$. Similarly, $\forall x : \exists y : f(x, y)$ may be modified by the use of a Skolem function such that $\forall x f(x, g(x))$, where $g(x)$ returns one of the y previously asserted to exist. The logical content is identical, albeit of a different flavour. The result is that all variables in Prolog are universally quantified. So, no quantifiers are written at all.

Prolog is first-order logic. That is, Prolog does not allow variable predicates. This means that functional equations are difficult to express within the spirit of Prolog logic. There are, however, some options involving formal expression manipulation, with unification reduction.

Unification-reduction of Horn clauses is called resolution. It was noticed by Robinson that under the right conditions resolution of horn clauses can be linear in the number of Horn clauses. But this is only true for the completely pure binary logic situation, which leads to a rather large number of horn clauses for describing the problem. Prolog tries the horn clauses in a specific order. Permuting the Horn clauses can lead to non-termination, or variation of response from a Prolog program.

On finite trees, the distinction between breadth-first and depth-first search is a technicality of the order of the solutions. Prolog uses depth-first search partly because it requires less scratch space, but also because solutions are usually fairly deep on the search tree. Thus, if the programmer makes an effort to ensure that the solutions are on branches that will be searched first, the speed of the program is greatly increased.

On infinite trees, depth-first and breadth-first search are fundamentally different. Depth-first can get caught in an infinite-length branch, and never get back to the top again. It is easy to create infinite search trees in Prolog, especially since sometimes there are an infinity of solutions. If Prolog was based on breadth-first it would be much more reliable, but it would also be a lot slower.

Prolog has no functions. Actually, apart from some syntactic troubles this causes no great difficulty. We simply replace $fact(3) = 6$ by $fact(3,6)$. In essence, the core entity in Prolog is the relation rather than the function, but since a function is a special case of a relation this is not important. On the other hand, this puts a greater burden on the pure and honest Prolog programmer, since searching all the projections of the relation should be made to work correctly.

The built-in arithmetic in Prolog is slow and clumsy, and does not pattern match properly. The excuse I've heard is that Prolog is not a numeric processing language, but it would take little effort to put in the effect. There are standard ways of enumerating the solution sets. It is an interesting exercise in Prolog programming to build up an efficient set of clauses to define correctly backtracking arithmetic.

With all these problems however, the one thing it does have going for it is the unification reduction, which is clean and very powerful. This feature alone is enough to write a good Prolog program. Throw away all the logic, and use only pure unification reduction, and many things can be easily written.

What about the original concept of logic programming? A Prolog program can nicely realise dynamic logic. But it is usually best to see the correct logical behaviour of a Prolog program as being a design criteria, rather than as an aid to design.

Exercise 11: Prolog in Java

Find a systematic way to translate a Prolog back-tracking tree scan into Java, not using any simulation, but using while-loop conditions, together with the lazy evaluating properties of && and ||.

Hints and explanation:

An expression such as   p1 && (p2 || p3)   tries p1 first, if false it stops, otherwise it tries p2; if true it returns true, if false it tries p3. Thus, a loop such as

```
while(p1&&(p2||p3)) print(result)
```

will print result for each time a path is found in the tree. If the predicates set the state of some variable each time, then result can indicate the values that have been found.

The problem with this is if the predicates are recursive, how do we develop the required variables?

```
while(p1(&x)&&(p2(&x)||p3(&x))) print(x);
```

where x is a structure that contains all the required variables. The predicates can do something similar with local variables on the stack.

```
p1(&x)
{
y = new thing(x);
while(p3(&y)||p4(&y)) return true;
return false;
}
```

The principle is to find a translation into Java that is as simple and close to the structure of Prolog as possible. And the faster it runs, the more points you get. Does your implementation run faster than Prolog itself?

Notion 95: Functions in Prolog

In its simplest form, a Prolog predicate describes a relation. By responding Yes or No it indicates whether or not a given tuple is in the relation. A function add(x,y) is a special case of a relation, so we can naturally express it as set of tuples (x,y,add(x,y)). The fact that add(2,3)=5 is expressed as add(2,3,5) in Prolog. Apart from some syntactic clumsiness, this causes no great hardship.

In English we do ask questions such as "Does 3 add 4 equal 7?" In Prolog this is "add(3,4,7)", and the response is Yes or No. But we can also ask questions with place holders, or variable symbols. Such as "3 add 4 equals what?" In this case, what is 7. But for "3 add what equals what", we have an infinite list of answers: 3+0=3, 3+1=4, etc. In Prolog, we can easily be more precise with our pronouns, such as distinguishing between add(3,X,X) and add(3,X,Y), but the principle is the same. In practice, in Prolog it is the listing of the set of solutions, rather than the yes–no answers, that is useful.

The built-in arithmetic in Prolog, however, does not work in the Prolog style. In fact, Prolog arithmetic is rather badly thought out, does not back-track, and is not a relation. A Prolog predicate add(X,Y,Z) can be called in eight modes, depending on which arguments are variable. When none are variable it should just answer yes or no. When one is variable, it should give the one possible numerical answer. When two are variable, there is a simple infinite list of options. When all three are variable, a two-dimensional solution space is expressed.

The definition of subtraction is sub(X,Y,Z) :- add(Y,Z,X), so there is no need for a separate inverse operation. This is characteristic of Prolog. In principle, F(3,X) can always be called as F(X,3), and thus the inverse of a function is implicit with the function. However, although in principle Prolog is supposed to work this out, in practice, explicit checking for which variables are instantiated is advised.

Integer multiplication mul(X,Y,Z) is well defined, but the number of solutions to mul(X,Y,12) is finite. Division is implicit with multiplication. If there are no solutions, then the predicate will indicate this.

Notion 96: Arithmetic in Prolog

How do we achieve back-tracking arithmetic in Prolog? Here we discuss
a very pure form, which is interesting for its discussion of the nature of
Prolog. A pure version based on binary notation would be more efficient.
But if you need an efficient solution, then a completely different approach
using meta-logic is advised.

We code $0 = 0$, $1 = s(0)$, $2 = s(s(0)$, $3 = s(s(s(0)))$ ...

Addition in Prolog for this representation is

```
add(X,0,X).
add(X,s(Y),Z) :- add(X,Y,s(Z)).
```

The query add(X,Y,s(0)) produces the list

```
(X,Y) = (0,s(0)),(s(0),0).
```

And the infinite list

```
(Y,Z) = (0,s(0)), (s(0),s(s(0))), (s(s(0)),s(s(s(0)))) ...
```

is produced by add(s(0),Y,Z).

However, it responds to add(X,s(0),Z) with $(X,Z)=(V,s(V))$ — correct
enough but not very helpful. When Prolog finds a syntactic solution
with a free variable it does not look for others. But we wanted integer
answers. The problem is partly that add is a little too general, for
example, add(fred,0,fred) is true.

Changing the program to insist on non-negative integers,

```
int(0).
int(s(X)) :- int(X).
add(X,0,X) :- int(X).
add(X,s(Y),Z) :- add(X,Y,s(Z)).
```

The program now responds well to each case so far discussed, but for
add(X,Y,Z) we get a list in which Y is always 0.

A standard trick for this is exemplified by modifying the last clause to

```
add(X,s(Y),Z) :- add(Y,X,s(Z))
```

to scramble the arguments. But this does not produce the correct response in this case.

The purpose of the int(X) predicate is not simply to indicate that X is an integer, but also to respond to the query int(X) with a nicely ordered list of options. This notion of a Prolog predicate as a *generator* or enumerator of solutions is very important, and is a large part of programming in Prolog.

In similar manner, the add(X,Y,Z) predicate is not simply to answer the question of whether X+Y=Z, but rather to generate the various solution spaces in a reasonable order; in particular, to not miss any, and not list any twice.

The following program works as required.

```
int(0).
int(s(X)) :- int(X).

lte(Z,Z).
lte(X,s(Z)) : lte(X,Z).

qadd(0,Z,Z).
qadd(s(X),Y,Z) :- qadd(X,s(Y),Z);

add(X,Y,Z) :- int(Z),lte(X,Z),qadd(X,Y,Z).
```

The operation is as follows: int generates the integers in the order 0, s(0), etc. And lte generates all the integers less than or equal to Z, as long as Z actually has a value. This is established by the fact that it is called after int(Z) in the definition of add(X,Y,Z). Now if Z has a value, then qadd(X,Y,Z) just lists all the pairs (0,Z),(1,Z-1) etc.

However, this does seem to remove some of the intuitive semantics from the nature of the addition operation.

Notion 97: Meta-Logic in Prolog

If the clauses in a Prolog program are correct when interpreted as pure logic, then the program will not produce incorrect results. Unfortunately, it might not produce any results at all. A Prolog program defines a search tree. All solutions are on the tree, but an infinite branch with no solutions can trap Prolog preventing the discovery of those solutions. The pragmatic correctness of a Prolog program depends on meta-logical factors such as the order and multiplicity of clauses, and specific choice logically equivalent clauses.

Often because there is no true negation operator, a programmer may be aware that no further solutions are possible but be unable to cast this as a logical condition. Instead the cut and fail operators can be used.

The clause `solns(X,Y) :- check(X),!,fail.`, states that if check is true, then no further solutions exist for Y. The fail operator is always false. The cut (!) operator instructs Prolog not to back-track past that point, it has no simple meaning as a logical condition. If it is used when no further solutions exist, then it does nothing other than improve the searching strategy.

A very simple demonstration is `a(2) :- !. a(2)`. The cut prevents Prolog from back-tracking to find the second occurrence of the solution to `a(X)`, thus assuring that each solution occurs exactly once.

The clause `var(X)` is true if X has not been bound to a value. The algorithmic behaviour of a predicate may be very different in cases of different binding states. The work required to verify `add(1,2,3)` is very different from that required to determine the infinite set of solutions to `add(X,1,Y)`.

The use of cut, fail, and var can be organised so that the logical content of the program is is unaffected, however, doing so requires care, and means that the correspondence between the pure logical program and the Prolog program has been made more obscure. If used contrary to logic, then these meta-logical operators can turn the Prolog program into something that bears little if any resemblance to the original logical constructions.

Exercise 12: Meta-Logic and Prolog

If the tree scan in Prolog was indefinitely fast, and based on a breadth-first search, then there would be no problems in extracting all the solutions correctly. But it is based on a depth-first search (so that programming tricks can make it run faster). Thus, meta-logical commands, such as

!	=	do not backtrack passed this point
fail	=	always returns false
var(X)	=	true if X is currently unbound
not(G)	=	try the goal, respond oppositely if it halts

are required for many applications, either for efficiency, or to make it possible at all. If used carefully, cut, fail, var, and not do not change the logic of the predicates they are used in.

1. Write transitivity into a predicate. That is, have some base information, such as f(a,b), f(b,c), and have Prolog produce a true response when such things as f(a,c) are in the transitive closure of the part of the relation actually specified.

   Can you do this without meta-logic?

2. Write arithmetic in Prolog, using the inbuilt arithmetic.

   Hint: Check explicitly for the 8 cases of instantiation. Generate the required solutions from knowledge of algebra. Try to do this efficiently, so that there are no unnecessary scans through the integers to find a single solution that could have been computed directly.

3. Given a predicate, P, which returns a sequence of elements X1, X2 and so on, write LP that calls P to produce the actual list of all these elements.

   Or prove that it can't be done.

Notion 98: What Is HTML Code?

As Peabody might have said,
Sherman, set the wayback machine for hyper-link.

Text can refer to other text. Ancient Greek books on geometry referred to other ancient Greek books on geometry. Thus was born the concept of hypertext.

However, it took a while to follow one of these references (hyper-links in modern terminology). You might have to send your slave off to the next city to retrieve a copy of the required document. But combine this idea with computers and the internet, and we get a copy of the referenced document in seconds. In practice, this idea is expanded out into a two-way real-time graphical communication medium. The generic notion is that by typing, pointing, clicking and dragging on a graphic image we can exchange information.

The second half of HTML (Hyper-Text Markup Language) refers to the way in which the virtual machine, the hyper-media graphics page, is to be described (paradoxically, in plain, old-fashioned text). A mark-up language describes how text and images will be laid out on a page.

Although not universally true, it is very broadly the case that the basis of computer files is some form of ASCII-encoded plain text. This code specifies upper- and lower-case Latin characters without any fonts. Traditionally, the font is chosen by the display device.

Very quickly an interest in specifying at least such attributes as bold or italic became strong. Programs such as WordPerfect allowed such codes as ^B to delimit a section of text to be displayed as bold. It was nothing other than a shorthand for *please display this in bold*.

Originally, we simply had plain hyper-text. That is, plain text, with links, and some related images. But quickly an interest in being able to specify other attributes of text emerged. The idea arose of specifying the attribute by enclosing the text in generic compound brackets. Such brackets have been used for related purposes in other contexts, so the choice was not unprecedented.

The cat sat on the mat.

The **cat** sat on the mat.

An attribute can be given to text that already has attributes.

The cat sat on the mat.

*The **cat** sat* on the mat.

Part of the reason behind these compound brackets, called tags, was that there were too many of these to give specific neat codes, another part was to allow for indefinite expansion in a regular manner. Tags that were not understood could just be ignored.

The basic hyper-link is referred to by

<a href=myExample.html>myExample</a>

Tags include italics, bold, heading, comment, colour, blinking, font size, image and tabular format.

Some attributes do not naturally refer to text, and occur at a particular spot on the page, such as a carriage return, or a horizontal line.

For these HTML uses just an open tag on its own.

 for a line break.

<hr> for a horizontal rule.

Because of the confusion, in looking for a close tag for a tag the interpreter does not understand it has been suggested that some other format, such as <br/> should be used for tags that occur singly instead of in pairs. There is a general trend to more formal and less forgiving HTML. Most likely the trend was inevitable.

Notion 99: Illogical markup language

A word processor is a program that can right-justify text
that cannot be justified in any other way.

At one point the idea was that the information given should be independent of the media. So, the `<b>` tag might be used to cause voice output to be read louder than average.

However, people do not work this way.

In practice, web-page designers have gone out of their way to find ways to bring back specific graphic control: for example the tabular format. There are programs that produce the details of a specific graphic and chop it into small pieces for use as the background of all the various cells in a table.

A similar perversity is the trend to sending a text message as a bit-mapped graphics image.

But the truth is, it is a lot harder to design a format that will work well in many media, and people do not want to put the effort in; especially since they are probably motivated by one specific medium, and a lack of time. Even if you do put the effort in, it might be easier to check the media type and transmit an entirely different page.

Many designers object to the idea of the user being able to reorganise the page; they do not see the ability to send plain text to be given a font as a good ideal. Their ideal is that the user should observe exactly, and only, what they want the user to observe.

Anyway, some media have characteristics that just do not translate. The notion of a carriage return in plain text does not translate to anything in spoken words. A pause perhaps, but it just does not feel the same. The idea of a Scottish accent in spoken words is difficult, at best, to translate into formatted text, and *gey naurby* impossible in plain text.

Notion 100: HTML Forgive and Forget

HTML interpreters are usually very forgiving.

A classic example is the `<p>` .. `</p>` tag. Since these do not nest, you can't have a paragraph inside another paragraph, the usual interpretation of opening a new paragraph before closing the last one is an implicit close of the previous one. Thus, many HTML documents have been written with just the `<p>` tag and not the `</p>`. [31]

HTML can, and should be more forgiving because, typically, there is very little relation between the parts. If a paragraph has something difficult to interpret in it, at worst it can just be dumped, and the next paragraph considered.

This is assisted by the relative lack of long-range effects in HTML code, no variables, no data storage, no function definitions means that the effect of a piece of code is local to its occurrence.

Half a paragraph is better than none, at least a lot of the time. As long as you did not put any ...

...half a routine in Java is unlikely to do anything even vaguely resembling the original intention. There is a much stronger relation between HTML code and the intended output than there is with most other languages.

A variety of extensions, such as program scripts, are introduced by tags intended to be ignored by browsers that do not recognise them.

If an image is not available, a browser will provide a small icon to show that an image should have been there, and continue with the rest of the processing. It is also possible to declare a textual alt parameter in the image tag, which replaces the image if the image cannot be found or displayed (for example on a plain text screen).

---

[31]But talk on the street is that close tags may be enforced in the future.

Notion 101: Expanding Beyond Recognition

In vanilla HTML there are no variables, and no long-range effects. However, typically HTML is not served in its vanilla flavour; javascript, vb-script, cgi, php, jsp, and so on all make HTML a basic data element to be bandied around.

In practice HTML code is used as the input and output of other systems, and also calls other languages, such as Java applets.

The HTML document needs to use the applet tag.

```
<applet code=myExample.class
        width=550
        height=350
>MyExample</applet>
```

The original Java code should extend the applet class.

```java
import java.applet.Applet;
import java.awt.Graphics;
public class thing extends Applet
{
 public void paint(Graphics g)
  {
   g.drawRect(0,0,size().width-1,size().height-1);
  }
}
```

Much of the original capacity of Java is still available, depending on the client security model, including the opening of other windows (popups) and the writing of files. Thus, a web page can perform in ways completely beyond HTML itself. However, the class file for this code is sent to the client's machine, so it is not a good idea to put any unencrypted secrets in it.

Chapter 6

Arithmetic Computation

Numbers are one of the most extensively developed formal structures that human beings have. Int and Float types are used extensively in programs. But the types provided in many languages do not really correspond in any nice way to the neat formal structure.

An understanding of the formal structures, and the differences on entering the orthodox language arena, can help to avoid a lot of obscure bugs in software.

Notion 102: Natural Arithmetic

Today, commonly known algorithms are easily used for basic arithmetic operations on natural numbers.

Addition: We are given two rows of digits, x and y. The $z = x + y$ row is computed as the sum of x and y, digit by digit. The c row is auxiliary working space.

$\cdots$	c_{i+1}	c_i	$\cdots$	0	1	0
$\cdots$	x_{i+1}	x_i	$\cdots$	2	3	9
$\cdots$	y_{i+1}	y_i	$\cdots$	1	2	1
$\cdots$	z_{i+1}	z_i	$\cdots$	3	6	0

The value of z_i depends on x_i, y_i and c_i, and can be tabulated completely without any reference to any semantics of the digit strings. A similar table is easily constructed for the carry c_{i+1}.

x\y	0	1	2	3	4	5	6	7	8	9
0	0	1	2	3	4	5	6	7	8	9
1	1	2	3	4	5	6	7	8	9	0
2	2	3	4	5	6	7	8	9	0	1
3	3	4	5	6	7	8	9	0	1	2
4	4	5	6	7	8	9	0	1	2	3
5	5	6	7	8	9	0	1	2	3	4
6	6	7	8	9	0	1	2	3	4	5
7	7	8	9	0	1	2	3	4	5	6
8	8	9	0	1	2	3	4	5	6	7
9	9	0	1	2	3	4	5	6	7	8

x\y	0	1	2	3	4	5	6	7	8	9
0	1	2	3	4	5	6	7	8	9	0
1	2	3	4	5	6	7	8	9	0	1
2	3	4	5	6	7	8	9	0	1	2
3	4	5	6	7	8	9	0	1	2	3
4	5	6	7	8	9	0	1	2	3	4
5	6	7	8	9	0	1	2	3	4	5
6	7	8	9	0	1	2	3	4	5	6
7	8	9	0	1	2	3	4	5	6	7
8	9	0	1	2	3	4	5	6	7	8
9	0	1	2	3	4	5	6	7	8	9

This is one of a class of similar algorithms. Allowing the carry to be an arbitrary digit, each algorithm is characterised by the 2,000 one-digit entries in the sum and carry tables. Counting, we find we have 10^2000 algorithms. This is an astronomically large but nevertheless finite number, so it is clear that not all computable operations on natural numbers can be expressed in this manner.

The addition is characterised by $10c_{i+1} + z_i = x_i + y_i + c_i$ which has a unique solution for digits. Analogously, the subtraction uses $-10c_{i+1} + z_i = x_i - y_i - c_i$.

$\cdots$	c_{i+1}	c_i	$\cdots$	0	1	0
$\cdots$	x_{i+1}	x_i	$\cdots$	2	3	1
$\cdots$	y_{i+1}	y_i	$\cdots$	1	2	9
$\cdots$	z_{i+1}	z_i	$\cdots$	1	0	2

There are two versions of this algorithm in use today. One, as above, and another in which a borrow (the carry) is subtracted from x_i, which causes a cascade of borrow operations when there is a sequence of 0s in x. Thus, this variant, which is common in English-speaking countries, is not a local algorithm. Although not commonly in use, an addition algorithm exists in which the carry is added immediately, potentially causing a cascade of carries when there is a sequence of 9s.

The subtraction and addition algorithms are matched in pairs; this is no coincidence. The essential relation is that $x - y = x + (-y)$. The addition algorithm is a formal definition of an operation on an infinite digit string, well defined even if the string is not eventually always 0. The 9's complement of y is $p_i = 9 - y_i$. Adding $p_i + y_i = 9$, adding 1 to this obtains 0. Thus, $p + y + 1 = 0$, and $-y = p + 1$. So any addition algorithm can be changed to a dual subtraction algorithm by incorporating 9s complementation. This is the limiting case of n-digit modulo arithmetic (see page 217).

Multiplication is a common example of an operation that falls out of this scope, although if the carry is allowed to be an arbitrary integer this limitation vanishes. The reason is more the power of an integer register (see page 38) than a restriction on the complexity of multiplication. The layout of the algorithm above is recognised as the architecture of a one-way three-tape Turing machine (see page 26).

Since z represents the natural number $\sum_{i=0}^{\infty} z_i 10^i$, the carry operation $(z'_{i+1}, z'_i) = (z_{i+1} + 1, z_i - 10)$ does not change the numeric value of z. Starting with z_0 and working to the left with one pass, we may normalise z, by repeated carrying, so that each z_i is a digit.

With the use of a second, normalisation, pass, we can express the addition as $z_i = x_i + y_i$. Similarity, $z_i = x_i - y_i$, with normalisation, expresses a correct subtraction algorithm. Convolution is $z_i = \sum_{i=0}^{j} x_i y_{j-i}$, this is the core of polynomial multiplication. Convolution followed by normalisation is a conceptually clean method for multiplication.

Finally, if the discrete Fourier transformation is used, both before and after, then multiplication is expressed as $z_i = x_i \times y_i$.

Notion 103: Modulo Arithmetic

Especially in computing, it is natural to think of a natural number as a sequence of digits. In the case of full natural arithmetic (see page 215), this register is infinite to the left. Moving through the digits of a natural number from right to left, we will find that they are eventually always 0. However, there is a suggestion that an infinite string of 9s is equivalent to -1. This idea can be promoted more strongly within the context of finite length register arithmetic.

Suppose that we have two 3-digit base-10 numbers, and we add them.

$$
\begin{array}{r}
{\scriptstyle 1\,1\,0} \\
158 \\
+965 \\
\hline
1\,123
\end{array}
$$

This results in a 4-digit base-10 number.

However, if we only have space for three digits, as may well be the case in a computer program, then we just drop the upper carry, and obtain

1	1	0
1	5	8
9	6	5
1	2	3

which is the arithmetic that occurs in a 3-digit register, showing the carry as full-size digits in its own carry-register.

The definitive property of -1 is that $1 + (-1) = 0$. That is, -1 is that which when incremented becomes 0. Now consider this ...

1	1	0
9	9	9
0	0	1
0	0	0

If we limit ourselves to sufficiently small integers, then the result from the fixed-digit register arithmetic is the same as that for the integer result. The above shows that we can also model -1 within this register arithmetic, as a string of all 9's. Further work shows that 998 is -2 and so on.

More generally, if the register has n digits, then adding 10^n will make no difference, so $y - x = y + (10^n - x)$. So we may equate $-x$ and $10^n - x$. In practice this works. This can also be expressed as $(10^n - 1) - x + 1$. Going back to the register ...

0	0	0
9	9	9
0	2	3
9	7	6

We subtract the number from a row of nines, generating all 0 carries. Then we subtract 1, to obtain the required negative.

A register with a google of digits is quite sufficient for all practical applications of arithmetic, so an overflow will never occur. In this case, a register of all 9's really does behave as -1. We can think of arithmetic on finite natural numbers as being on sequences that continue to the left with all 0s. Then integers are those sequences that either continue with all 0's, for positive numbers, or all 9's, for negative numbers.

However, we do not have to store an infinite number of 0's or 9's, we simply note that the upper digit is repeating, and state what it is. The rules for arithmetic on these sequences should be clear.

Returning to the finite-size register, we have of course an instance of modulo arithmetic. More generally, if we have an n-digit register storing numbers base-b, then the arithmetic is modulo b^n. The ideas of register and modulo arithmetic are essentially the same concept.

Notion 104: Integer Arithmetic

Given an understanding of natural arithmetic, it is possible to build up, in an algorithmic manner, integer arithmetic. The essential factor is to include, for each n, a $-n$, such that $n + (-n) = 0$.

A standard method begins by stating that the pair (a_1, a_2) of natural numbers represents the integer $a_1 - a_2$. It follows by definition that $(a_1, a_2) = (b_1, b_2)$ exactly when $a_1 - a_2 = b_1 - b_2$. This is restated as $a_1 + b_2 = a_2 + b_1$. The latter form uses only operations that are known from the natural numbers.

Using this result as a definition, without any circularity, we have built up an integer datatype from natural numbers. At least we have equality. Equality is a non-trivial operation, more than just checking the individual components for equality. This is typical. Equality of abstract types needs to be defined.

In a similar manner, $(a_1, a_2) \times (b_1, b_2)$ means $(a_1 - a_2) \times (b_1 - b_2)$ which is $(a_1 b_1 + a_2 b_2) - (a_1 b_2 + a_2 b_1)$ From which we get the definition $(a_1, a_2) \times (b_1, b_2) = (a_1 b_1 + a_2 b_2, a_1 b_2 + a_2 b_1)$. Again, we have an algorithm for suitable manipulation using only the operations over the natural numbers.

Summarising, and adding a couple more operations,

$$
\begin{aligned}
(a_1, a_2) = (b_1, b_2) \quad &= \quad a_1 + b_2 = a_2 + b_1 \\
(a_1, a_2) - (b_1, b_2) \quad &= \quad (a_1 + b_2, a_2 + b_1) \\
(a_1, a_2) + (b_1, b_2) \quad &= \quad (a_1 + b_1, a_2 + b_2) \\
(a_1, a_2) * (b_1, b_2) \quad &= \quad (a_1 b_1 + a_2 b_2, a_1 b_2 + a_2 b_1) \\
-(a_1, a_2) \quad &= \quad (a_2, a_1)
\end{aligned}
$$

Division is not included because the integers are not closed under it. Mod and div operations could be but are not quite so straightforward.

However, while these operations are strictly correct, as can be verified by appropriate work in the algebra of real natural numbers, the elements tend to get rapidly larger, without bound.

To combat this we introduce the idea of normalisation.

If $a \geq b$, then $a - b$ is well defined just within natural numbers. Thus, $(a, b) = (a - b, 0)$, and $(b, a) = (0, a - b)$. A slightly cleaner way of putting this is that $(a + 1, b + 1) = (a, b)$, for all natural numbers, a and b, which leads to the same conclusion; we can reduce at least one of the numbers to 0.

This makes it look very much like just storing a sign bit, $(0, a)$ is a negative, $(a, 0)$ is a positive. Combining this with a bit of Boolean algebra would yield an alternative integer datatype. In practice this is a good call, but it does mean no canonical form. In the above, $(0, 0)$ is the unique 0, while with a sign bit we have the potential for ± 0.

The above illustrates many of the most important aspects of building up a new datatype from tuples of old ones. The new operations are defined as compounds of the old ones. Equality needs to be defined, and a canonical form is useful, but not required. The external algebraic character of the operations is what is required. The specifics of the internal structure are not so important.

A very common and powerful technique, this is the idea of abstract datatypes, and the idea of modularity and encapsulation. It can be a very powerful technique for building robust software quickly. When the conditions of the code change, the required modifications are normally clear. Occasionally, the modifications required will lead to a very inefficient implementation, because the new operations go strongly against the grain of the original concept. But this problem may appear in any code, and is not the effect of the encapsulation itself, only a limitation on the scope of problems it can solve.

Further, the cleaner the code the easier it is for optimising compilers to produce a fast (and dirty) version of the code for actual execution, but applying code transformations. Compilers are a lot better than humans at applying multiple code-transformations correctly, which is why the compiled high-level code may be more reliable that the low-level code written by a human.

Unless, perhaps, that human applies a very rigorous discipline.

Notion 105: Rational Arithmetic

Following on from the concept of integers as pairs of natural numbers (see page 219), we can develop rational numbers, a/b, as pairs of integers.

Let (a, b) stand for a/b, where a is an integer, and b is a positive integer. The latter requirement is due partly to the problem of division by zero, and partly to an issue of normalising signs.

Then using the normal rules of fraction arithmetic,

$$
\begin{aligned}
(a, b) \quad \times \quad (c, d) \quad &= \quad (ac, bd) \\
(a, b) \quad \div \quad (c, d) \quad &= \quad (ad, bc) \\
(a, b) \quad + \quad (c, d) \quad &= \quad (ad + bc, bd) \\
(a, b) \quad - \quad (c, d) \quad &= \quad (ad - bc, bd)
\end{aligned}
$$

These rules are more normally typeset as

$$
\begin{aligned}
\frac{a}{b} \quad \times \quad \frac{c}{d} \quad &= \quad \frac{ac}{bd} \\
\frac{a}{b} \quad \div \quad \frac{c}{d} \quad &= \quad \frac{ad}{bc} \\
\frac{a}{b} \quad + \quad \frac{c}{d} \quad &= \quad \frac{ad + bc}{bd} \\
\frac{a}{b} \quad - \quad \frac{c}{d} \quad &= \quad \frac{ad - bc}{bd}
\end{aligned}
$$

but are identical in meaning.

Equality is tested by $(a, b) = (c, d)$ when $ac = bd$.

Again the point is that all the operations use only the operations of addition, subtraction and multiplication, over the integers.

Normalisation is obtained by dividing out the greatest common divisor:

$$(a, b) = (a/\gcd(a, b), b/\gcd(a, b))$$

This is more traditionally referred to as reducing to lowest form.

Exercise 13: Arithmetic

Many operations on numbers can be performed by a single pass along the number(s), generating a single digit for each digit, and carrying a single digit as state. Addition and subtraction are two well known examples.

Develop algorithms in this style.

1. Divide a number by 2 in base 10.

   Hint: Start at the most significant digit.

2. Test for divisibility by 2 in base 7.

   Hint: Use arithmetic modulo 2.

3. Divide a number by 2 in base 7.

4. Multiply a number by 9 in base 10.

5. Determine the remainder after division by 11 in base 10.

A rational number implementation might have limited precision — for example, an int over an int. If the numbers get too big, then the result can't be represented exactly.

6. Write rational arithmetic add, sub, mul, and div. Check for overflow conditions. Write so that, if the result is representable it must be determined (think about dividing out the gcd), and errors will be detected before they occur without ever performing an operation that would generate a numeric error.

7. Write limited precision rational arithmetic which returns the closest representable rational to the actual answer, even when the actual answer is not representable.

Notion 106: Complex Arithmetic

When a binary operation is not defined for all elements of a number system, we say that the system is not closed under the operation. Looking at the extension of a number system to include negatives (see page 219), or ratios (see page 221), we see that the common approach is to do so by including a formal pair of numbers (a, b) that stands for $a \circ b$, where $\circ$ is the operation that we wish to close. Of course division was not entirely closed over the rationals, but is defined as long as the divisor is non-zero.

In the same way, a unary operator can be closed by including some structure that represents the application of that operator. The idea of generating the natural numbers, by starting with 0 and then constantly applying $+1$, is a special case; although it does have the logical complication that the set is defined inductively.

One standard extension is to add a square root. While some square roots exist within the rationals, most do not (For example, the famous case of $\sqrt{2}$). But it is not enough to add just the square root, we also need to be able to do standard arithmetic on them. For this we are back to pairs of numbers.

If we set up a pair (a, b) to mean $a + b\sqrt{2}$, then we quickly find that

$$(a_1, a_2) + (b_1, b_2) = (a_1 + b_1, a_2, b_2)$$

$$(a_1, a_2) + (b_1, b_2) = (a_1 + b_1, a_2, b_2)$$

Multiplication is a bit more difficult, but simple algebra will suffice.

$$(a_1 + a_2\sqrt{2}) \times (b_1 + b_2\sqrt{2}) = (a_1 b_1 + 2 a_2 b_2 + (a_2 b_1 + a_1 b_2)\sqrt{2})$$

Thus, the rule is

$$(a_1, a_2) \times (b_1, b_2) = (a_1 b_1 + 2 a_2 b_2, a_2 b_1 + a_1 b_2)$$

At this point, we are not sure that this is the *only* rule for arithmetic, since one number might be represented by multiple ordered pairs.

Looking for equality, $a_1 + b_1\sqrt{2} = a_2 + b_2\sqrt{2}$ means $(a_1 - a_2) = (b_2 - b_1)\sqrt{2}$ but $\sqrt{2}$ is not rational, we need $b_1 = b_2$, and $a_1 = a_2$. So equality is simple, there is only one form for each number.

$$(a_1, a_2) = (b_1, b_2) \text{ when } a_1 = b_1 \text{ and } a_2 = b_2$$

Division is a little more complicated, but inspection shows that

$$(a_1, a_2) \times (a_1, -a_2) = (a_1^2 - 2a_2^2, 0)$$

$$(a_1, a_2)^{-1} = (a_1/(a_1^2 - 2a_2^2), a_2/(a_1^2 - 2a_2^2))$$

And division follows from $a/b = a \times 1/b$.

Checking the algebra it is clear that the exact number under the surd is not significant. In particular, the special case of $\sqrt{-1}$ obtains the rule for complex multiplication.

$$(a_1, a_2) \times (b_1, b_2) = (a_1 b_1 - a_2 b_2, a_2 b_1 + a_1 b_2)$$

It is also more than a curious coincidence that

$$\begin{bmatrix} a_1 & pa_2 \\ a_2 & a_1 \end{bmatrix} \begin{bmatrix} b_1 & pb_2 \\ b_2 & b_1 \end{bmatrix} = \begin{bmatrix} a_1 b_1 + pa_2 b_2 & p(a_1 b_2 + a_2 b_1) \\ a_2 b_1 + a_1 b_2 & a_1 b_1 + pa_2 b_2 \end{bmatrix}$$

This shows that special case matrix multiplication can be used to provide an extension, including square-roots of a numbering system. A more full discussion of this takes us rapidly into more sophisticated matters of linear algebra, abstract algebra, extension fields, and the solution of polynomials.

The intention of this discussion is to make some of the options known, and the direction that can be taken to develop code, apparent.

Applying this to the rationals obtains the rational version of complex numbers, not the complex extension of real numbers, which is non-computable (see page 151). One thing missing from our development here is the method for taking the square-root of $a_1 + \sqrt{p}a_2$ (see page 225).

Notion 107: Exact Arithmetic

Fixed precision floating-point representation is not exact.

$$0.66666 \times 3 = 1.99998$$

which is close, but not exactly 2.

A similar problem arises with fixed-precision integer or rational arithmetic, but it is possible (see page 221) to get around this by appropriate data structures. It is also possible to include square roots into consideration (see page 223).

Ignoring for the moment the square roots of negative numbers, what if we want a numbering system that includes, for example, all integer roots of positive quantities?

Firstly, to find a square root,

$$(a_1 + a_2\sqrt{p})^2 = b_1 + b_2\sqrt{p}$$

$$a_1^2 + pa_2^2 + 2a_1a_2\sqrt{p} = b_1 + b_2\sqrt{p}$$

Which is equivalent to solving $a_1^2 + pa_2^2 = b_1$ and $2a_1a_2 = b_2$ simultaneously. By substituting $a_1^2 = b_1 - pa_2^2$ into $2a_1^2a_2^2 = b_2^2$, we obtain $4pa_2^4 - 4b_1a_2^2 + b_2^2 = 0$, from which using standard technique we get the solution ...

$$a_1^2 = \frac{b_1 \pm \sqrt{b_1^2 - pb_2^2}}{2p}$$

But if we extend the system to include $\sqrt[3]{p}$, then we find that we have numbers of the form

$$a_0 + a_2\sqrt[3]{p} + a_2\sqrt[3]{p^2}$$

The algebra is rapidly getting deeper.

In fact it is possible by using this approach to include the solution to any finite polynomial over the original number system. But to do so requires non-trivial use of the algebra of field extensions.

Similarly, we can include π, the famous ratio of the diameter to the circumference of a circle in Euclidean space. But in this case we find that we have $a_0 + a_1\pi + a_2\pi^2 + a_3\pi^2 + \cdots + a_n\pi^n$, without any particular limit on n.

Nevertheless, we can continue to work with this

$$(a_0 + a_1\pi) + (b_0 + b_1\pi) = (a_0 + b_0) + (a_1 + b_1)\pi$$

$$(a_0 + a_1\pi) \times (b_0 + b_1\pi) = (a_0 b_0) + (a_0 b_1 + b_1 a_0)\pi + (a_1 b_1)\pi^2$$

These expressions can become very large; megabytes of memory are easily generated in only mildly non-trivial applications.

Our motivation for going to this effort is that the floating-point numbers, which are not exact, are often not sufficient. Especially in geometric algorithms, such as have to be used in computer-aided design packages. For the package to be geometrically correct, we need to know exactly, without error, whether $a > b$ and other similar logical conditions. This can only be done by using exact arithmetic in the above basic style.

Alternatively, the floating-point algorithms can be fixed up with a lot of special case logic, and very careful study of the exact impact of all the approximations. But this is not the easy way out. A lot of sophisticated analysis is required, and there always remain cases in which the approximation is insufficient to obtain the desired answer.

The trade-off is that approximate arithmetic is fast but wrong, (sometimes spectacularly so) and exact arithmetic is right but slow (sometimes spectacularly so). Practical solutions usually involve a bit of both, together with an acceptance of some non-zero level of errors in the system.

Research into the problem continues. But it is likely that there will never be a neat solution (see page 151)

Notion 108: Showing That a Power Loop Works

Consider this code:

```
n = m; b = 1; a = x;
while(n) { b *= n%2 ? a : 1; a *= a; n /= 2; }
```

All the variables are integer, and as a *pre-condition*, $m \geq 0$.

Will the loop terminate?

Yes: The loop runs until `n==0`. Before the loop starts `n==m`, which is either 0, or some positive integer. If `n>0`, then `n/2` is *strictly* less than `n`, but still positive. Thus, `n` is a positive integer that strictly reduces. So `n` is positive as long as the loop runs, but eventually `n==0` and the loop stops.

Can we tell if the loop is correct?

No: because we do not know what it is supposed to do.

It is a vital point, but one that is sometimes missed. Further we can never in any absolute sense prove that the program is just what we wanted, we can only prove that an operation expressed in a manner with no means of computation indicated, is equivalent to another expressed explicitly as a computation.

Now, I tell you that the computation is intended to be $b = x^m$.

By this I mean that the *final* value of b is x^m. How do we proceed with a proof? A generic technique is to prove a loop invariant. Picking an invariant can be difficult if you do not already have one. But, the difficulty is that you are not aware of the principle on which the loop was constructed. Normally, when you design a loop you have in mind *why* the loop works. With a bit of practice you can turn this into a loop invariant.

In this case my original inspiration was looking at the binary expansion of m. Suppose that $m = 10110$ in binary, we want to construct x^10110. We can build $n = 2^5 + 2^3 + 2^2$, so $x^m = x^{2^5} * x^{2^3} * x^{2^2}$.

This produces the following half-step:

```
b=1;
for(i=0;i<=digits(m);i++)if(digit(i,m)) b*=pow(x,pow(2,i));
```

But we need the powers of x, so we repeatedly square.

```
a=x; b=1;
for(i=0;i<=digits(m);i++) {a*=a; if(digit(i,m)) b*=a;}
```

and in the loop given we are blanking out the digits of m.

```
a=x; b=1; n=m
for(i=0;n;i++) {a*=a; if(n%2) b*=a; n /= 2;}
```

Now, the digits in m that we have taken into account are the digits that have been blanked out of n_i that is, the part we have computed is $m - 2^i n_i$. Checking, when $i = 0$, we get $m - m = 0$ has been computed. So, all the time $x^m = b_i x^{2^i n_i}$. But we also need to know that the value of a is correct, with $a_i = x^{2^i}$. These two expressions form our invariant. By inspection they are both true when $n = m$, $i = 0$, $b = 1$ and $a = x$. For an inductive proof we need, $b_{i+1} = x^{m-2^{i+1}n_{i+1}}$ and $a_{i+1} = x^{2^{i+1}}$.

The latter is easy, $a_{i+1} = (x^{2^i})^2 = x^{2*2^i} = x^{2^{i+1}}$.

Now, let $n_i = 2p_i + q_i$, with $q_i = 0, 1$, then $n_{i+1} = p_i$, and

$$b_{i+1} = b_i a_i^{q_i} = (x^{m-2^i(2p_i+q_i)})(x^{2^i q_i}) = x^{m-2^{i+1}p_i} = x^{m-2^{i+1}n_{i+1}}$$

This proves the invariant.

The invariant is true initially, so it will be true when the loop halts. At this time $n = 0$, and so $x^m = bx^{2^i 0} = b$. This is the required result. This method is based on the equality $x^{2p+q} = (x^p)^2 x^q$.

```
pow(x,0) = 1
pow(x,n) = (n%2?x:1)*pow(x,n/2)
```

It is faster than method using the equality $x^m = x * x^{m-1}$.
For 100-digit n, used in cryptography, it is astronomically faster.

Notion 109: When Is a Proof Not a Proof?

Consider the following numerical code. What does it do?

```c
#include <stdio.h>
#define e 0.000000000001

main()
{
double x=2.0;

while(x*x>2.0+e || x*x<2.0-e)
  {
  x = (x*x+2)/(2*x);
  printf("%10.20f^2 = %10.20f\n",x,x*x);
  }
printf("%10.20f^2 = %10.20f\n",x,x*x);
}
```

Look at the loop condition. For the loop to terminate the condition must be false when tested. No further commands are executed before the loop stops, and also no assignments occur in the loop test, thus at the second print statement, the negation of the test must be true, i.e., 2-e =< x*x =< 2+e, which states that x must be close to the square root of two.

Thus ... **if** the loop terminates, then the result is a number that is close to a square root of two. But that is a big if.

How do we show that the loop must terminate?

Look at the loop transformation

$$x \to \frac{x^2 + 2}{2x}$$

Clearly, if $x > 0$, then $\frac{x^2+2}{2x} > 0$.

$$\left(\tfrac{x^2+2}{2x}\right)^2 > 2 \quad \equiv \quad x^4 + 4x^2 + 4 > 8x^2$$
$$\equiv \quad x^4 - 4x^2 + 4 > 0$$
$$\equiv \quad (x^2 - 2)^2 > 0$$

from which it is clear that

$$\forall x \in \mathbb{R} : \left(\frac{x^2 + 2}{2x}\right)^2 \geq 2$$

So, $x > 0$ and $x^2 > 2$ are both loop invariants. If we start with positive x such that $x^2 \leq 2$, then this condition will always be true.

Now that you have this clearly in mind, we run the program.

```
1.50000000000000000000^2 = 2.25000000000000000000
1.41666666666666674068^2 = 2.00694444444444464182
1.41421568627450988664^2 = 2.00000600730488287127
1.41421356237468986983^2 = 2.00000000000451061410
1.41421356237309492343^2 = 1.99999999999999955591
1.41421356237309492343^2 = 1.99999999999999955591
```

If the previous proof is true, then why is x^2 less than 2?

The answer is that floating-point arithmetic is not the same thing as real arithmetic. The two are distinctly different, and careful coding is often required to correct for this type of problem, and sometimes even careful coding is not enough, and some other approach entirely is required.

In this case the result is still a good approximation to the square root of 2, even though it turns out to be less than would be possible with the real-valued memory assumption. The reason the algorithm still works is that the original iteration on which it is based is very stable under the presence of noise. Small fluctuations in the computation do not affect the general tendency of x^2 to converge to 2, but this should be proved (see page 231).

But many other computations are not so stable, so it was through luck rather than good management that the above naive approach works.

Notion 110: Real-Valued Memory

A program loop iterates a real values x by the rule $x \to \dfrac{x^2 + 2}{2x}$

Static values of x are obtained by looking at $x = (x^2 + 2)/(2x)$, so $2x^2 = x^2 + 2$, and $x^2 = 2$. The only fixed points are the positive and negative square root of 2. How does the distance between x^2 and 2 update?

$$x \to \frac{x^2 + 2}{2x} \quad \equiv \quad x^2 - 2 \to \left(\frac{x^2 + 2}{2x} \right)^2 - 2$$

We show that x^2 keeps getting closer to 2. We know (see page 229), all the x values after the first will be at least 2. We want to know when x_{i+1} is closer (above) 2, than is x_i. On the last line the left-hand side increases monotonically above $x^2 = 1/3$, and substituting $x^2 = 5/3$ yields 16/9. So at least for $x^2 > 5/3$ the inequality is satisfied. This is enough, for real-valued memory, to say that the inequality is always satisfied. x always gets closer to 2. Since x^2 is always decreasing, always above 2, and only static if $x^2 = 2$, it is clear that x^2 will approach the value 2.

$$x^2 - 2 > \left(\frac{x^2 + 2}{2x} \right)^2 - 2$$

$$x^2 > \frac{(x^2 + 2)^2}{(2x)^2}$$

$$4x^4 > x^4 + 2x^2 + 4$$

$$3x^4 > 2x^2 + 4$$

$$3x^4 - 2x^2 - 4 > 0$$

$$9x^4 - 6x^2 - 12 > 0$$

$$(x^2 - \frac{1}{3})^2 > \frac{13}{9}$$

We have shown that if $x_0 = 2$, then $(\forall i \in \mathbf{Z}^+ : x_i^2 > x_{i+1}^2 > 2)$. And we have shown that $x^2 \to 2$, as the loop runs, so that this loop computes better and better approximations to the square root of 2.

Unfortunately, this analysis assumed real memory. In a digital computer, this is never the case. The conclusions that floating-point numbers will act the same is not justified, and in this case, is false.

Notion 111: Cellular Matrix Multiplication

We have a cell that takes numeric input s from
the top and x from the right, and produces
numeric output $s + ax$ from the bottom and
x on the left. The value a is a parameter of
the cell type, and we do not otherwise specify
how this is determined.

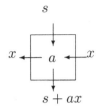

We place a group of these in a square grid.

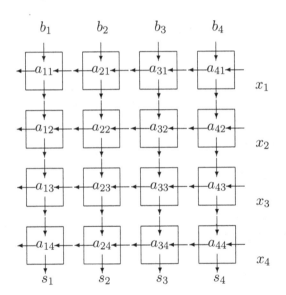

The row input is x_j, and
the column input is b_i,
each cell has state a_{ij}.
When the system has set-
tled down, the output s_i
is the sum $\left(\sum a_{ij}x_j\right) + b_j$,
which is a matrix multipli-
cation. This works even
if there is no synchronisa-
tion signal.

$$s = Ax + b$$

It takes a linear amount of time for the matrix multiplication to settle
down. Thus, with this hardware available to a desktop computer, it
is possible to load the matrix in n^2 time, which is as good as it gets,
but afterwards to transform a large number of vectors by affine transformation, in linear time. In matrix algorithms for computer graphics,
this can be a very large saving. Often there are a large quantity of
vectors, representing objects, to which it is desired to apply the same
transformation, so that the object is shifted as a solid piece.

Notion 13: Heron's Formula

The area of a triangle with side lengths a, b, and c, is

$$\sqrt{s(s-a)(s-b)(s-c)} \text{ where } s = (a+b+c)/2$$

This is Heron's formula, and it is found in many basic books on geometry. This formula can be directly implemented in C code.

```
double a = 1234568.0;
double b = 1234567.0;
double c = 1.01;
double s = (a+b+c)/2;
double area = sqrt(s*(s-a)*(s-b)*(s-c));
printf("Area = %lf\n",(double)area);
```

From this code we get the area 87515.03125 but, if we change the data type to float, we get 0.0000 instead.

The following results were produced.

c value	float area	double area
1.010	0.000000	87515.074765
2.009	1069166.875000	1075577.036082
2.099	1069166.750000	1139185.579129
2.999	1745942.125000	1745287.360123
10.00	55211548.000000	61418970.075344

While we might have believed the double result if we had seen it on its own, the fact that the float result is different (and sometimes radically so) gives doubt to the issue of how many decimal places we really have.

Generically, the problem can be pinned down to the fact that Heron's formula was derived on the assumption of real-valued variables. The algebra of real numbers simply does not apply to floats (for example floating-point multiplication is not associative). The suggestion that this is "just" round-off error seems to imply that we should get approximately the right answer, but this is not always the case. It is unwarranted to assume that a transliteration of a real result to a float expression will produce viable code for the problem at hand.

Different expressions, equivalent under real algebra, will produce different floating-point responses. Sometimes it is possible to get a result that is closer to the desired result by rearranging the formula so that we are not adding big numbers and small numbers, such as in $a + b + c$ or $s - c$, above. For this specific case, an approach here is to multiply out the terms in the brackets, substituting $(a + b + c)/2$ for s. The result is the following:

```
area = sqrt((c*c*c*c) +
            (c*c*(b+a)*(b+a)) +
            (c*c*(b-a)*(b-a)) -
            ((b-a)*(b-a)*(b+a)*(b+a)))/4;

printf("Area = %lf\n",(double)area);
```

For $c = 1.01$ this produced 87515.031250 for float, and 87515.075748 for double, a much closer result (but how do we know if it is correct?).

Floating-point numbers are a subset of the rationals, which are a subset of the reals. For any given real we may look for the one or two closest floating-point numbers to that real. A simple ideal for a floating-point algorithm is to obtain the closest floating-point number to the actual real solution to an equation.

However, floating-point arithmetic is a thing unto itself. It is not interval arithmetic, and not simply approximate real arithmetic. It is possible that a floating-point number might solve, under floating-point arithmetic, an equation, without being the real-valued solution, or the closest approximation to it. It is possible for it to be desired that the floating-point answer has the algebraic character of the real solution, rather than being as close as possible to it.

Typically, when replacing a real expression by floating-point, there will not be one floating-point expression that best approximates the real in all cases. Rather, different expressions will have their own domain. Thus, the generic floating-point algorithm is a combination of multiple logical tests, selecting the appropriate formula for the current domain.

Naive floating-point algorithms may produce *just floating-point noise*.

Chapter 7

Repetitive Computation

In which we learn that most of our programming constructs are just variations on repeating a single operation while a condition is true, or until a condition is false.

That there is little distinction in thinking required between recursive and iterative programming. That both can be discarded for other techniques, which reflect the notion of repeat and test.

Notion 112: The Use of Recursion

From the beginning, C was designed to be recursive. We can write C
programs in a manner that is very similar to Haskell or Scheme:

```
fact x = if x>0 then x * (fact (x-1)) else 1
```

```
(define (fact x) (if (> x 0) (* x (fact (- x 1))) 1))
```

```
fact(x){return x ? x * fact(x-1) :  1 ; }
```

In C, in analogy to `int x[3]={6,5,4};`, and `thing x={2,"cat"}` it
would be more consistent to use an assignment operator in the definition
of functions ...

```
int f(int x)={return x*x;}
```

to emphasise that we are initialising the value of the variable `f`.

Transliteration of the definition of the sum operator into C yields:

```
int sum(int a, int b, int (*f)(int))
                {return b-a+1 ? f(b) + sum(a,b-1,f) : 0;}
```

This is correct for $a \leq b$ and can be used for sums with small ranges.
Unfortunately, C and Java compilers typically do not use optimisations
for recursive code. Thus, for a large range the above will cause a stack
crash, or an out of bounds error. (For example, on the compiler I use, a
sum of 20,000 terms is ok, but 30,000 gets a segmentation fault.)

The exact same definition in MIT-scheme:

```
(define
  (sum a b f)
  (if (= b (- a 1)) 0 (+ (f b) (sum a (- b 1) f))))
)
```

works up to about 40,000 recursions.[32]

---

[32]More in mzscheme from Rice University.

But a variant that carries the sum with it, as an argument:

```
(define
  (sum s a b f)
  (if (= b (- a 1)) s (sum (+ s (f b)) a (- b 1) f))
)
```

succeeded in evaluating (sum 0 1 10000000 f),
the sum of 10 million elements.

Just like the design of iterative code, the correct design of recursive code is a subject in itself. However, most of the reasoning in well-designed code can be transliterated into iteration and recursion equally. Because iterative code is taught more at lower levels, the programmer may develop the delusion that the unfamiliar recursion is more difficult. But well-written recursive code is normally closer to the specification, easier to prove, easier to design, and loses nothing in efficiency.

To the programmer who has concentrated on iteration, the mind-set for recursion is unfamiliar. But this no more indicates trouble with recursion than saying that you find it easier to read in English than in French says anything about the complexity of the French language. Once you have learned both, you become more independent of a specific language. Once you have learned iteration and tail recursion you can see that the difference is largely one of syntax. Beyond tail recursion things become more complex, because the problems that are being tackled are more complex. Often a simple recursive implementation exists, when a lot of work is required to convert it to an iterative loop.

It is of historical interest that in the 1970s it was fair to say that recursion compiled slower on a Von Neumann machine (but not on a stack machine). And since Von Neumann machines were the major commercial technology, and languages like C were specifically designed to compile easily onto these machines, they had the advantage. However, since the mid 1990s the compiler technology has closed the gap, and (for example) the Stalin scheme compiler, mzscheme from Rice University, or the Glasgow Haskell compiler, provide perfectly viable environments in which to create serious applications from recursive code.

Theoretical Introduction to Programming

Notion 113: Doing Without the While Loop

Look at the summation code in C, as a while-loop:

```
{int t=0, i=a; while(i<=b) {t = t+f(i); i++;}; return t;}
```

The code clearly splits into initialisation, looping and return code. Look at the loop code specifically.

We may rewrite it as

```
if(i>b) return t; else {t+=f(i);i++; }
while(i<=b) {t = t+f(i); i++;}; return t;
```

and again as

```
if(i>b) return t; else {t+=f(i);i++;}
if(i>b) return t; else {t+=f(i);i++;}
while(i<=b) {t = t+f(i); i++;}; return t;
```

In fact we could repeat the if statement as many times as we want, without affecting the computational behaviour of the code. This leads us to the point that, as code fragments

```
{while(i<=b) {t = t+f(i); i++;}; return t;}
```

is the same as

```
{if(i>b) return t; else {t+=f(i);i++;}
while(i<=b) {t = t+f(i); i++;}; return t;}
```

So ignoring the meaning of the while-loop, and replacing it by a code fragment variable C(i,b,t,f), we know that

```
C(i,b,t,f) =
{
if(i>b) return t;
else {t+=f(i);i++;} return C(i,b,t,f);
}
```

But this is a recursive definition of a function. We could use this as our code. We do not actually *need* a while-loop at all, as long as we have recursive definition.

This is part of the process of deriving code. We begin with code that we do not know how to implement (the while-loop), and we examined its properties to determine what code would actually produce this effect. Technically, we have only proved correctness given termination; however, it is fairly clear, and easy to prove that the code will actually terminate (as long as the equivalent while-loop would). We have our recursive routine. This algebra-of-code flavour is typical of the taste of recursive programming.

As a slight (but significant) variation, we do not actually need to assign the variables as long as we know exactly what effect the local code has on them.

We can write, in C code, the equivalent:

```
sum(int i, int b, int t, int (*f)(int ))
{if(i>b) return t; else return sum(i+1,b,t+f(i),f);}
```

This becomes

```
sum(int i, int b, int t, int (*f)(int ))
            {return i>b ? t : sum(i+1,b,t+f(i),f);}
```

Compare this with the Scheme code for the same thing (see page 236). The variable i performs the logical function of a, in enabling us to know when to stop, otherwise the code is identical in meaning.

This sum actually computes

$$\text{sum(i,b,t,f)} = t + \sum_{j=i}^{b} f(j)$$

Our original concept of a sum is the special case $t = 0$. But the recursive properties of the generalisation are more amenable to pragmatic programming. The discovery of suitable generalisation is a significant part of recursive program design.

Notion 114: Defining the Generic While-Loop

Any piece of code contains within it the names of a number of variables defined outside itself, but to which it refers. An arbitrary such piece of code may be symbolised as code(x,y,z), making the use of variable names explicit.

A fairly abstract while loop is expressed as

```
x = a; y = b; z = c;
while(test(x,y,z)) body(x,y,z);
```

Given any piece of deterministic code referring only to variables x, y, and z, the final value of (x,y,z) is fully determined by the initial value. For each initial value there is exactly one final value. Clearly, any such code may be replaced by a pure function,[33] called the transfer function, and a multiple assignment.

$$(x,y,z)=code(x,y,z)$$

We need to allow the inclusion of extra variables representing machine-state information that is often left implicit. In the C code fragment x=&y, we need to have access to the symbol table. In the most general[34] case the transfer function takes the entire machine state as its argument. By encapsulating *all* the memory being referred to as variables in a single record, X=(x,y,z), we can express a fully generic while-loop.

```
X=A ; while(test(X)) X=body(X)
```

Determining *exactly* what is the transfer function of a piece of code can require a little thought. However, in practice it is often a good way to debug. The reason for the difficulty in determining the transfer function is often a lack of understanding of the problem at hand, a lack that might lead to bugs. Working out what the code *actually* does can be a clue as to why it is not doing what you want, and also how to modify it so that it does.

---

[33] A function with no side effects, a mathematical function.
[34] Perhaps I mean "desperate", but the point is, it can be done.

We can expand the generic while-loop as the equivalent code:

```
X=A ; if(test(X)) X=body(X) ; while(test(X)) X=body(X)
```

The inserted conditional will not execute the body if the test is false, and if it makes the test false by executing the body, then the while-loop will not run. The conditional has simply replaced the first run through the while-loop.

If the conditional does not run, then the value of X afterwards is unchanged. Otherwise it is modified to body(X) and fed back into the while loop. Thus, the while code satisfies the following recurrence relation:

```
while(test,body,X) =

        if(test(X)) then X else while(test,body,body(X))
```

which can actually be used as a definition of the while-loop.

```
data myWhile(bool t(data), data b(data), data x)
{
 return t(x) ? myWhile(t,b,b(x)) : x;
}
```

In C and Java a test might have a side effect. In this case, we can split the test into a pure test test(X) and a command rest(X), so that the initial test is the same as t=test(X) ; rest(X) ; return t. It is important that the test is done first, or using pure functions, with compound assignment (t,X)=(test(X),rest(X)). Since the transformation might destroy the distinction that the test is computing.

Iteration can be given natural and precise meaning by recursion.

Exercise 14: Code Without the While-Loop

It is possible to write a generic while-loop using recursion in C, or Java, and so write software without any use of inbuilt iteration. Write the generic while-loop in C, or Java, and using this write the following functions.

1. `gcd(n,m)`

   The greatest common divisor of two positive integers.

   Hint: `gcd(n,m)` = `gcd(n%m,m%n)`, `gcd(0,n)=n`

2. `fact(n)`

   The factorial function, $f_0 = 1$, $f_n = n f_{n-1}$.

3. `maxnum(a,n,m)`

   The maximum of `a[n]` .. `a[m]` where `n` $\leq$ `m` are positive integers.

4. `sort(a,n,m)`

   Sorts in place `a[n]` .. `a[m]`, where `n` $\leq$ `m` are positive integers.

5. `fib(n)`

   The Fibonacci sequence, $f_0 = 0$, $f_1 = 1$, $f_n = f_{n-1} + f_{n-2}$.

   Hint, use $f(n, a, b)$ which computes the nth element in the generalised Fibonacci sequence starting $f_0 = a$, $f_1 = b$.

6. `cmd()`

   An infinite loop that asks for input, and repeats the input enclosed in square brackets. Include a termination condition, in which the entry "stop" will halt the program.

   What is going to go wrong with this loop?

Notion 14: Tail Recursion and Loop Design

Tail recursion is recursive definition where the return value from a recursive call is just returned. Such as the following:

```
fact(t,n) = !n ? t : fact(t*n,n-1)
```

as opposed to

```
fact(n) = !n ? 1 : n*fact(n-1)
```

There is a close analogy between these two code fragments. The return value of the latter is used to avoid the requirement for an accumulating parameter in the former.

The equivalent while-loop is: `while(!n){t=t*n; n=n-1;}`

Given a generic loop, with side effects,

```
while(test(a,b,c)) body(a,b,c)
```

we can rewrite it, side effects and all, as

```
fn(a,b,c) = test(a,b,c) ? body(a,b,c),fn(a,b,c) : (a,b,c)
```

It requires significant thought to produce a tail recursion — to go

from   `fib(n) = (n<=1) ? 1 : fib(n-1) + fib(n-2)`

to   `fact(n,a,b)= n ? fib(n-1,b,a+b) : a`

but the thought is identical for the loop, bookkeeping of the partial results to avoid storing them on the stack.

Some loops are really recursion in a weak disguise; they are iterative depth-first search in an array. It has not avoided stacks; it has made the stack a datatype instead of an implicit feature of the function calls.

Notion 115: Design of the Power Function

We want to write some code to compute x^n, but how? We could say that $x^n = x * x * x \ldots * x$. But, the ellipsis is meaningless. We need to be able to formalise the intended *and so on* in the definition. A loop {for(t=1,i=0;i<n;i++) t*=x;} comes to mind. This gives exact meaning, but only if we know what the for-loop means. We can formalise this intuition by saying that $x^n = x^{n-1} * x$. This is a more precise way of saying that we compute x^n by multiplying 1, by x, n times. This is the heart of the recursive routine pow(x,n)= n ? x*pow(x,n-1)) : 1. It is no coincidence that after the ellipsis we write $*x$, since we already have in mind that x^n is defined as the end of a sequence beginning $1, x, x^2, x^3$, and terminating in x^n, in which each element is defined as $*x$ of the previous. By specifying the ellipsis, we have already understood the recursive definition of the power function.

It is clear that such a computation requires $n - 1$ calls to the $*$ operator in order to compute x^n. It may be important to reduce this to make computation faster. As an example, if we compute x^4, by computing $a = x * x$ and then $b = a * a$, we see that $b == x^4$ has been computed with 2 instead of 3 calls to $*$. Obviously this may be extended to compute x^{2^n} in n steps, a potentially vast improvement on 2^n steps. This is based on the idea that $x^{2n} = x^n * x^n$. To deal with odd numbers we note that $x^5 = x^2 * x^5$. This can be formalised as $x^n = x^{\frac{n}{2}} * x^{\frac{n+1}{2}}$. (The division also truncates the result to an integer). This gives us a recursive definition, pow(x,n) = n ? pow(x,n/2) * pow(x,(n+1)/2) : 1. This gives us a new way to look at x^n, but does not actually reduce our computational effort. The problem is exemplified in that in the computation of pow(x,2n) we compute pow(x,n) *twice*, thus spoiling our potential advantage.

We get an idea from picking out the bit that is being duplicated, i.e., rewrite the routine as

pow(x,n) = n ? pow(x,n/2)*pow(x,n/2)*(n%2 ? x : 1).

This leads to the following code:

pow(x,n)

```
{
if(n==0) return 1; a = pow(x,n/2);
if(x%2) return a*a; return a*a*x;
}
```

This is much more efficient than the original approach, and can be written in C as

```
pow(x,n){int a; return !n?0: (a=pow(x,n/2)),a*a*(n%2?1:x);}
```

Now, how do we write a loop to do the same thing? We can translate back to a loop from the recursive definition. We need to introduce a new variable to store the value that would otherwise be stored on the return stack. Let us call this t. Now, we construct our loop to keep information about a decomposition $a^b = x^n * t$. (The loop, based on the same logic as the recursive routine, will be just as efficient.)

```
t = 1; n = b; x = a;   // initially a^b == x^n*t

// if n==0 then x^n==1, so a^b==t, and we can stop
// inside the loop we need to change the data

while(n>0)
{
// x^(2m+1)*t==x^(2m)*(xt),
// so if n is odd, transfer one x to t,
if(n%2){t*=x; n--;}
x*=x;                  // here n will be even,
n/=2;                  // so x^n*t == (x*x)^(n/2)*t
}

// at this point t == a^b
```

The n-- is redundant. while(n){t*=n%2?x:1;x*=x;n/=2;} would also work.

Notion 116: Powers by Multiplication

The values of the variables used are the *state* of the computation. The *final state* is the state just after the computation ends. The *initial state* is the state just before the computation begins. Suppose we have $t = a$, $x = b$ and $n = c$, then (a, b, c) is the initial state. To compute b^c we can use a loop: `t=1; while(n!=0){ t=t*x; n=n-1; }`. This looks about right. We decrement n, and multiply t by x, computing x, x^2, x^3, and so on. But, what about this code: `t=x; while(n!=0){t=t*x; n=n-1;}`? They both look superficially about right, how can we tell in an objective manner?

We could try testing, if we start with $n = 1$ and run the second loop then afterwards $t = b^2$, which is wrong, so we know the second code is not correct. The same test does not eliminate the first code, but no amount of testing will establish its correctness. To emphasise this consider the code `t=1; while(n!=0){someCode();}` Testing 1,000 cases, do we know that this loop will work? No! We have no idea what `someCode()` does. It could be `someCode(){return y>132412 ?  1 :   pow(x,n);}`. You need to look at the structure of the code to answer this question.

We see that the initial value of t is $1 = x^0$ is a power of x. Now, $x^m \times x = x^{m+1}$, another power of x. No matter how many times we multiply t by x it will always be a power of x. This is an *invariant* of the loop. An invariant is something that does not change. A loop invariant is something that is true after the body of the loop, if it was true before. Thus, an invariant that is true before is also true once the loop stops. This thinking is occurring inside your head, possibly subconsciously, when you become confident that the loop will work after testing a couple of cases. Why does a test or two convince us that it works? To make this question more significant, think about code that finds the area of a polygon. You could try a lot of cases, and still not feel very confident.

Each time the body of the loop is executed, t is multiplied by x, and n is decremented by 1. The decrements count the number of times that t is multiplied by x. This gives us the confidence that once n is reduced to 0, t has been multiplied by x roughly n, plus or minus a couple of times. At the end of the loop execution, $t = x^m$, where $m = n + p$, and

p is some unknown constant. Thus, testing even just one case should tell us whether $p = 0$ as required.

n	t
m	1
$m-1$	x
$m-2$	x^2
$m-3$	x^3
$m-4$	x^5
$m-5$	x^5
$\vdots$	$\vdots$
$m-m$	x^m

Looking at the body of the loop we find we have $body(\mathtt{n}, \mathtt{t}) == (\mathtt{n}-1, \mathtt{t}*\mathtt{x})$ This produces a sequence of values which can be tabulated as below. The pattern is fairly clear, and we see that at the time that $\mathtt{n} == 0$, we have $\mathtt{t} = \mathtt{x}^m$, which is the value that we need to compute.

To show this we use a loop invariant and true. Initially $\mathtt{t} = 1$ and $\mathtt{n} = m$, so $\mathtt{t} * \mathtt{x}^{\mathtt{n}} = a^m$. This may seem trivial, but if we look further we find, for example, that $\mathtt{t} = \mathtt{x}^5$ and $n = m - 5$, then $\mathtt{t}\mathtt{x}^{\mathtt{n}-5} = a^5 a^{\mathtt{n}-5} = a^m$. So, $\mathtt{t}\mathtt{x}^{\mathtt{n}} = a^m$ is true at this point also. Consider any point in the computation just before the computation enters the body of the loop. Suppose that $\mathtt{t} = p$ beforehand and $\mathtt{n} = q$, and that $p * \mathtt{x}^q = a^m$, then after applying the body, we have $\mathtt{t} = p * \mathtt{x}$ and $\mathtt{n} = q - 1$, so $\mathtt{t} * \mathtt{x}^{\mathtt{n}} = p * \mathtt{x} * \mathtt{x}^{q-1} = p * \mathtt{x}^q$, is indeed a^m, since that is where we started. Thus, the assertion that $\mathtt{t}\mathtt{x}^{\mathtt{n}} = a^m$ is true initially and cannot be made false by executing the body of the loop. That is, $\mathtt{t}\mathtt{x}^{\mathtt{n}} = a^m$ is an invariant of the loop and true.

The value of $\mathtt{t} * \mathtt{x}^{\mathtt{n}}$ is a^m initially. Whatever the actual values of $\mathtt{t}$ and $\mathtt{n}$ are after the loop, we know that $\mathtt{t} * \mathtt{x}^{\mathtt{n}} = a^m$. Looking at the loop test in `t=1; while(n!=0){t=t*x; n=n-1;}`, when the loop finishes, $\mathtt{n}$ must be 0. Substituting this value into the invariant, we find that $\mathtt{t} * \mathtt{x}^0 = a^m$, but $\mathtt{x}^0 == 1$, so $\mathtt{t} = \mathtt{t} * 1 = a^m$, as required.

This all just makes the thoughts in your head, regarding this code, more conscious and formal, so that we can write it down on a piece of paper and examine the reasoning for correctness. The key is an appropriate invariant. This can be hard to find. But, if it is your code, then typically the invariant will be the thought that you have as to *why* the code will work. If you truly have no idea how or why it should work, you are advised to reconsider the design of the loop.

Notion 117: Computing Powers by Squaring

We can compute powers with the following loop:

```
t=1; n=m; while(n!=0){ t=t*x; n=n-1; }.
```

Before, during, and after the loop, $x^m = tx^n$. The code works because decrementing n reverses the effect of multiplying t by x. The loop establishes a lock-step between these operations.

```
if(n%2) {n--;t=x;} else t=1; while(n>0){t=t*x*x; n=n-2;}
```

So, n is even before entering the loop. Thus, the lock-step still occurs; the loop does each operation twice. Our previous reasoning still works. This loop will run about twice as fast as the previous one.

The while-loop is a form of recursion. The first code fragment works using $x^n = x^{n-1} * x$; the second, $x^{2n} = x^{2(n-1)}x^2$. Both of these are recursive properties of the power function. In fact, any transformation on (t, x, n) that preserves the value of tx^n and eventually drives n to 0 is the basis of a correct loop.

So, we ask, how can we make n drop to zero faster?

$(t, x, n) \rightarrow (t, x^2, n/2)$ has the effect $tx^n \rightarrow t(x^2)^{n/2} = tx^n$. So this preserves tx^n. But, n does not remain an integer, and although it approaches 0, it only reaches 0 after an infinite number of steps. Of course, floating-point arithmetic would also result in errors in the computation. However, if n was an even integer, then this operation is ok.

Consider the following loop body:

$$(t, x, n) \rightarrow n\%2 \ ? \ (tx, x, n-1) : (t, x^2, n/2)$$

In each case this transformation preserves the value of tx^n, and $tx^n = a^m$ is an invariant of the loop body. Once the loop terminates at $n = 0$, the required value will be stored in t. Each time n is either divided by 2, or decremented by 1, so it becomes strictly smaller, and will eventually reach 0.

The loop can be expressed directly in C code as follows:

```
x = a;
n = m;
t = 1;
while(n!=0) if(n%2) {t=t*x;n=n-1;} else {x=x*x;n=n/2;}
```

But, the following also works on the similar logic:

```
x = a;
n = m;
t = 1;
while(n!=0) {t*=(n%2)?x:1;x*=x;n/=2;}
```

Each time, multiply t by $x^{n\%2}$, square x, and halve n, dropping any remainder. This makes use of the fact that each time n is decremented, the next time it will be halved.

$$(t, x, n) \rightarrow (tx^{n\%2}, x^2, n/2)$$

Continuing, we could base a powers algorithm on division by 3 or higher.

$$(t, x, n) \rightarrow (tx^{n\%3}, x^3, n/3)$$

but with the difficulty that we need to be able to compute 1, x, and $x * x$. As the modulus becomes larger, so does the code.

The effort in the design of a loop to compute powers is in the discovery and selection of a suitable transformation of a tuple of variables. Transliteration to code, as C, Java, or Haskell, is a matter of knowing the syntax. The loop is proved by a simple substitution, regardless of the language in which it is written.

With a clear concept of abstract datatype this idea applies very broadly.

Notion 118: Language or Algorithm?

We can compute powers in many ways (see page 248).

The core concept is language independent. Even shifting all the way from C to Prolog makes very little difference in the logic required. Here are the multiply and square algorithms algorithms in C, Java, Haskell, and Prolog, to emphasise this.

C: (result computed in t)

```
t=1; x=a; n=m;
while(n!=0) {t*=x; n--;}

t=1; x=a; n=m;
while(n!=0) {t*=(n%2)?x:1;x*=x;n/=2;}
```

Java: (result computed in t)

```
t=1; x=a; n=m;
while(n!=0) {t*=x; n--;}

t=1; x=a; n=m;
while(n!=0) {t*=(n%2)?x:1;x*=x;n/=2;}
```

Haskell: (pow x n is x^n)

```
pow x n = aux 1 x n

aux t x 0 = t
aux t x n = aux (t*x) x (n-1)

aux t x 0 = t
aux t x n = aux t*(x^(n mod 2)) x^2 (n div 2)
```

The C and Java codes are identical. In Haskell, by a standard process, the loop body becomes the computation of the arguments in the recursive call. The distinction between the languages is mainly one of syntax and is easy to automate. But the distinction between the algorithms is deeper logic, and very hard to automate.

In Prolog, the same information is placed into the conditions on the variables in the new goal.

Prolog with pow(x,n,r) means that $x^n = r$.

```
pow(x,n,r) :- aux(t,x,n,r).

aux(t,x,0,t).
aux(t,x,n,r) :- td is t * x, nd is n-1, aux(td,x,nd,r).

aux(t,x,0,t).
aux(t,x,n,r) :- even(n),
                xd is x*x, nd is n div 2, aux(td,x,nd,r).
aux(t,x,n,r) :- odd(n),
                td is t*x, nd is n -1, aux(td,x,nd,r).
```

The core logic is the same across all these languages.

We have a state (t, x, n) which we give the initial value of $(1, b, c)$. Thus, initially $tx^n = b^c$. We apply a transformation $(t, x, n) \rightarrow \mathsf{body}(t, x, n)$, which preserves the truth of the assertion $tx^n = b^c$. This assertion remains true while the loop runs, and is true as the loop terminates. Since the loop test must be false after termination of the loop, we know that $n = 0$, and thus $t = b^c$. The loop body must eventually reduce n to 0, and it must preserve the invariant, but otherwise we are free to choose from many options.

$$(t, x, n) \rightarrow (tx, x, n - 1)$$
$$(t, x, n) \rightarrow (tx^2, x, n - 2) - \text{needs a precheck for odd } n$$
$$(t, x, n) \rightarrow \text{if even } n \text{ then } (t, x^2, n/2) \text{ else } (tx, x, n - 1)$$
$$(t, x, n) \rightarrow (tx^{n \bmod 2}, x^2, n \text{ div } 2)$$
$$(t, x, n) \rightarrow (tx^{n \bmod 3}, x^3, n \text{ div } 3)$$

Whatever mechanism is used — iteration, recursion, or reduction — for the repetition, the underlying logic is identical across languages.

Exercise 15: Language or Algorithm

The core of a number of algorithms is an algebraic thought involving a transformation of a tuple that it repeated until a condition is true (or false). The transformation is based on an equality that the quantity being computed satisfies generically. The distinction between different algorithms for the same thing can be much greater than the same algorithm in different languages.

Keeping the same logical structure, transliterate each of the following into Haskell, Prolog, and Scheme, so that the relation is clear.

Find the tuple transformation, the invariant, and the equality, on which each of these is based.

For the power function:

```
t=1; x=a; n=m;
while(n!=0) { t*=(n%3)==2?x*x:(n%3?x:1); x*=x*x; n/=3; }
```

```
t=1; x=a; n=m;
if(n%2) { t=x; n--; } while(n!=0) { t*=x; n-=2; }
```

```
t=1; x=a; n=m;
while(n!=0) { if(n%3) { t*=x; n--; } else { x*=x*x; n/=3; } }
```

For factorial:

```
t=1;for(i=1;i<=n;i++) t*=i;
```

```
t=1;for(i=n;i>=1;i--) t*=i;
```

Hint: Keep the loop control variable in the recursion.

Notion 119: Repetitive Program Design

A generic while-loop can be written as

```
X = A ; while(test(X)) X = body(X)
```

The equivalent recursive definition is

```
myfunc(X) = if test(X) then myfunc(body(X)) else X
```

The value being computed by the call: `X = myfunc(A)`

When examined carefully, the while-loop is just a special syntax for a recursive definition. The body of the loop calls the body again, until the test is false. While-loops exist because they are easy to compile. Likewise any tail recursion. The while-loop is defined as *if the test is true repeat this on the new data*, the recursive definition literally says this, with no special syntax. Both the loop and the recursion transliterate to English as *to compute the value, initialise the data, if the test is true, then modify the data and repeat, otherwise just stop.*

When designing a repetitive program, an iterative loop, or a tail recursion, we need to identify three things.

1. The initial value.
2. The operation to be repeated.
3. The termination condition.

Being clear about these things helps to reduce errors in code. Once they are known, it is straightforward to realise them as either a tail recursion or an iterative loop.

More significantly, since we debug more code than we write, analysing given code in these terms helps us to identify what the code is really doing. Once we know this, it is easier to determine why it is not doing what it is supposed to, and what we need to change to make it work to specification.

Notion 120: Recursive Code Compilation

There is an old myth that recursive code is slow to execute. This myth is false, and based on a straw-man argument. The pure performance of an algorithm depends only on its underlying logic. Any distinction in pragmatic performance between iterative and recursive definition is an effect of compiler technique. A good compiler will generate identical assembly code for the same underlying logic. Any distinction between an iteration and a simple in-line tail recursion is artificial.

Consider the two methods for computing x^n. One is iterative, the other is recursive.

```
pow(x,n){int t=1;while(n){x=x;n=n-1;t=t*x;};return t;}
```

```
pow(x,n)=powa(x,n,1) where powa(x,n,t)=n?powa(x,n-1,t*x):t
```

How will these be compiled? It is often supposed that the loop would be analogous to the left-hand, and the recursion to the right-hand, assembler code below.

```
                                      pow:   cmp  n,0
                 mov  1,t                    beq  end
        start:   cmp  n,0                     call mul x,t
                 beq  end                     dec  n
                 call mul x,t                 push x
                 dec  n                       push n
                 jmp start                    push t
          end:   push t                       call pow
                 ret                   end:   push t
                                              ret
```

The core operations are the same, but the recursion is slower and uses more memory due to stack handling and subroutine calls. However, the pre-call copies of x, n, and t are not referred to after the call, so there is no need to save them; we can mechanically replace the push and call with a single jump instruction.

```
pow:    cmp n,0
        beq end
        call mul x,t
        dec n
        jmp pow
end:    push t
        ret
```

The compiled code is identical to the standard for a loop. You can't tell from looking at the compiled code whether the original was a loop or an in-line tail recursive routine. The use of a jmp is *not* a while-loop. The jmp and cmp structure is a compiler technique for implementing a while-loop. The same approach works for tail recursion because a loop and a tail recursion are just two ways of saying the same thing. It is semantically valid to implement a while-loop using push and call, rather than jmp and cmp. The compiler determines which technique is used.

I originally heard of this technique as *tail recursion removal* in the context of Scheme code compilation, where it has existed for decades. Later I heard it referred to as *last call optimisation*, since it can be used as a generic method, destroying the stack frame *before* making the next call, if possible, instead of afterwards. Tail recursion optimisation then comes along for the ride. But the fullest natural generalisation is more subtle. Some mechanics of this are entangled in the compilation of monad code in Haskell.

As for other types of recursion, such as fact(n) = n*fact(n-1), with use of a knowledge of the associativity of multiplication, a compiler can compile this to code that does not use the stack. The code fn(x) = r(f(g(x)) can be compiled with a double use of jmp and cmp. But, the more general, fn(x) = r(x,fn(g(x))), in lieu of an advanced use of case specific code algebra, would require a stack structure. Both recursion and iteration can be written efficiently and inefficiently; it is the underlying logic (and the compiler) that determines the resources used in practice.

Notion 121: Functions as Data

What is the following partial Java code doing?

```
abstract int2int{abstract int at(int x);}
abstract int2intfn{abstract int2int at(int x);}
new int2int(){int at(int x){return x*x;}}
new int2intfn(){int2int at(int x){ ... }}
```

The two assertions: $f(x) = x^2$ and $f = \lambda x.x^2$ have the same meaning.

The "λ" may be read as *a function that takes*, and the "." may be read as *and returns*. Thus, $g = \lambda x.x + 2$ is read as g *is a function that takes* x *and returns* $x+2$. At first this seems to be just syntactic sugar. But, a significant aspect of lambda expressions is that we can use them directly as in: $(\lambda x.x^2)(6) = 36$.

A function may be compound just like data. If I defined $f(x) = x + 3$, then the value of $f(y + 5)$ is $y + 8$. The argument being a compound expression is no problem. Likewise, if I define $\texttt{twice} = \lambda f.\lambda x.f(f(x))$, I am saying that `twice` is a function that takes a function, and returns the composition of the function with itself. Thus, `(twice f)(3) = 9`. Or more generally, `(twice f) = (lambda x .  x+6)`. The function being compound is no problem. The same reasoning by substitution of the definition applies in each case, for argument and for function.

Typically, in programming, code for a function is written, thus making the function compound. Later the function is applied. This is largely a syntactic matter. Instead of writing `int f(int x){return x*x;}` and then evaluating `f(6)==36`, we might write in-line code and evaluate it directly:

`[(int x){return x*x;}](6) == 36.`

We can write expressions with numbers, and we can define numbers by some relation that they satisfy. For example, $\phi = 1/\phi + 1$ defines two numbers, one of which is the golden proportion. In the same way, we can write expressions with functions and define functions by relations that they satisfy.

Given $hyperfact(f) = \lambda x.$ if $x == 0$ then 1 else $x * f(x-1)$

We can look at the value of $hyperfact(\lambda x.0)$, which is a function that returns 1 if $x == 0$, and 0 otherwise. Now if we feed this back into the hyperfact, we get something that returns 1 if $x == 0$ and 1 if $x == 1$; otherwise it returns 0. Continuing this process, we see we are generating the factorial function. Not only does $hyperfact(fact) = fact$ but repeated application of hyperfact converges on fact, in the same way that repeated application of $x \rightarrow (x + a/x)/2$ results in x converging on the square root of a.

Similarly, the exponential function is the only continuous function that satisfies $f(x + y) = f(x)f(y)$. The gamma function, the continuous interpolation of factorial, satisfies, $\Gamma(x) = x\Gamma(x-1)$. These equations in an unknown function are specifications for a program.

The type of reasoning, using substitution of definition to compute the value of the expression, is no different when we do work out a numerical answer than when the answer is a pair of numbers, a string, an array, or a function. However, in my pedagogical experience, there is a psychological hurdle for students to overcome in making this realisation. Perhaps the key is to realise that we compute with a *representation* of the number, pair, array or function, and thus in all cases we merely compute with the expressions, rather than the data entity itself. It does not matter that the function is an infinite structure, since the representation is a finite expression we can work with.

So, what was the Java code doing? It was defining the types required to encapsulate a single method in a class as an abstract function type, enabling us to say `f.at(3)==6`, but also to say `twice.at(f).at(3)==9`. While functions are not first class in Java, this simple-to-define abstract type is very easy to manipulate, allowing us to treat functions as data in a surprising variety of ways.

Notion 122: Lambda Expressions in Java

Programs can be built from loops or recursion. A lack of one can be compensated for by a use of the other. But if both loops and recursion are avoided, general programming is still possible if you remember that functions are data.

A lambda expression, $(\lambda x \ y.x^2 + y)$, defines a function in the computational sense. The list of arguments is followed by the code for computing the result. The code has place holders for the arguments. This is precisely the mechanism for function definition in most common languages.

In functional languages such as Haskell and Scheme, functions can be arguments and return values. More importantly new functions can be constructed at run-time. In Java, this is not possible. But the ability to overwrite methods when constructing new instances produces almost the same effect.

But, we need lazy evaluation. For example, define a basic conditional `myIf(c,v,a)return c?v:a;`. If we call `myIf(x!=0,a/x,0)` since all the arguments are evaluated, an arithmetic error that this code was intended to prevent would occur. The inbuilt `if` decides whether or not to evaluate its arguments.

We avoid this with a *thunk*, a function not yet applied to an argument. We apply the function only when we *really* need to. The result of application might be a function. We do not try to work out what it is until someone either asks for its value, or asks for it to be applied.

We also need a function type `Function`, which in this case is built with a separate body and apply method. This is mainly to be compatible with the manner in which the thunk was structured. Because it has to have a parent in common with `Thunk` I have created the `Lambda` class to contain both. In a similar vein, the `Datum` class exists to act as completely evaluated data.

The lambda class contains the value and apply methods so that I can pass around thunks, functions, and datums to all the same routines, without worrying which they are. In the code, when an apply method is called, the exact code that is executed depends on the dynamic type of the object at the time — it might be the thunk or the function code. If it is the datum code, then this is an error in the usage.

This exercise illustrates the nature Java, and shows that logic can be used to produce unexpected code, and expands your horizons. The factorial and Fibonacci functions can, of course, be implemented much more simply. But, this type of code, and reasoning, is required in computer algebra packages.

```
// a generic lambda abstraction with evaluation
abstract class Lambda
{
abstract Lambda apply(Lambda l);
abstract int Value();
}

// an actual value that we are looking for
abstract class Datum extends Lambda
{
public Datum(int x){value=x;}
Lambda apply(Lambda l){return null;}
int Value(){return value;} int value;
}

// an action without an argument
abstract class Function extends Lambda
{
Lambda apply(Lambda data){return fn(data);}
int Value(){return 0;} abstract Lambda fn(Lambda l);
}

// an action, with argument, waiting to happen
abstract class Thunk extends Lambda
{
public Thunk(Lambda this_fn, Lambda this_data)
       {fn=this_fn;data=this_data;}
Lambda apply(Lambda arg)
       {return (fn.apply(data)).apply(arg);}
int Value()
    {return fn.apply(data).Value();}
Lambda fn; Lambda data;
}
```

Notion 123: The Y-combinator definition

Having constructed in Java (see page 258) a basic engine for reducing functional expressions, an engine that evaluates when it must, we are free to use a wide variety of functional techniques in our Java code.

We derive a non-recursive definition of factorial by starting with the normal recursive definition:

$\mathtt{fact} = \lambda x.(x == 0?1 : x * \mathtt{fact}(x-1))$

and abstracting it as hyperfactorial:

$\mathtt{hyperfact} = \lambda f.\lambda x.(x == 0?1 : x * f(x-1))$

The second is obtained in a simple-minded manner from the first. The process is called lambda abstraction. The right-hand side of the recursive definition is an expression with a single free variable $\mathtt{fact}$. We simply construct a lambda expression that binds this free variable, turning $\mathtt{f}$ from the symbol being defined, to being an argument of a new symbol. It is now no longer a recursive definition. But of course it also no longer defines the factorial function either.

The key is to recognise that the definition of a function is also an equation that it satisfies. In simple cases, such as $\mathtt{f(x)=x+3}$, this is obvious, trivial. In more subtle cases such as $\mathtt{f(x+y)=f(x)f(y)}$, there is no obvious way of determining the value and indeed there is more than one solution. But a standard recursive definition such as factorial is both a non-trivial equation,

```
f(x) = if x==0 then 1 else x*f(x-1)
```

and provides the means to determine $\mathtt{f(1)=1*f(0)=1}$ and so on, by repeated substitution. There can only be one function that satisfies this definition. Factorial is defined by the axiom $\mathtt{hyperfact(fact) == fact}$

The definition of a definition is
an equation that is satisfied by exactly one entity.

The nature of the Y-combinator is that it finds fixed points.

Thus, Y(hyperfact) is a fixed point of hyperfact,

that is, hyperfact(Y(hyperfact)) = Y(hyperfact).

The question is, how does it work? How does the Y-combinator work out the fixed point. Surely it must be a complex piece of code that looks at the definition of its argument function and does some heavy duty logical analysis to determine the fixed point?

No, in reality it is very simple, for the following reason:

Let $f(x) = (x + a/x)/2$, then $f(\sqrt{a}) = \sqrt{a}$.

We generate the sequence $2, f(2), f(f(2)), f^3(2), f^4(2) \ldots$..

None of these are $\sqrt{a}$, but they get closer and closer to it.

Now $f(f^n(2)) = f^{n+1}(2)$, so for $n = \infty$, $f(f^\infty(2)) = f^{\infty+1}(2) = f^\infty(2)$. Thus, $f^\infty(2)$ is a fixed point of f. With a bit of extra work it is possible to say that this must be that $f^\infty(2) = \sqrt{a}$. Admittedly, there are some details skipped in this, but the essential intuition is correct.

Thus, the value of $Y(f)$ is essentially $f^\infty(\lambda x.0)$,
where the actual value of the argument $\lambda x.0$ was not really important.

The technique by which Y computes $f^\infty(\lambda x.0)$ is reconstruction.

$Y = \lambda f.(\lambda f(gg))(\lambda f(gg))$

This almost comes into the "dirty trick" category, the value of Yf is defined to be $f(Yf)$. Recursion is avoided by having the structure of Y being repetitive, so that Y can be rebuilt from part of itself. Such a technique seems almost too simple to work, more like mathematics humour than a derivation. But the conclusion is correct, and the Java code demonstrates that the direct implementation of these ideas works well enough to be used as a method of computation.

Notion 15: Y-combinator in Java

This program implements the Y-combinator using a Java code implementation of a lambda reduction engine (see page 258). The Y-combinator
is a generic operator for constructing, without the use of loops or recursion, functions commonly expected to require loops or recursion. The
Y-combinator is not an encapsulation of loops or recursion, since it uses
neither in its own definition.

In pragmatic terms, we give the Y-combinator the right-hand side of the
recursive definition that we wanted to write, and it gives us the function
we would have defined. Thus, it can be seen as a mechanism for avoiding
the direct syntax of recursion. But, in detail it means a lot more.

```
class Combinators // function construction operators
{

// Half f = L g . f (g g)
static Lambda half(final Lambda f)
{
return
new Function()
  {
  Lambda fn(Lambda g)
          { return new Thunk(f,new Thunk(g,g){}){}; }
  };
}

//  Y = L f . (L g . f ( g g ) ) (L g . f ( g g ) )

static Lambda y(final Lambda f)
        { return new Thunk(half(f),half(f)){}; }
}
```

Notion 124: Y-combinator factorial

Although this clearly contains the essence of the factorial function, it does not require any loops or recursion in its own definition

```
static Lambda hyperfact =
new Function()
{

Lambda fn(final Lambda f)
{
return new Function()
 {
 Lambda fn(Lambda data)
  {
  if(data.Value()==0) return new Datum(1){};
  else return
  new Datum
   (
    data.Value() *
         (f.apply(new Datum(data.Value()-1){}))).Value()
   ){};
  }
 };
}

};
```

Now define non-recursive factorial using the Y-combinator:

```
static Lambda nrfact = Combinators.y(hyperfact);

// a wrapper function so we can have int factorial
static int fact(int x)
{
return ((Datum)(nrfact.apply(new Datum(x){}))).value;
}
```

Notion 125: Y-combinator Fibonacci

Now let's define Fibonacci. I have formatted the definition to try to emphasise certain points. There is a pre- and a post-amble, independent of what we are defining. There is a central function definition that should look familiar; here the definition is based on the $f(n) = f(n-1)+f(n-2)$ definition. But, note clearly, there is NO recursion here (or loops). This shows that the logic of Fibonacci is independent of the exact method by which it is being implemented.

```
static Lambda hyperfibo =
new Function()
    {Lambda fn(final Lambda f)
     {return new Function()
      {
       Lambda fn(Lambda data)
       {
          if(data.Value()<2) return new Datum(1){};

          return new Datum
             (
             f.apply(new Datum(data.Value()-1){}).Value() +
             f.apply(new Datum(data.Value()-2){}).Value()
             ){};
       }
      };
     }
    };
```

Now we get the non-repetitive Fibonacci using the Y-combinator:

```
static Lambda nrfibo = Combinators.y(hyperfibo);
```

```
// a wrapper function so we can have int Fibonacci
static int fibo(int x)
{
return ((Datum)(nrfibo.apply(new Datum(x){}))).Value();
}
```

Chapter 8

Temporal Interaction

In which we learn that when you are code you are never alone. That the universe evolves in time and software execution requires temporal interaction between many parts.

Code executes in time. The universe evolves through time. We might not understand what that means, but the implications for the nature of code we write are strong. In particular, a pure function is timeless and an interactive program has irreversible side effects. Once the paper is printed, it can't be unprinted.

Edsger Dijkstra refers to it as the problem of the mosquito and the elephant. If you start with two tiny programs and let them interact you can find you have an enormous and complex beast on your hands.

But this is the nature of any program that must interact with the universe, and there are many nice solutions to various problems that involve multiple programs running at the same time.

The technicalities of the distinction between multi-programming, multi-threading, parallel programming, multi-tasking, and other similar terms and concepts are not the issue here. The question is simply, what happens when two programs interact? Or a program interacts with the outside universe?

Notion 126: Virtual Interaction

A side effect can always be expressed as a change in the state of the machine, and thus as a pure function of that state. Without loss of generality, we consider only flow control, variable assignment, and pure functions in this discussion.

Temporal interaction between external entities and a program is often said to be contrary to the pure functional approach. In practice, peripheral devices certainly can be a problem, but this is more typically due to the subtle nature of the state of these devices, and the operations on them, rather than a conceptual conflict. The states and operations do not fit well into the restricted data types allowed by many contemporary computer languages. (Haskell is one exception.)

Because time has only one dimension, a pure device is a sequence of events. A serial output port is a sequence of character transmission events. This sequence is modified only by extension. Once a character has been sent, the program cannot go back in time to unsend it.

The state of a raster screen is an array of coloured pixels. The screen may be written, read, and rewritten, creating a sequence of whole screen states. A raster screen is an array of sequences of colours embedded in time. As it is for a serial port the program cannot go back in time to unchange the screen. We can view the screen in different bases. A vector screen is more naturally a sequence of line and circle writing events.

All output devices (and variables) are sequences of states. A state is a possible current output to be viewed, and the sequence can only be extended, never shortened or otherwise changed.

Although it is often used, we need no special syntax for any output device. If `cout` represents a character stream output device, then the syntax `cout += "some more output"` is usable and has clear semantics. Logically, this is the meaning of `cout << "some more output"` in C++. The value of `cout` could be the list of all characters so far output.

Implementation might allow reading characters such as `c[0]`. It might buffer the last n characters, and `+=` drop characters. It might allow overwriting. But since, physically we can't unwrite or truncate the stream, this breaks the synchronicity between the physical device and the language construct.

It is likewise for an input device. One entity's input is another entity's output.[35] For you to listen to me, I must be talking. An input stream is a sequence, and `c=cin` reads the next character, or perhaps all characters not yet read. The value changes, but we did not change it. We are learning that we are not alone in the universe.[36] The axiom that `{a=x;b=x}` has the post-condition `a==b`, is not admitted.

Computation is naturally multi-threaded. Input and output streams involve the interaction between two threads. Likewise, any variable is an interactive stream — if only between a program and itself.[37]

```
T1 = { c=cin      ; something(c) }
T2 = { cin=cin+x ; something(x) }
```

The second thread might be a person typing at a keyboard, or clicking with a mouse. Or the low-level thread that reads the keyboard, and writes characters into a buffer. The command `c=cin` changes `cin`. Let `cin<<1` be an expression with the value obtained by dropping the first character. Thus, `"this"<<1 == "his"`. We also have `cin<<n`, for non-negative integer n, and further let `"this">>1 == "s"`, and `1<<"this"` be `"t"`.

The read operation is really two operations:

```
{c=(1<<cin); cin=(cin<<1)}
```

Taken exactly as stated, if two threads read the keyboard at the same time, it is possible that they will both read the current character, and the next character will be thrown away without being noticed. This is a real problem, not an artifact of this model. The quintessential problem in the virtual universe is that nothing is ever moved, only copied and deleted.

---

[35] Shades of Wittgenstein's disproof of solipsism.
[36] Actually, I am a solipsist, but do not let that spoil the story.
[37] Wittgenstein's disproof of solipsism refuted.

Notion 127: Incorruptible Operations

For a thread to update the value of a variable it must read the variable,
compute the new value, and write this value into the variable. Normally,
these operations occur at different times. The execution of multiple
threads is analogous to a public job board, on which jobs are listed.
Someone comes and copies information into a notebook and goes away.
Another someone comes and deletes the job note. But if in the meantime
yet another someone has come by, they might also pick up the same job
note. The single input has been read twice, an erroneous duplication.

Two threads will drop two symbols, but the first might be read twice
and the second not at all.

```
T1 = {c1=(1<<cin)              ; cin=(cin<<1)              }
T2 = {            c2=(1<<cin) ;              cin=(cin<<1)}
```

The stream `cin` is extended only by a dedicated thread reading the physical keyboard register. Suppose `cin="this"`. Conditions on the machine
state are expressed as conditions on variables. Each condition is true
or false between and indeterminate during commands. We interlace the
commands and conditions, listing between commands only conditions
that are true in that interval.

```
                    -- here cin=="this"
T1: c1=(1<<cin);
                    -- here c1=='t' and cin=="this"
T2: c2=(1<<cin);
                    -- here c1=='t' and c2=='t' and cin=="this"
T1: cin=(cin<<1);
                    -- here c1=='t' and c2=='t' and cin=="his"
T2: cin=(cin<<1);
                    -- here c1=='t' and c2=='t' and cin=="is"
```

One possible interlacing of the thread execution is shown. The data
has become corrupted. The 't' has been read twice, and the 'h' not at
all. The input has been corrupted by the concurrent behaviour of the
threads. There is interference between the threads. If the read as a
whole had no duration, this would not occur, but giving the parts zero
duration would not solve the problem.

In a single-cpu desktop machine, there are indivisible operations; anything that takes only one machine cycle is indivisible. In digital time, it has no duration. But most operations take multiple machine cycles. Even writing a value into a multi-byte variable can be corrupted by the action of another thread.

If all commands require non-trivial pre-conditions to establish the desired post-condition, then it can be impossible to establish any post condition. We need some command, like assignment in serial code, which establishes a post-condition regardless. But even with indivisible simple assignment we may have corruption; many algorithms require related modification to multiple variables. We need some method for protecting compound operations.

For this discussion, we assume that assignment of tuples is indivisible. The semantics of $(a,b)=(x,y)$ is distinct from $a=x;b=y$. In the latter, there might be a period of time between the two assignment, allowing interference. In the former, all values on the right are computed before the assignment. $(x,y)=(y,x)$ really does swap x and y.

But use of compound expressions might lead to corruption.

$$(a,b)=(f(x),g(y)) \equiv \{(t1=f(x) \ || \ t2=g(y)) \ ; \ (a,b)=(t1,t2)\}$$

where t1 and t2 are variables that are not affected by any other thread, and || (which is read as *in parallel with*) indicates the concurrent execution of the two assignments. x=a+b does not have the post condition x==a+b. It is equivalent to {(t1=a || t2=b) ; t3=t1+t2 ; x=t3}.

In c,cin=(1<<cin),(cin<<1), cin might be changed between the evaluation of (1<<cin) and (cin<<1). For a practical solution of this, especially at low machine level, an indivisible read-modify-write cycle is provided. We might express this as c <- cin; where <- is an indivisible operation that copies the first character of cin into c and also deletes it from cin itself.

The study of multi thread code begins with an examination of software mechanisms that can provide compound protection, given only the indivisibility of simple assignment, and some basic arithmetic.

Notion 128: Temporal Computing

Temporal means to do with time.

It is axiomatic that a computer exists in space and evolves in time.

This is so obvious that it is often overlooked. But, to explore the behaviour of a generic digital computer, with a view to pragmatic application, we must take into account the physical aspect of the machine.

Some pragmatic computational limits are due to physical law (thermodynamics, quantum theory, special relativity, the atomic theory of matter), rather than deriving from logical limitations. Most of the spatial matters can be ignored in practical terms, once limitations on speed and memory size have been accounted for. The physical aspect that is the hardest to ignore is time. It is this one aspect that we will admit into our discussion. We have no choice if we want to be even vaguely practical about applying our theory to a real machine. An algorithm, by definition, starts with the problem and ends with the solution. We use time to compute, we interact with our machines in time. An infinitesimal computer is acceptable, an instantaneous one is incomprehensible.

But we will abstract the temporal nature whereever practical.

By design intent, contemporary computers are discrete-state machines. This means that we can identify a sequence of definite states that the machine passes through as it evolves. A bit in memory is intended to have only two states, 0 and 1. The value of a bit is either 0 or 1, but not both.

This is not the only way to build a computer. There is such a thing as an analogue computer in which variables have states that lie on a continuum. But this is not the type of computer that you are likely to be dealing with, and is not the type of computer that we are discussing here.

If we look closely at the operation of a physical digital computer we will see that the discrete nature of the states is only an approximation, but we take it that the machine is designed with the intent of being a valid implementation of a discrete-state machine, and work with the assumption that our machine is functioning correctly. It is an axiom of our theory that the machine may be considered to be a discrete-state machine.

Ignoring the details of peripherals such as screens, magnetic disks, tapes, CDs, and so on, we take it that the state of the machine is naturally described as a binary memory cell. For example, a desktop machine might have 1,024 Mb of RAM. This is $1,024 \times 2^{20}$ bytes, which is a total of 2^{30} bits, which is roughly 10,000,000,000 bits. Each bit can have two states, so 1 bit has two states, 2 bits have $4 = 2 \times 2$ states, 3 bits have $8 = 2 \times 2 \times 2$ states total, and so on, so that n bits have 2^n states. Thus the total size of the state space for the contemporary computer is

$$2^{10,000,000,0000}$$

which is way too big to write down in plain decimal notation.

If the machine is operating at 10 Ghz = 10,000,000,000 instructions per second, then it might explore around 2^{30} states per second. At this rate the time taken to touch each state just once is many times longer than the estimated time for which the universe is likely to have been in existence.

Nevertheless, it is quite easy for us to comprehend any one of these states in terms of the value of each byte in memory, and to envisage a transition of the state as changing the value of a number of bytes.

The machine has a discrete state (a finite integer) as a function of time, and operates at a finite speed. Thus, in any finite interval of time there is at most a finite number of state changes. We can model the temporal aspect of the machine by the times of the changes in state. The state changes are instantaneous events, and occur with finite density, at a definite time. Since nothing changes in between, we have little interest in the intervals and can scale our image so that each interval is the same. At this point we can largely ignore the intervals and talk simply of the sequence of states or state changes.

Notion 129: Multi-Threaded Code

A computer executing software in memory is like a person following instructions on paper. At each moment the person is at a particular location in the instructions and they remember a number of previously obtained results. Multi-threaded execution is analogous to a group of people all working from written instructions. Each person remembers a different collection of previous results, known as their current environment. They may also be concentrating at different locations, and, due to their differing environments, responding differently even to the same instructions.

The multi-threading concept in software abstracts the computational aspect of this by admitting a data structure (often called a thread, task, or process) which stores a location in the code, and a collection of variable bindings. The semantics is that each thread is like a person operating on the store of shared instructions. In practice, some code is used only by a single thread, and is part of its private environment.

Treating a point of execution as a data structure may cause a jolt. In single-threaded code there is only one thread, and the programmer does not ever have to think about it explicitly. But the thread is there nevertheless. In particular, an explicit choice is made of where to start in the list of instructions. In C, it is at the main routine, in Java it is the main method, in an applet it is the init method, in Haskell the main function. In multi-threaded code, there is no obvious default choice of start point or number of threads. So multi-threaded code typically starts with a single thread and the ability to create new threads. The program has to indicate explicitly the entry point for each new thread as it is created. It is useful to have a method to indicate explicitly the initial state of the variable bindings for each thread. However, this latter facility is not always provided.

Generically, multi-threaded code is very much more complicated than single-threaded code. Two parallel routines multiply in complexity of execution, while two serial routines only add. If we are not careful in writing multi-threaded code we may find that the code produces extremely peculiar effects that cannot be viewed as a combination of the external behaviours of the individual routines.

Notion 130: Graphs of State Machines

Consider again the state machine that has been used $00 \rightarrow 01$
several times elsewhere and whose transitions are listed $01 \rightarrow 10$
here. The states deterministically run in the sequence $10 \rightarrow 10$
$11 \rightarrow 00 \rightarrow 01 \rightarrow 10$, then the state 10 loops on itself. $11 \rightarrow 00$

We can draw a network that represents this machine; each link is between two states, and is drawn as a line, each state is indicated in a little circle. The edges show the possible transitions.

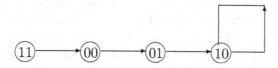

If we physically run, in parallel, two state machines whose transitions occur at random points in time, and which do not in anyway interact, then the chance of actually getting two transitions at once is zero. Thus, in practice each transition is either a transition of one machine, or a transition of the other. This is also the case in a multitasking single processor, since only one task is running at a time. So, the transitions of the two processes together conform to the notion of a direct product (see page 113) (independent parallel composition) of these two state machines. We obtain the following diagram.

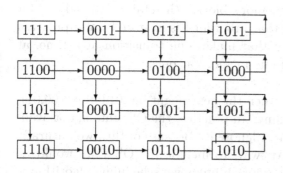

Each row is a copy of state machine 1, and each column is a copy of state machine 2. If we factor the graph (see page 111) by combining each row into a single node, then we obtain state machine 2. If we factor by combining columns, then we get state machine 1.

Notion 131: Direct Thread Composition

A single isolated piece of software running on a desktop machine has been allocated a memory block for all its local variables. This memory is the state of the program. By ignoring memory changes outside this block we see that the program is a virtual state machine. The memory inside the block is the state machine's state. In principle, we may list for each state of the memory block the state the memory would be in after the program has single stepped.

On a desktop machine with 1024 Mb of RAM, our code might be allocated 16 Mb. That is $2^{\wedge}(2^{\wedge}24)$ states, while the full machine has vastly more. If a second independent program runs in its own 16 Mb of RAM, then the two programs can be composed, conceptually, into one whose state is the pair of memory blocks of the individual programs. The number of states of the two programs together is the product, $2^{\wedge}(2^{\wedge}24) \times 2^{\wedge}(2^{\wedge}24) = 2^{\wedge}(2^{\wedge}25)$ of the individual state counts. Once again the total is vastly more[38] than for the single program. In practice, the state transitions for 1 Kb of RAM are prohibitively many to list explicitly.

But, with 2 bits of memory and deterministic software, we can list the transitions. For each state we indicate the next. If the memory block is in the state on the left then the next state will be the state on the right.

```
00 -> 01
01 -> 10
10 -> 10
11 -> 00
```

With two copies in disjoint memory blocks, the state is (ab,cd) — for example, (01,10) — meaning that program 1 is in state 01 and program 2 is in state 10. Given a cpu that makes one transition at a time, at most one program will change its memory at once.

If the current state is (00,00), then the next might be (01,00) or (00,01), depending on the cpu scheduling. In practice, the OS state is not available to the program, so we must ignore it. Because of this, we naturally discover non-determinism. Anyway, to include the OS state would be to overspecialise. Programming for an unknown scheduling algorithm is pragmatically the same as programming a non-deterministic machine. It must work under all permutations.

---

[38]Even if it does not look it, check the effect of the 24+1 carefully.

The complete table is on the right. Check that you see how this table was created. I have dropped the parentheses and commas, notating (00,00) as 0000. Apart from abbreviation, the reason for this will be more apparent later (see page 276) when we look at less direct products of state machines. The table is very regular; the machines are identical. You could independently choose the virtual machine and then choose the transition. When the two machines are distinct the structure is almost as regular, since the transitions available to one machine are not affected by the state of the other.

```
0. 0000 -> 0100 or 0001
1. 0001 -> 0101 or 0010
2. 0010 -> 0110 or 0010
3. 0011 -> 0111 or 0000

4. 0100 -> 1000 or 0101
5. 0101 -> 1001 or 0110
6. 0110 -> 1010 or 0110
7. 0111 -> 1011 or 0100

8. 1000 -> 1000 or 1001
9. 1001 -> 1001 or 1010
A. 1010 -> 1010 or 1010
B. 1011 -> 1011 or 1000

C. 1100 -> 0000 or 1101
D. 1101 -> 0001 or 1110
E. 1110 -> 0010 or 1110
F. 1111 -> 0011 or 1100
```

```
0. 00xx -> 01xx or 00xx
1. 00xx -> 01xx or 00xx
2. 00xx -> 01xx or 00xx
3. 00xx -> 01xx or 00xx
```

If in the above table we blank out the state of the second machine, using xx, we get a table of 16 entries of which the first four are listed here.

Extracting distinct entries we obtain a list of four.

```
00xx -> 01xx or 00xx
01xx -> 10xx or 01xx
10xx -> 10xx or 10xx
11xx -> 00xx or 11xx
```

Except for xx this is the transition table for a single machine.

It did not have to be. But because the two programs are running in separate blocks, the transitions of one do not affect the state of the other.

Ignoring the state of one returns the transition table of the other. Fixing the state of one returns the transition table of the other. This type of composition is called the direct product, or pure parallel composition, of threads. It models a lack of any real interaction. The two programs might as well be on opposite sides of the universe.

Notion 132: Concurrent Thread Interference

Consider again the two virtual machines (see page 274) which we call threads. But now the two threads are not entirely independent. The second bit of the first memory block is the same bit of memory as the first bit of the second block. So in each state `(ab,cd)` we have `b==c`, since they are physically the same bit of memory. Thus, the state can be written with three bits instead of four, `abbd==abd`. The transitions can be computed in essentially the same manner as before, by considering transitions for the first machine involving only the first two bits, and the second machine involving only the last two bits.

```
000 -> 010 or 001
001 -> 011 or 010
010 -> 100 or 010
011 -> 101 or 000
100 -> 100 or 101
101 -> 101 or 110
110 -> 000 or 110
111 -> 001 or 100
```

```
00 -> 01
01 -> 10
10 -> 10
11 -> 00
```

In a pure parallel combination, we can view the original machine by blanking out the other memory. But, in this case if we view only the first two bits of the joint memory block, blanking out the third bit, we get a machine with a transition table different from the original. The effect of giving two machines overlapping memory is to create two new machines.

```
00x -> 01x or 00x
00x -> 01x or 01x
01x -> 10x or 01x
01x -> 10x or 00x
10x -> 10x or 10x
10x -> 10x or 11x
11x -> 00x or 11x
11x -> 00x or 10x
```

```
00 -> 01 or 00
01 -> 10 or 01 or 00
10 -> 10 or 11
11 -> 00 or 11 or 10
```

When we blank out some memory and look only at part of it, we are forming a factor of the original machine. If a product does not return the original machines on factoring in this way, then we can validly say that some interference has occurred. Often, but not always, when this was intentional, the two factors will be submachines of the original machines.

In this case we get two new machines which we can just accept, and ask what type of a product the full machine is of the two factors. It is not a pure parallel product, since the number of states is 8, while pure product would have 16. In particular, the transitions of the two machines are interlocked. If the product is in the state 000, and the second machine goes to state 11, then the first has gone either to state 01 or 11. There is a degree of cooperation required between the machine in order to change state. Fundamentally new behaviour may appear (see page 288).

Perhaps not obviously, this situation is one that every programmer is very familiar with. When we have a variable such as x, and a program { code1 ; x++ ; code2 }, then in order for the program to progress from the start of the second to the start of the third command, it must cooperate with the x-machine. We have viewed an integer variable as part of the state of a program. But now we can view it as a machine itself, which responds to x++ by moving one step around a large loop. But it must do so in cooperation with transitions in the main program that are marked with x++.

In a product we usually start with transitions that are transitions in one, or both, machines. The direct product takes only those in one machine; the lock-step product takes only those on which both machines agree. More generally, it is required that the machines agree on some transitions, but not others. Labelling the transitions, we might say that only those in which x++ is coupled with an increment on the x-machine are acceptable. And that x>0 needs the single loop on the x machine.

A program using n bits of memory has 2^n states but typically only reaches a small fraction of these. For pure products, the set of states actually accessed is the product of the states accessed by the components. But with interference the states may be more or less. When a bit is set, T_1 does a lot; otherwise it does nothing. T_2 sets this bit, greatly expanding the states reached with the bit initially clear. Alternatively, if T_1 is an n-bit counter, and overlaps with another n-bit counter, T_2, by one bit, then the total states accessible can't be more than $2^{(2n-2)}$, rather than the direct product 2^{2n}.

We know that $10 * 10^{1000} = 10^{1001}$ without writing out the digits of the numbers. Likewise, we do not have to list transitions exhaustively. We can define transition tables as combinations of other transition tables. We can compute with formal products. These products are like joins in database theory, and they have their own logic.

Notion 133: Control Structures

We are used to structures such as
`if(x>6) code1 else code2`
and may have heard of the idea of a flow
chart. We know that any block code structure can be written as a flow chart. But can
any flow chart be written as block code?
The answer is that any flow chart can be
simulated by block code, but it can't always be written down in a transliterative
fashion. Flow charts are in this sense more
expressive.

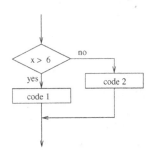

A flow chart is a network in which each node is a conditional and each
edge is a command. This rather random example shows the flow chart on
the left, and the equivalent code on the right. This illustrates a general
technique to convert a flow network into code with branch instructions.

But what about block-structured code?

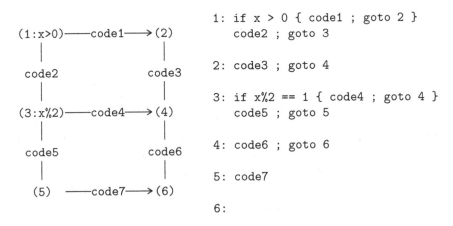

```
1: if x > 0 { code1 ; goto 2 }
   code2 ; goto 3

2: code3 ; goto 4

3: if x%2 == 1 { code4 ; goto 4 }
   code5 ; goto 5

4: code6 ; goto 6

5: code7

6:
```

When block-structured design was first considered, the problem of possible limitation was a concern. A theorem was proved that all programs
could be written in a block-structured manner. And thus the concerns
were eliminated. But it is not possible to duplicate the above flow of
control via block structured flow control. The two distinct paths for
getting to code6 make it impossible. A technical proof is more complex,
but the way in which attempts fail is instructive.

The first code is as close it gets, but we duplicate `code6`. The second code uses the flag `t`, which is hidden non-block control structure.

```
if(x>0)
    code1 ;                    t=0
    code3 ;                    if(x>0)
    code6                          code1 ; code3 ; t=1
else                           else
    code2 ;                        code2 ;
    if(x%2==1)                     if(x%2==1)
        code4 ;                        code4 ; t=1
        code6                      else
    else                               code5 ; code7
        code5 ;                    if(t==1) code6;
        code7
```

Direct implementation of the graph (`t` stores the state) shows that a `goto` structure can be simulated in block structured code.

```
t=1
while(t!=6)
    if(t==1) if(x>0)     code1 ; t=2 else code2 ; t=3
    if(t==2)             code3 ; t=4
    if(t==3) if(x%2==1)  code4 ; t=4 else code5 ; t=5
    if(t==4)             code6 ; t=6
    if(t==5)             code7 ; t=6
end
```

This is the core of the proof that block structure is sufficient; by using auxiliary variables we can simulate any flow network. But this is lip-service only. The spirit of block structure is a style, not a language. By simulating a Von Neumann machine, we can produce the behaviour of any spaghetti code within the confines of a block-structured language. This does not prevent it from being spaghetti.

A computation is a flow graph, the edges are serial code, and the nodes are decision points; there is a hidden state. Each link of the graph indicates a state change. A pure computation has no state other than the points (there might be many) of activity. It would have been nice if all computations could be transliterated into a simple, finite, block-structured language, but they cannot — not without loosing their spirit.

The flow network is the natural form of a computation.

Notion 134: Thread Point of Execution

Part of the state of a thread, such as

```
T : command1 ; command2 ; command3
```

is the information about where it is in its execution. Given that each command is indivisible, T has four execution locations.

1   at the beginning before command1,
2   between command1 and command2,
3   between command2 and command3,
4   at the end after command3.

Each thread is a graph of execution locations linked by the commands.

It is important, and not always this trivial, to know all the points of execution. If a command, as written, is not indivisible, there may be hidden points of execution.

The code

```
x=(2*y)+1
```

is typically shorthand for

```
{t1=2*y ; t2=t1+1 ; x=t2}
```

or similar. Typically, the evaluation of a compound expression has many actual points of execution that must be taken into account in the analysis of multiple threads.

If arithmetic and assignment are indivisible, which is typical for machine datatypes, then this expansion might give us the correct points. But, we need to know what the compiler is doing with our code. Did it compile it precisely as written, or did it use algebraic manipulation to change it into an equivalent? Did it change it into reverse polish? In practice, we need to write code so that the precise decomposition by the compiler does not invalidate our code.

Notion 135: The Transition Network

A single thread of code such as

$$|^0 \ \text{t=x} \ |^1 \ ; \ \text{x=y} \ |^2 \ ; \ \text{y=t} \ |^3$$

is a transition network in which the nodes are the points between the commands where execution might rest. On a desktop computer, the nodes correspond to an instant of time, and the edges to the duration of the command. But, with incorruptible commands, we may think of the machine as resting on the nodes, inactive, and then executing a command in no time.

Each variable is another transition machine with states which are the values that the variable can hold. The transitions of the variable and the thread execution are locked together, so that, for example, a transition across the command x++ will only occur in conjunction with a change of value of the variable x.

The network in this case,

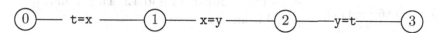

is a simple linear network, but other code,

$$|^0 \ \text{while(i<10)} \ |^1 \ \text{i=i+1} \ |^2 \ ; \ |^3 \qquad\qquad \text{may have loops in it} \ldots$$

```
 (2)——————————(0)—— i>=10 ——————(3)

  i=i+1      i<10

               (1)
```

Some of the edges are annotated with a logical condition. A logical condition is a transition that must be performed in conjunction with the universe at large. That is, if the universe agrees that i<10, then the edge to the left may be traversed.

Notion 16: Interacting Thread Example

Consider the following two thread networks.

T1: $\mid^0$ t=x $\mid^1$; x=y $\mid^2$; y=t $\mid^3$

T2: $\mid^0$ x=6 $\mid^1$

(0)——t=x——(1)——x=y——(2)——y=t——(3)

(0)——x=6——(1)

The states of thread T1 are $\{0,1,2,3\}$ and the states of T2 are $\{0,1\}$. The parallel composition of these is T3=T1∥T2. The states of T3 are $\{(0,0),(1,0),(2,0),(3,0),(0,1),(1,1),(2,1),(3,1)\}$.

```
(00)——x=6——(01)
 |            |
t=x          t=x
 |            |
(10)——x=6——(11)
 |            |
x=y          x=y
 |            |
(20)——x=6——(21)
 |            |
y=t          y=t
 |            |
(30)——x=6——(31)
```

The network for T3 is on the left. Transitions occur top-left to bottom-right. The thread starts in state (00) and ends (eventually) in state (31). Unlike T1 and T2, T3 has multiple paths from start to finish.

At high-level (ignoring t), T1 swaps x and y and T2 sets x to 6. We might hope that the combination will produce some logical combination of these two effects, the order making a difference.

$$(x,y)=(6,x) \text{ or } (x,y)=(y,6)$$

There are four paths. Across the top and down the right is T2;T1 down the left and across the bottom is T1;T2. Both of which produce logical combinations of effects. The problem is that there are two other rungs, where T2 breaks into the action of T1. It is not obvious that these will result in a transformation equivalent to one of the two serial combinations.

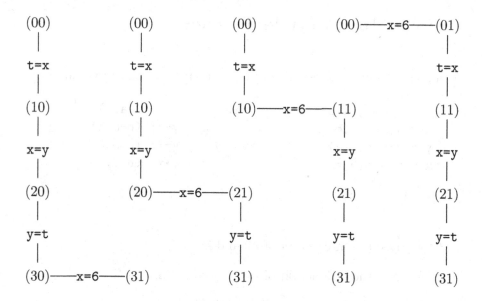

The third rung leads to t=x; x=y; x=6; y=t;,

(0,23,45) t=x (23,23,45) x=y (23,45,45) x=6 (23,6,45) y=t (23,6,23)

The net effect is (x,y)=(x,6), which is the same as T2;T1.

The second rung leads to t=x; x=6; x=y; y=t;,

(0,23,45) t=x (23,23,45) x=6 (23,6,45) x=y (23,45,45) y=t (23,45,23)

The net effect is (x,y)=(y,x). The effect of x=6 has been lost.

Accidentally, the effect of T1||T2 is the same as T1, leading to the thought that the effect might always be one of T1, T2, T1||T2, or T2||T1. However, this is untrue in general. The effects might have little relation to any combination of the logical effects of the individual threads.

Normally, threads have so many states that exhaustive analysis would be exhausting. However, for communications protocols which will be reused numerous times, have a relatively low number of states, and high relia-bility requirement, automated explicit listing to check is recommended.

Exercise 16: Multiple Threads

A numerical swap can occur with or without an auxiliary variable.

```
S1:            (_,a,b)          S2:                (a,b)
   t = y;  (b,a,b)                 x = y-x;  (b-a,b)
   y = x;  (b,a,a)                 y = y-x;  (b-a,a)
   x = t   (b,b,a)                 x = y+x   (b,a)
```

Also let A = {x=6}

1. Analyse the interaction of S2 and A.

2. Analyse the interaction of two copies of S2.

3. Analyse the interaction of S1 with S2.

Some attempt can be made to protect the thread S1 from the interaction of other threads by using an auxiliary variable to flag activity.

```
S3 = { while(t) ; t=1 ; S2 ; t=0; }
```

4. Analyse the interaction of two copies of S3.

5. Analyse the interaction of three threads made from the three commands in S2 taken separately. What is the chance that a correct swap will occur?

Notion 136: High-Level Interference

Although it is possible (see page 276), and for some purposes desirable to express the state of a program in binary, the explicit application of this to a program written in a higher-level language can then be obscure or difficult.

But we do not need to express every thing as binary patterns to see what is happening, we simply say that thread T1 accesses variables a, b, c, and d, and thread T2 accesses variables c, d, e, and f. Then the state of the parallel composition of the two threads is (a,b,c,d,e,f). The transitions do not have to be indicated explicitly as a table.

For example, x -> x+1

is short-hand notation for a whole large number of transitions. In this way extensive and complex transitions can be expressed in a simple compact notation. We can compose x -> x+1 with x -> 2*x, which interfere because of using the same variable.

```
0 -> 1
1 -> 2
2 -> 3
  :
2^n-1 -> 0
```

Although good studies of the problem can be done at this level, there is one caveat. We have to make sure that the machine does not split these operations into multiple suboperations. If it does, then the states visited by the composition might move outside the range of those suggested by the above approach. That is, we need to keep track of what is genuinely an indivisible operation.

We have come full circle. We began with an increment, and went through the enormous state space of a desktop computer, through state transition tables and parallel composition, all the way back to saying

$$x=x+1$$

The point of the exercise, a point which is vitally central to increasing understanding of programming, is that we have learned a new, and much more precise, way of explaining what we mean by x=x+1, and a method for relating it directly to a real physical computer with spatial extent and temporal character.

Notion 137: Incorruptible Commands Again

A digital computer performs action in sequence.

For multi-threaded code the actions are selected from various threads
one at a time. The selection is assumed to be fair; any thread which can
run will eventually (before the end of the universe). Subsequences of
primitive machine actions make higher-level commands. The command
x=6 is not usually a single machine instruction. Just the reference to x
may require several machine cycles. But we assume that the language
implementation establishes certain commands as incorruptible. So the
command x=6, even though it takes multiple machine cycles, establishes
the truth of the condition x==6 for at least an instant. In the parallel
command x=6||x=7, each thread is multiple machine cycles.

These two commands are interlaced by the action of the machine,

```
                                  t1              t2
      |----------(x=6) - - - - - -|
           |- - - - -(x=7)- ----------|
```

By assumption assignment is incorruptible, so at time t1 we have (x==6)
and at time t2 we have (x==7). Perhaps, during the initial phase of x=7
it is computing the references. At the end of x=6 the machine does a
single load instruction into the variable x, so for an instant, (x==6), but
then x=7 completes, also doing a load into x; and thus (x==7), which
will continue to be true from now on, if no other commands are executed.

But what if the two instructions terminated at exactly the same time? There is
no value of x that is consistent with the assumption that assignment is incorruptible.
We deduce that incorruptible commands
do not finish at the same time. Thus, we
can validly express the action of the entire machine as a sequence of incorruptible
commands.

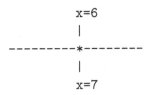

This decision can be interpreted as an arbitrary choice between

either of which is logically consistent.

An incorruptible command is certain to produce its definitive post-condition. Given no incorruptible commands we cannot write any incorruptible commands. Programming is a process of combining small incorruptible commands into larger, composite commands that are also incorruptible. It is a logical contradiction for conflicting incorruptible commands to finish simultaneously. If two incorruptible commands do not interfere, then their relative time of execution is immaterial.

We model the action of the computer as a sequence of incorruptible commands, each of which occurs instantly and none of which occur at the same time. A further technical requirement is that in any finite period of time at most a finite number of actions occur (possibly none).

We model the action of a thread as a sequence of incorruptible actions. The action of a machine running both threads is some interlacing of two sequences of individual thread actions, the incorruptible actions. But, the trace of one thread taken from a composition might be impossible as a trace for the thread on its own. Interference between threads is due to inappropriate interlacing of the commands in the code.

Without some assumption of incorruptibility, we could not be sure of our programs at all. In principle, it is impossible to be sure that any two commands do not interfere. A long time ago, it is said, someone managed to crash a mainframe computer by executing instructions that caused the part of the machine nearest the fire detector to get hot, shutting down the computer.

But, in practice we can make the violations sufficiently rare.

Notion 138: Thread Interaction

Any variable represents an interaction in the same manner as an input or output command. Like any input or output channel, each variable actually stands for the sequence of values assigned to it during the course of the program execution. Each time we look at the value of the variable, we are reading the most recent input. By definition the old values are not available.

This is most clear when we consider two threads that can access the same variable. One thread might write the value into the variable, and the other read it out. Even if there is only one thread, the effect is the same, in so far as the state of the variable is not determined locally in the code, and so the thread is interacting with itself across time. When threads that share variables are combined in parallel they might not form a pure parallel composition.

```
T1 = { t=x ; x=y ; y=t ; t=x ; x=y ; y=t ; }
T2 = { x=x+1 ; }
```

T1 has seven execution states and T2 has 2; there are 14 states for the parallel combination, and seven possible traces. Rather than analyse this as a theoretical exercise, we place them in two threads that loop forever, repeating the actions.

The thread thing1 swaps the variable x with the variable y, and then swaps them back; a net total non-operation. The second thread thing2 repeatedly increments x.

```
thing1: while(true) T1;
thing2: while(true) T2;
```

We examine a Java code fragment (see page 290) which illustrates some of the concepts. The Java code implements a process formed by parallel composition of implementation of the two threads, using a single function that chooses between acting like thread 1 or thread 2, depending on the configuration parameter. The assumptions of incorruptibility in this example, and the Java code may be distinct. But, this does not show up in the empirical data.

A test run produced the data on the right. t is not shown, and c is a counter that counts the number of increments.

If the two threads were (x,y)=(y,x) and (x,y)=(x+1,y) as incorruptible actions, then we should find that x+y==c. But inspection of the data shows that x+y is about c/2 as we near the end of the trace.

Detailed examination shows that x+y increments and decrements by more than 1 at a time. The actual changes in x+y occur somewhat randomly. This behaviour would not occur in the threads specified. Since x is incremented, the only thing that can happen is that the effect of the increment is lost. This could cause a single decrement. What we are looking at is an effect of the complex interactions between the three threads involved (the third thread is the main thread that prints out the values).

```
x,y,c == 0,0,0
x,y,c == 1,0,1
x,y,c == 0,0,2
x,y,c == 0,0,3
x,y,c == 1,0,4
x,y,c == 1,0,5
x,y,c == 0,0,6
x,y,c == 1,1,7
x,y,c == 1,2,8
x,y,c == 1,2,9
x,y,c == 1,3,10
x,y,c == 4,3,11
x,y,c == 1,5,12
x,y,c == 1,1,13
x,y,c == 1,7,14
x,y,c == 7,1,15
x,y,c == 1,1,16
x,y,c == 8,1,17
x,y,c == 9,1,18
x,y,c == 1,1,19
x,y,c == 1,9,20
x,y,c == 2,9,21
```

In the specification of the JVM the machine code instructions ought to be incorruptible. But there is no assurance of any incorruptible commands at high-level. Thus, in Java, it is possible for variable reading, writing, and increment to interfere. For example, the JVM must look up the address of a variable, and then fetch the information. So variable read and write are not indivisible.

These interactions are not normally the desired behaviour. The study of multi-threaded code considered many attempts to avoid these problems. In Java, the simplest way around is to declare a synchronised method. Then the JVM assures that only one thread at a time will be executing in this method and that once a thread has entered this code, it will not be disturbed by another thread until it leaves the code.

This simple mechanism resolves a lot of low-level problems. But how does the JVM achieve this in the first place?

Notion 17: Interacting Java Code

```java
import java.io.*;
import java.util.*;
import java.text.*;
import java.lang.Thread.*;

class thing extends Thread implements Runnable
{
 static int t, x = 0, y = 0, c = 0;
 Boolean swap;

 public thing(Boolean a){swap = a;}

 public void run()
 {
 if(swap)
  while(true)
  {
   t=x; x=y; y=t;
   t=x; x=y; y=t;
  }
 else
  while(true)
  {
   x = x + 1; c = c+ 1;
   try{sleep(100);}catch(InterruptedException e){}
  }
 }
}
```

```
class conflict
{
 static thing thing1 = new thing(true);
 static thing thing2 = new thing(false);

 static public void main(String args[])
 {
  int i,j;

  thing1.start(); thing2.start();

  while(true)
  {
  for(i=0;i<10000;i++) for(j=0;j<1000;j++);
  System.out.println("x,y,c == ");
  System.out.println(thing.x+","+thing.y+","+thing.c);
  }
 }
}
```

Notion 139: Pure String Interaction

A pure function has no side effects. We can purify an impure function by the superficially simple method of including all the implicit data explicitly in the arguments, without otherwise modifying the code. But interactive code can be subtle

The routine `getch()` that reads characters from the keyboard has a side effect. It has no arguments, and yet the return value can vary from call to call. Where is the implicit data to explicitly include? The data is the sequence of keystrokes from the user, past and future. How can we provide that which does not yet exist?

Perhaps we do not need to. A program reads a sequence of input characters from the keyboard; it writes a sequence of output characters to the screen. If we glance at the computer afterwards, we see a string-to-string function. The Hello-World program is `p(s)="Hello World"`. A program that echoes its input is the identity function `p(s)=s`. Each character input appears unchanged on the output.

Both the input and output are potentially infinite. If we waited for the entire input before producing the first character of output, we might wait forever. But, we do not normally need the entire input string to compute an output prefix. A simple program indefinitely repeats a prompt-read-write sequence. We type, the program reads, then writes. In the simplest case `p(s1+s2)=p(s1)+p(s2)` where `s1` is a specific completed input after which the user expects a response.

A command line calculator takes a single expression on one line. It determines the value of the expression and prints it out. Before each input, it writes out a prompt to the user. If the expression reduction is `value`, then the string function is defined recursively. We use utilities `top`, which returns the shortest prefix to which a response is required, and `pop`, which returns the rest of the input string.

```
calc(s) = "p: " + top(s) + value(top(s)) + calc(pop(s))
```

As a string to string function this is correct. But, the Hello-World program can immediately write out its entire greeting without waiting for any input. There is a whiff of a problem. What if we had wanted it to wait? We want the prompt to appear, for us to type and then have a response from the program before continuing. How do we include the temporal part of the interaction?

One short solution is that the computer prints out exactly as much of the output as it can compute. For calc(s) before any input prints the prompt "p: ", as top(s) is being input, calc echos each character, and when top(s) is completed, calc can output value(top(s)).

This is the semantics of the Haskell interact function.

```
top [ ] = [ ] ; top (a:b) = [a]
pop [ ] = [ ] ; pop (a:b) = b
val a = "\n["++a++"]\n"
cal s = "p: " ++ (top s) ++ (val (top s)) ++ (cal (pop s))
```

The above program works as expected with interact calc.

Why the empty string clauses? What if the empty string clauses were left out? This is a typical bug for a novice programmer. There would be no prompt, until the first character is struck. Since [ ] does not match (a:b), the program must wait for a character before deciding whether to generate the prompt, or an exceptional condition. This non-appearance of the prompt tends to surprise; it is a very rare type of bug for a C or Java program. But it is explicable in the above simple terms. Bugs in Haskell may be strongly distinct from bugs in Java. But they are clear if you understand the semantics.

This type of programming tends to make explicit that your program is parsing the input string, thus making it clear that every program defines a language. It also strongly separates interaction from pure data manipulation. There are drawbacks, but in practice, they tend to come from handle changes in the specification, rather than from defining the string to string function. This approach promotes much cleaner thought, and even when writing in C or Java it can be beneficial to think the code through as above.

Exercise 17: Pure String Interaction

Even if you are not going to write the program rigorously that way, it is a good idea to consider your input software as a language parser. The simplest place to test this approach explicitly is the HUGS command line. Get a copy of this running and then try the following:

Write a program that —

1. Prints out the hello-world greeting.

2. Echos what you type.

3. Echos 30 characters and then stops.

4. Replaces each character with an x.

5. Prompts for you name and then prints it.

6. Interacts in a loop until you type stop.

It is the last two that really test your ability at this type of programming. In particular, get the prompts to come out at exactly the right time with respect to your input; and for the loop, make sure that no prompt is printed after the code has read the stop command.

After you have got this right once, the basic issues should be fairly clear. But, it is usually a good idea then to practice with a reasonably large program.

7. Implement a command line calculator.

8. Add persistent variable definitions to your calculator.

9. Add command line editing to your calculator.

Notion 140: Showing That a Parser Works

A tokeniser is a part of a parser that takes the input string and splits it into a sequence of substrings. Appending all the substrings reproduces the input.

A tokeniser satisfies the axiom: `fold (++) (tokenise s) == s`

We might (but do not have to) define a tokeniser in terms of a token function that splits off the leading token.

A token function is one that satisfies the axioms:

```
token s = (a,b) => s = a++b
token s = ([ ],b) => s == [ ]
```

We can define tokenise from token by

```
tokenise [ ] = ["eof"]
tokenise s = aux (token s)
          where aux (a,b) = a : (tokenise b)
```

We must prove this is a tokeniser. Since, `tokenise [ ] == [ ]`, the axiom is true for the empty list. Suppose the axiom is true for all lists of length less than the length of a given list `s/=[ ]`. If we call `tokenise s`, we know that `a++b==s`, so,

```
fold (++) (tokenise s) =  a ++ (fold (++) (tokenise b))
```

Now, by the token axiom `a/=[ ]` and `a++b == s` and since

```
a/=[ ], length(a)>0, and length(b) = length(s)-length(a)
```

so `length(b) < length(s)`.

Thus, by the inductive hypothesis, `fold (++) (tokenise b) == b`

We have established the required axiom for tokenise by substitution of the program into the specification, and mechanical reduction.

Notion 141: Mutual Exclusion

A central problem in the interaction between threads is that only certain operations are given to us as being indivisible, but for correct operation of compound commands, we often require that some of the variables not be touched by any other thread while a given thread is updating them. A very simple example is the swap, mentioned earlier.

The solution {t=x ; x=y ; y=t} to the problem of swapping two values does not work in general. If x and y are variables that must be accessed by other threads, then it is possible that some other thread might have interfered, the interlacing on the right, resulting in the loss of the effect of x=a.

```
1:   t=x;
2:   x=a;
1:   x=y;
1:   y=t;
```

How can we modify the code to solve this problem? A flag indicating that the thread wants exclusive access to the variables might produce some effect. T1: f=true; t=x ; x=y ; y=t; f=false. Any other thread that wants to use x and y must check the flag first to see if it is ok to proceed. T2: while(f); x=a.

This will not work against a deliberately antagonistic thread. But, it is accidental interference that we are avoiding here. Antagonistic interference prevention requires environmental assistance, for example, if the variables can only be accessed through a set of operating-system-protected functions, then the functions can check the mutex protocol.

Unfortunately, even for nice threads, this might be interlaced as on the right, with the flag being checked just before T1 does the swap, but with the assignment occurring later, during the swap. We have just changed the problem from one of the indivisibility of the swap, to one of the indivisibility of the test-and-set operation in the second thread.

```
T2:  while(f);
T1:  f=true;
T1:  t=x;
T2:  x=a;
T1:  x=y;
T1:  y=t;
T1:  f=false;
```

If we could just make sure that either T2 is doing the assignment, or T1 is doing the swap, but not both, then we could solve the problem. The exclusion of one thread from access to some of its code, while another thread is running some critical code, leads to this problem often being termed as one of mutual exclusion of two (or more threads).

The test-and-set is significant. An indivisible test-and-set could be expanded into a generic mutex protocol that would work for any number of threads. The one and only thread that succeeds in setting the variable gains access to the code that requires exclusive access.

T1 and T2 might be trying to run any code with mutual exclusive access. The generic situation is

```
T1: while(true) { NCS1 ; CS1 ; }
T2: while(true) { NCS2 ; CS2 ; }
```

where CS1, known as the critical section of thread 1, is the code, as above, which swaps x and y, that is, CS1: t=x;x=y;y=t; and NCS1 is the so-called *non-critical* section of thread T1, which is whatever else thread T1 is doing when it is not affecting the values of x and y. Similarly CS2 is known as the critical section of thread T2; it is the code as above where T2 affects the value of x, that is, CS2: x=a, and NCS2 is the non-critical section of thread T2, which is whatever else thread T2 is doing when it is not affecting the value of x.

The problem of mutual exclusion stated in this context is usually seen as the problem of determining entry and exit protocols for both threads as follows:

```
T1': while(true) { NCS1 ; entry1 ; CS1 ; exit1 ; }
T2': while(true) { NCS2 ; entry2 ; CS2 ; exit2 ; }
```

The entry and exit protocols guard the execution of CS1 and CS2, so that at most one thread is executing its critical section at any given time.

Notion 142: Good Mutual Exclusion

Due to the perversity of logic, the requirement that at most one thread is in its critical section at any given time is not enough. The protocol `entry:  while(true);` satisfies this requirement, but it is of no practical use. We need some more appropriate criteria for mutual exclusion, so we can determine rigorously whether given protocols are correct.

It has been found through decades of experience that in practice protocols for multi-threaded interaction require solid proofs, there is a history of supposedly thoroughly examined protocols being later determined to be flawed, letting something undesired happen. In a more general situation, this is a major problem today. Computer security systems are typically applications of multi-threaded operation, if only because the code is running on multiple machines, and so cannot be clocked synchronously.

While the development of actual protocols is fraught with difficulty, the development of suitable conditions to be satisfied is reasonably straightforward, after a bit of thought, and a bit of experience with the things that can go generically wrong.

1. Always at most one thread is executing its critical section.
2. If both are in the protocol, eventually one will leave.
3. If exactly one is in the protocol, eventually it will leave.
4. If a thread enters the protocol, it will execute its critical section.

The above informal statements do not constitute a fully rigorous description, but the intent should be reasonably clear. It is commonly considered that any proffered protocol that establishes the above conditions is a good protocol, however, a warning is required due the word "eventually". If something eventually happens, it might still not happen for the next million years. Attempts to change such criteria to use a phrase such as "within a second" are generally inappropriate for certain systems, it being hard to decide what exact time period should be used, but also, while "eventually" can sometimes be proved, "within 1 second" can be extremely difficult to demonstrate. The manner of failure to prove "eventually" can also often show a bug in the protocol.

Notion 143: A Partial Mutex Protocol

There is a simple mutual exclusion protocol which does not work in general, but does work under the extra condition that each thread frequently enters the protocol. This condition is true frequently enough in practice to make this approach useful, but it is very limited. It is fairly easy to implement and to demonstrate. To do so, we assume that simple assignment is indivisible.

But, this protocol, or any other, does not work if the protocol variables can be modified other than by entering the protocol code.

```
T1= while(true) { NCS1 ; while(x)  ;  CS1 ; x=true  }
T2= while(true) { NCS2 ; while(!x) ;  CS2 ; x=false }
```

Examine the flow of execution. The variable x is Boolean and so is exclusively either true or false. If it is true when the threads are started, and T2 enters the protocol, then T2 will be blocked indefinitely. If thread T1 now, or otherwise, enters the protocol, it will be let through. It is clear that at most one thread can be blocked in its protocol at any time. When thread T1 has finished its critical section, it will set x=true, so thread T1 now can't execute its critical section again until T2 has executed its critical section.

From this basic discussion (and the assumption that x is not used in either critical section), it is clear that the execution of critical sections will alternate. Thread T1 will execute its critical section, and then thread T2 will, and then T1 again, and so on.

The central problem with this protocol is that it contradicts criterion 3 (see page 298). If each thread randomly and frequently attempted to execute its critical section, especially if one did so at a different rate to the other, then it is apparent that frequently one thread would be waiting for the other thread to take its turn. This characteristic makes this otherwise very neat and solid solution typically not useful in practice.

However, we now have reason to suppose that it might actually be possible to produce a mutual exclusion protocol that satisfies all the criteria.

Notion 144: Guarded Commands

The normal conditional command is formed as follows:

```
if(cond1) command1 else
if(cond2) command2 else
if(cond3) command3
```

There are multiple conditions, if at least one is true then the command corresponding to the first true condition is executed. We require that the conditions be pure, with no side effects. There is no default case. If none of the conditions are true, then no code is executed. This is similar in effect to adding the clause if(true) skip.

Could we have a while command that has multiple conditions?

```
while(cond1) command1 else
while(cond2) command2 else
while(cond3) command3
```

If at least one is true, then the command corresponding to the first true condition is executed, and the loop restarted. This construct has some syntactic advantages over the nesting of an if-statement inside a while-loop that would normally be required. It has direct application to event driven code, in which a loop waits for something to happen and takes different actions depending on what has occurred.

The combination of a condition and a command, condition->command, is called a guarded command. In our pure context, the condition is a statement, it is a logical assertion and has no imperative semantics. This helps untangle the conditional from the imperative and makes it easier to analyse what a program is doing. A single guarded command amounts to a blocking task that waits for the condition to be true, and then executes its command. A guarded command, however, will not usually appear on its own, but rather it will appear inside an if or a do compound command.

For the pure if command we introduce a new syntax:

```
if [ cond1->command1 ; cond2->command2 ; cond3->command3 ]
```

This is very much like the scheme `cond` command; no action is taken unless there is a condition that is true. For our pure if, there is no significance to the order in which the guarded command occurs. To prove that a program works with a guarded if command, we must prove that it will work no matter which path is taken, as long as the corresponding condition is true. In this way, a proof can handle many different implementations as one. Also our pure if blocks. That means that the if statement will not execute until at least one of the conditions is true. A pure if will only skip if there is an explicit skip clause.

The normal C or Java conditional is

```
if (cond) command == if [ cond->command ; !cond->skip ]
```

Or, with an else clause

```
if (cond) cmd1 else cmd2 == if [ cond->cmd1 ; !cond->cmd2 ]
```

The other type of compound command is the do command. It is the pure form of the while command from C or Java.

```
do [ cond1->command1 ; cond2->command2 ; cond3->command3 ]
```

It looks a lot like the if command, but its semantics are distinctly different. Firstly, if none of the conditions are true, then it can skip. However, as long as at least one of the conditions is true, it continues to execute some command for which the condition is true.

The do command will also be denoted as

```
[ cond1 -> cmd1 ; cond2 -> cmd2 ; cond3 -> cmd3 ; ]
```

The post-condition of the pure do is the negation of the conjunction of the conditions. `!cond1 and !cond2`

The post-condition of the pure if is the disjunction of the conditional post conditions of the commands. If condi establishes pcondi given cmdi, then we have `pcond1 or pcond2`. The condition that activated the command may have been made false again by the command.

Notion 18: A Small Sorting Example

What does the following code,

```
do [ q1>q2 -> (q1,q2)=(q2,q1) ]
```

do?

We will go through this example in tedious detail to illustrate the concept; in practice analysing this loop would be done by inspection.

This is a loop containing exactly one guarded command. Look at the effect that the command has on the truth of the guard. If the guard is true on entry into the loop, then the only way in which the loop may exit is that the command, or repeated execution of it, must make the guard condition false.

Let us see if this is true, we require

$$(q1>q2) \xrightarrow{\quad (q1,q2)=(q2,q1) \quad} q1>q2$$

Or in English, if the condition (q1>q2) is true just before the execution of the command (q1,q2)=(q2,q1), then the condition (q1>q2) must be false just after.

To determine this we consider the nature of equality. What is the definitive property of equality? We could say that x==y means that x and y are the same thing, or have the same value, but this is just playing with words. The definitive property of equality is

$$\forall E : (x == y) \Rightarrow (E(x) == E(y)).$$

In English, if x==y, then anything done with x should get the same result as doing the same thing with y. A simple assignment has a related effect:

$$P(y) \xrightarrow{\quad x=y \quad} P(x)$$

This requires that P does not contain any hidden references to x or y, so P(x) is an expression in x, with no reference to y, and P(y) is an expression in y with no reference to x. For example, if P(q) was q!=x, then we could have y!=x before the assignment, in which case, we would be have x!=x as the condition afterward.

A similar effect is established by multiple assignment:

```
If P(a,b) is true just before (x,y)=(a,b)
then P(x,y) is true just after
```

with similar constraints on the occurrence of x and y in P.

This also applies in the case of a swap of two values: If P(a,b) is true just before (a,b)=(b,a) then P(b,a) is true just after.

Illustrating this with the above case we see that

$$(q1>q2) \quad \xrightarrow{\quad (q1,q2)=(q2,q1) \quad} \quad (q2>q1) \quad \Rightarrow \text{ not } (q1>q2)$$

Where (q2>q1) has been obtained from (q1>q2) by swapping the two symbols over.

The original loop is   [q1<q2 -> (q1,q2)=(q2,q1)]

From the above discussion, either (q1>q2) is false on entering the loop, and no action will be taken so the condition (q1>q2) will be false after the loop has exited; or (q1>q2) is true, in which case after the command has executed, (q1>q2) will be false.

Thus, we see that the loop will eventually terminate, after executing the swap either no times, or one time. If (q1=<q2) at the start, it will leave the variables as they are, and if (q1>q2) it will swap them, establishing the truth of (q1=<q2) as a post-condition.

In simple English, this program sorts a list of length 2.

Notion 19: A Longer Sorting Example

To extend from sorting a list of two elements (see page 302) to sorting an arbitrary finite list, it is instructive to see how a non-deterministic version of bubble sort operates.

We have an array of n+1 elements, a[0] .. a[n], the following C code implements a version of bubble sort on this array:

```
for(i=0;i<n;i++)
  for(j=i;j<n;j++)
    if(a[j]>a[j+1]) {t=a[j];a[j]=a[j+1];a[j]=t;}
```

To show that this code sorts an array we have to be clear about what is meant by a sorted array. An array is sorted in ascending order, if the elements are "in-order", that is, if we lay the array out by placing the first element down, and then the second element to the right of the first, and the third to the right of the second, and so on, then as we look at them from left to right, we will see the elements getting bigger.

We make this precise by stating that

```
for each i,j in [0 .. n] : i<j => a[i]=<a[j]
                           i>j => a[i]>=a[j]
                           i=j => a[i]=a[j]
```

or, in words, an array sorted into ascending order is one in which the relation the values have to each other is the same as that which the corresponding indices have to each other (except that the elements in the array might be duplicated, producing a non-strict inequality on the right-hand side).

Also the frequency of occurrence of each value is unchanged after the code. It is intuitively reasonable that a swap, the only modification we perform on the entries in the array, does not change the frequencies. Other than this statement we will ignore this issue.

Given the list (4 2 3 1), consider the truth or falsity of the assertion that this list is sorted. We build up a table to show, for each pair of indices, whether the order of the elements is compatible.

A 1 indicates that the element values are compatible with the index values in the sense that
i<j and a[i]=<a[j], or i>j and a[i]>=a[j],
or i=j, in the latter case a[i] is automatically
equal to a[j].

	4	2	3	1
4	1	0	0	0
2	0	1	1	0
3	0	1	1	0
1	0	0	0	1

This matrix has six 0 entries. Each 0 entry stands for a condition of sortedness that is not satisfied. If there where no 0 entries the list would be sorted. We use the number of 0 entries as an indicator of how sorted the list is. The reason for using this indicator is that it has a nice property that allows us to use it to prove that our program works.

We examine the execution of a vaguer version of the bubble-sort code:

```
While there is a pair (i,j) such that i<j and a[i]>a[j]
    select a pair (i,j) such that i<j and a[i]>a[j]
        swap(a[i],a[j])
```

Looking at the definition of the above matrix, we see that the number of 0 entries is reduced by any swap of the type indicated in the body of the loop, since the number of 0 entries can't be less than zero, and is finite to begin with, then after no more than about n^2 swaps the number of 0 entries must have been reduced to none. At this point the above program will stop, and the list must be sorted.

We have proved the following pure do loop sorts the list.

```
[forall i,j in [0..n]:  (i<j and a[i]<a[j]) → swap(a,i,j)]
```

This code uses constructs that would be rather hard, or impossible, to implement efficiently. But the logic is very clear, and can be applied directly to other code fragments. In particular, any implementation of bubble sort will act in a way that the above do loop *could* act. Thus, since we have proved that the do loop works, we have proved that bubble sort works — not because of its details, but because of a fairly generic property of its code. The proof is much easier in this form.

This style of proof from an abstract pure non-deterministic version of the code is standard and an excellent return on the investment in generalisation. At once, it covers many different implimentations.

Notion 145: Blocking Commands

The pure if command gives us the essential ability to halt a thread until some condition is satisfied. In C, we write `while(x);`, to wait for a condition. Using the pure if we can rather write it as

```
if [ !x -> skip ]
```

Since the post-conditions of skip are the pre-conditions, we also know that straight after this statement has executed, the condition x must be false.

It is significant that the condition in the if is a pure statement. In C code we can have `while(i--);` in which case the number of times the condition is evaluated has an impact on the behaviour. The idea behind the pure if and do blocks is that the number of evaluations of the condition does not matter, and can be left as an implementation detail. Alternatively, the emphasis is that the condition really is just that: a condition that is either true or false, and has nothing to do with imperative programming at all.

We can now restate a partial mutex solution (see page 299) as

```
T1: NCS1 ; if [  x -> skip ] ; CS1 ; x=false ;
T2: NCS2 ; if [ !x -> skip ] ; CS2 ; x=true  ;
```

This could also be expressed as

```
T1: NCS1 ; if [  x ->  CS1 ] ; x=false ;
T2: NCS2 ; if [ !x ->  CS2 ] ; x=true  ;
```

However, the first form is conceptually preferable, due to its explicit separation of the entry protocol, keeping it in line with the generic idea of a solution to the problem of mutual exclusion.

Notion 146: Hardware Assistance

The core problem of mutex is that of making a physical entity. Physically we provide mutual exclusion by locking a room and having only one key. Short of deliberate attack, only the person with the key can get in. How do we create a virtual key that only one person can possess at a time and that will not accidentally duplicate?

If x==1, the key is on the hook, so set x=0 to take it. But between testing and taking, someone else may have grabbed the key, and we have a duplicate. We solve this with multiple assignment.

```
(t,x)=(x,0)
```

By definition, the assignments occur together, indivisible. If x==0, I have read it without modification; if x==1, then I uniquely have the key.

A physical token satisfies some axioms. There are n threads, T1 .. Tn, we have a token array t[1..n] how many tokens each thread has. We have a token store x, how many tokens are left in a virtual box.

1. The total number of tokens must be constant.
2. No thread may have a negative number of tokens.
3. The box cannot contain a negative number of tokens.

Translating this into a more precise formula we get

```
1.      x + sum(i=1,n) t[i]  == k
2.      foreach(i in 1..n) 0 =< t[i]
3.      0 =< x
```

The constant k is the number of tokens. We now need a get and put protocol, where get(y) will get a token from the box into y and put(y) will put a token into the box from y. If k==1, then we can use the pure if to create the required effect.

```
    get(y):  if [ x==1 -> (y,x)=(1,0) ]
    put(y):  if [ y==1 -> (y,x)=(0,1) ]
```

We must be sure that y is only accessed through put and get.

Notion 147: Proving That a Protocol Works

One method for mutex is to keep a count that acts like physical keys (see page 307). We consider proof technique for this type of property for 1 key only. A typical proof is more complex, but the techniques required are the same. Let x be the store of keys, and for each i in [1..n] let t[i] be the keys on loan to thread i.

The axioms are —

1.   x + sum(i=1,n) T[i] == k
2.   foreach(i in 1..n) 0 =< T[i]
3.   0 =< x

The putget protocol is —

```
get(j):   do [ t[j]==0 -> (t[j],x)=(x,t[j]) ]
put(j):   do [ x==0     -> (t[j],x)=(x,t[j]) ]
```

We are given that k==1, that t and x are only accessed within the putget protocol (if not, then all bets are off), that no two commands occur at the same time, and for all calls get(j) that j is in range.

We need to show that if (x + sum(i=1,n) t[i])==1 is at some point true, then it is true after the next execution of get(j) and of put(j).

```
  x + sum(i in [1..n]) t[i]
= (x + t[j]) + sum(i in [1..n]\j) t[i]
```

Now, both put and get swap x and t[j], thus x+t[j] is unchanged. The other variables are untouched, so the total is unchanged.

The non-negativity of the untouched variables is invariant of the call to put and get. Since the x and t[j] are swapped, if 0=<x before then 0=<t[j] afterwards, and vice versa.

Only put and get affect the variables in the axioms and the axioms are invariants of put and get. So, if the axioms are at one time true, they will be true always after that. The standard initialisation x=1 and t[i]=0 establishes the axioms true initially.

Notion 148: Two Partial Exclusion Protocols

Consider the following mutex protocol:

T1: $|^0$ w1=true $|^1$; while(w2) skip $|^2$; CS1 $|^3$; w1=false $|^4$

T2: $|^0$ w2=true $|^1$; while(w1) skip $|^2$; CS2 $|^3$; w2=false $|^4$

We assume that w1 and w2 are not touched in any other code, and both initially false. w1 is true exactly when T1 is at locations 1, 2 or 3. w1 indicates that T1 is executing the protocol. Similarly for w2 and T2. The loop condition is false immediately after the loop exits. So if T1 gets to 2, then w2 is false, and w1 is true. So, T2 is not in the protocol.

So, at most one thread is in the critical section at any one time. It is also apparent that neither thread will block if the other is not in the protocol. But if both threads arrive simultaneously at location 1, then w2 is true, and w1 is true, and so both threads block. Thus, this protocol does not entirely satisfy the conditions for a good mutual exclusion protocol.

Consider the following protocol:

T1: $|^0$ while(t!=1) skip $|^1$; CS1 $|^2$; t=2 $|^3$

T2: $|^0$ while(t!=2) skip $|^1$; CS2 $|^2$; t=1 $|^3$

where t is a binary valued variable with value 1 or 2 only.

If we start the threads both at location 3, with t=1, then T2 can't move from location 3 until T1 has returned to location 3. At this point t==2 and now T1 can't budge until T2 has gone around the loop. In this way, we are sure that at most one thread is in its critical section, and we can see that at most one thread can be blocked as well. The problem is that the threads must alternate. In particular, one thread may be blocked while the other is not in the protocol.

What we need is a way to combine these two protocols.

Notion 149: The Peterson Protocol

Looking at a couple of partial mutex protocols (see page 309) shows us that the problem is subtle, but also suggests that a solution might exist. We want to combine the logical properties of the two protocols[39]

```
         +                                    -
T1: w1=true ; while(w2 and t!=1) skip ; CS1 ; w1=false ; t=2 ;
T2: w2=true ; while(w1 and t!=2) skip ; CS2 ; w2=false ; t=1 ;
         +                                    -
```

This solves some problems, but suppose that T1 has been through once before, so t==2, and is currently in its critical section for the second time in a row. Then T2 comes and finds that t==2, and so drops out of the loop into CS2. If we use or instead of and, then the problem is that part of the post-condition of the loop for T1 is have t==1. Or in other words, the thread can only proceed if it is its turn.

Consider the following protocol:

T1: $|^0$ t=2 $|^1$; while(t!=1) skip $|^2$; CS1 $|^3$

T2: $|^0$ t=1 $|^1$; while(t!=2) skip $|^2$; CS2 $|^3$

This is essentially one of the previous protocols, but shifting the setting of the turn flag to the entry protocol. In action, if the threads are looping around many times this is all but indistinguishable, except in a minor way at the beginning. At the start both threads must attempt to enter the protocol before one will be allowed through.

Now we combine the two partial protocols in the following manner:

```
           +                              -
T1: w1 = true ; t=2; while(w2 and t!=1) skip ; CS1 ; w1=false
T2: w2 = true ; t=1; while(w1 and t!=2) skip ; CS2 ; w2=false
           +                              -
```

Intuitive argument: a thread wants exclusive access, it sets the turn indicator to the other thread, if there is no contention, then it goes through. If there is contention, then one of the threads was last to get

---

[39]This is where killer bees came from.

to execute the while-loop, this one will have deferred the turn. So only one of the threads will go through. When the one that got through has finished it turns off the contention, and the second thread goes through. Furthermore, if the first thread re-enters the protocol it will now be deferring to the second thread.

The essential difference between this and the protocol before that does not work is that a thread cannot enter the protocol without deferring to other threads. Thus, in all cases it will only go through if it is the last arrival or there is no contention.

The requirement for a good mutual exclusion protocol using basic operations on variables was noted in about 1960, but it was not until 1981, twenty years later, that a solution was found. This solution, the Peterson protocol, is neat and robust, but its history demonstrates how hard it is for humans to think about concurrent threads. We need to be trained to be able to do it, and we need to approach it with great caution. Since security protocols are typically multi-threaded in execution, and these protocols are becoming part of every application, as they are set up to operate over the internet, we see that the ability to handle multi-threaded code is becoming vital. Ready or not, that is the future of computing. There is a lot more to mutual exclusion than we are covering here (see note 4).

Since the turn flag can only be 1 or 2, it is effectively a Boolean variable. If we rewrite the Peterson protocol with this idea in mind we obtain

```
          +                              -
T1: x=true ; t=true  ; while(y and  t) skip ; CS1 ; x = false
T2: y=true ; t=false ; while(x and !t) skip ; CS2 ; y = false
          +                              -
```

This shows the basic issue behind the Peterson protocol. There is the flag for each thread, which is checked, but also a mutual flag that the threads set in an alternate manner.

Exercise: What problems are involved in expanding this solution to an n thread mutual exclusion protocol using an array w[i] of wait flags and a turn indicator $t \in [1..n]$?

Notion 150: The Decker Protocol

The core problem with the *defer all the time* partial protocol (see page 309) is that both threads might defer at the same time.

One way out is to add a tendency to drop contention:

```
T1: w1=true ; while(w2) {w1=false; w1=true} ;
    CS1 ;
    w1=false

T2: w2=true ; while(w1) {w2=false; w2=true} ;
    CS2 ;
    w2=false
```

If T1 is in CS1, then w2 must have been false when tested. But it was tested when w1 was true. So T2 was outside the protocol, or in the body of the loop, when this happened, and so will not execute CS2 until T1 leaves. But a fast-acting thread could get all the way through into its critical section, from outside the protocol, while a slow-acting thread is clearing and setting its flag. So a slow thread might be almost permanently blocked by a fast thread. The chance of testing w2 in the small time slot between two passes of the fast thread could be indefinitely small.

The slow thread is too deferential. It should only offer to defer if it is not its turn. So a thread checks a turn indicator.

```
T1: w1=true ; while(w2) if(t!=1) { w1=false; w1=true } ;
    CS1 ;
    w1=false ; t=2

T2: w2=true ; while(w1) if(t!=2) { w2=false; w2=true } ;
    CS2 ;
    w2=false ; t=1
```

In this case, the fast-acting thread can go through as many times as it wants, if the slow-acting thread is not interested. But once the slow-acting thread starts its protocol, it will prevent the fast-acting thread from re-entering its protocol.

But, this does not solve the problem. We still do not have the certainty that each thread will get a turn. If the fast thread does not defer for long enough, then the slow thread may take a long time to pick the small deferral time slot. The second thread will not go through, but will constantly be trying and backing off.

We could try putting a delay loop in the contention code that does not set the flag true until the other flag is false. If it is not your turn, and the other flag is true, then back off until the other flag is false. Since it is their turn the other thread will not defer, and will not go through. If it attempts to enter again it will not be its turn anymore.

Or, by adding in a random or increasing delay on contention, we can make sure that the first thread eventually runs its critical section. This is the ethernet protocol. For ethernet an attempt is made to transmit, if the signal is garbled, then contention is supposed, and the transmitter backs off for an increasing amount of time, until the line is clear.

It is often the case for concurrent work that we invoke the *fairness assumption* stating that any thread that can run indefinitely often will eventually be chosen to run. However, while this assumption has its uses, it is a good idea to keep in mind here the problem that a thread that waits too long for its turn might as well have not run. In practice, we need some limit to the amount of time the thread has to wait.

Full analysis of these situations in practice really needs some estimate of the probabilities. The fairness assumption is very close structurally to the idea that Kolmogorov tail properties have 0 or 1 probabilities. If the chance that the thread will be chosen to run does not tend to zero, then eventually, with probability one, the thread will run. However, the expected value of the time until it runs can be very high.

Small changes in the protocols, seemingly of no account, can make a big difference in the correctness. A very careful and formal analysis is indicated if the protocol must be correct.

Exercise: What problems are involved in expanding this solution to an n thread mutual exclusion protocol using an array w[i] of wait flags and a turn indicator $t \in [1..n]$?

Notion 151: Proving That a Protocol Works

One mutex approach is virtual keys that satisfy the axioms of physicality (see page 308). This is fairly easy to implement and prove for k=1 key, given compound assignment. But, the case for k>1 requires a little more work.

We might be tempted to use

```
get(j): if [ x>0 -> (T[j],x)=(T[j]+1,x-1) ]
```

It is clear that if the assignment command is indivisible, then the number of tokens is preserved, and neither x nor t[j] will become negative. It should also be clear how we might go about a more formal proof. The problem is that the evaluation of the x-1 and t[j]-1 will occur separately, and some other process might interfere between the arithmetic and the assignment.

```
do [ x==1 -> (y,x)=(1,0);
     x==2 -> (y,x)=(1,1);
     x==3 -> (y,x)=(1,2) ]
```

It is part of the semantics of the pure do that the command that is guarded will execute *when the condition is true*. That is, no interference could make the test false at the time that the command actually runs. This is especially significant if the command is indivisible. The above code works for k==3. But this solution requires new code for each new thread, and relies on a fairly sophisticated high-level construct.

Fortunately, some machines provide relevant hardware. For example the decrement and skip on zero instruction dsz(x,C) = if(x){x--; C}, is indivisible, if C is. So, dsz(x,y++) has the effect of transferring one unit from x to y if there is at least one unit in x at the time.

With this type of machine code a lot of other operations are easy, but without it keeping track of a conserved quantity can be subtle and complicated.

Chapter 9

Container Datatypes

You put something in, you get the same thing out later.

You put many things in, you get the same things out,
but not necessarily in the same order.

Maybe some things you put in you can never get back out.

But you never get out something you did not put in.

Or maybe you do.

Notion 152: Abstract Arrays

An array is a place where values can be stored, under a given index, and then later retrieved. This thinking about arrays is imperative. For a pure declarative approach we must restate this so that no values are changed. The process is easy and natural.

When we assign an integer variable we assign the whole thing.

```
x = 6
```

An array assignment assigns part of the array.

```
a[2] = 6
```

but when we initialise arrays in C, we assign the whole thing.

```
int a[3] = {23,45,12};
```

Think of the entire array at once in memory as a single data element. Just like an int, or a float or a char.

We might, instead of `a[2] = 6` say

```
a = {a[0],a[1],6}
```

It has the same meaning.

Just like records and functions, arrays are not normally first-class objects. We cannot just generate whatever array we want, even if we know exactly what it is that we want. We need to declare an array, and then fill it up, piece by piece. So, we consider extending the language with an abstract array datatype – an array that is a single structure that we can manipulate as a whole.

In both C and Java, the assignment a=b, where a and b are both arrays, would only assign a pointer. But in Haskell (and the equivalent in Scheme) it would assign the entire array, treating it as a single object. All we need is a mechanism for manipulating the structure.

If `a` is an array, `i` an index and `x` a value, then let `put(a,i,x)` be the array obtained by replacing the `i`th element of `a` with `x`.

Now instead of `a[2] = 6`, we say `a = put(a,i,x)`

Similarly, we have `get(a,i)`, to retrieve values.

Do not ask now, *why should we do this*. Such matters are discussed at considerable length elsewhere. The idea here is to free your mind. The question is, *can we do it*. The answer is yes, and it is not difficult. And now that we have a mechanism to modify an array, we can express the nature of array assignment precisely axiomatically.

```
get(put(a,i,x),i)=x
get(put(a,i,x),j)=get(a,j)
```
Assuming that i≠j.

Instead of `{a[2]=6 ; fn(a)}` we say `fn(put(a,2,6))`

This can be written in pure Prolog ...

```
equals(get(put(_,I,X),I),X).
equals(get(put(A,_,_),J),Y) :- equals(get(A,J),Y)
```

We have a piece of impure code with assignments of array elements. We can work out the new values that the array elements will have, and then express the value of the array as a whole using these pure functions. We can translate impure code into pure code that satisfies the axioms of substitution. This in turn admits a large quantity of sophisticated testing, proving and manipulation techniques. Reversing this, it may look here as though the array is being copied, leading to slow code, but this would only occur in a naive implementation. There exist efficient implementations of pure array manipulation that can be used within pure code, and run quickly. Haskell has this datatype available in standard libraries.

These axioms apply to more than just standard arrays, for example, we could have an array whose index set is the entire natural numbers. In fact, axiomatically, arrays are just functions. So this extension also applies to anything built from functions.

Notion 153: Pure Containers

The simplest container datatype to think about is the stack. A physical stack of cards on a desk acts this way. We can place a new card on the top of the stack, read the top card, or throw away the top card. These are put, get, and pop operations. This physical model inspires the stack axioms:

$$\text{get(put(e,s))} = e$$
$$\text{pop(put(e,s))} = s$$

A single variable in a program is also a container. It is rather like a stack in which there is no pop operation, you can put a new card on the top of the stack, but you cannot take it away. We can think of the old values of the variable still existing, but being impossible to access.

$$\text{get(put(e,s))} = e$$

The action on a stack or variable not constructed by put is undefined. That is, on an uninitialised variable, or empty stack. An empty element makes this explicit. A default first value for the variable is introduced by the axiom get(empty)=0. But we do not need to use the empty element. However, for queues, like at a supermarket, we need an empty instance. An element put on an empty queue is the next element to be got.

```
get(put(e,empty)) = e
get(put(e,s))     = get(s)
pop(put(e,empty)) = empty
pop(put(e,s))     = pop(s)
```

A deque is analogous to a deck of cards that we can pick up. We can place a new bottom card or top card, we can read the bottom or top, and we can throw away the bottom or top card. Thus, a deque acts like a stack if we attend to only one end, and acts like a queue in the manner in which the two ends interact.

```
lget(lput(e,s)) = e          lpop(lput(e,s)) = s
rget(rput(e,s)) = e          rpop(rput(e,s)) = s
lget(rput(empty,x)) = x    lpop(rput(empty,x)) = empty
rget(lput(empty,x)) = x    rpop(lput(empty,x)) = empty
lget(rput(e,s)) = lget(s) lpop(rput(e,s)) = rput(e,lpop(s))
rget(lput(e,s)) = rget(s) rpop(lput(e,s)) = lput(e,rpop(s))
```

Except for the somewhat spurious occurrence of the extra rput or lput in the last two axioms for a deque, the axioms for get and put are reflected by a dual for pop and put.

By picking the axioms for a deque, but throwing away the ones referring to pop, we obtain the axioms for a pair of variables. This can be generalised to include any indexed family of variables, of which an array is a special case.

```
get(i,put(i,e,s)) = e
get(j,put(i,e,s)) = get(i,s)
```

The above descriptions are both axiomatic and algorithmic. If used within a pure reduction system they would implement the desired behaviour. They are meant to be read from top to bottom, so that a more general case lower down is not used except when the expression does not satisfy the more specific case. This is the approach in Haskell, except that it does not allow complex expressions on the left of a definition. In Prolog, it would be required to place judicious cuts to make certain of correct operation.

Physically, the general notion of a container is that it contains a number of cells, each storing a value. A put creates a new cell, a pop destroys a cell, and a get reads a cell. The exact strategy by which the particular cells are selected defines the nature of the container.

For a regular container, every cell has an associated get and pop. If semiregular, pops and gets come in pairs associated with specific directly accessible cells. Every pop must have a means of addressing a cell, and so we can always augment the operations with the corresponding get. But there might be addressable cells for which there is no natural pop, for example, in an array.

Exercise 18: Abstract Arrays

An array with an infinite index set cannot be stored directly in finite memory. Even using only the range of the int type in C or Java the size is typically prohibitive. Sparse array technique assumes that only a finite number of the elements are interesting, and stores the (index,value) pairs explicitly. Alternatively, storing (upper, lower, value) triplets allows us to store large runs of the same value in a small space. Generalising this, we can store (interval, function) pairs, in which the upper or lower bound, or both, of the interval might be infinite, and the function is typically non-constant.

In Java a function can be passed by passing an implicit extension class with a single method, with a standard name; in C, use function pointers.

This exercise is to implement these basic ideas in Java, C, or both as desired. Remember to make sure that more recent assignments mask the earlier ones. The complexity of the code can be built up as indicated.

1. A sparse array built up as a linked list of (index,value) pairs will work even if the old index is not looked for, as a new one at the head of the list will mask the old.

2. A list of values with, each with an upper and lower bounds.

3. An interval type, so that we put(a,i,f), where i is an interval.

4. Let the interval type include open to the left and open to the right intervals.

5. Make a garbage collector that eliminates any intervals that are completely covered by later assignments.

6. Extend the garbage collector to shorten intervals that are covered on one end.

Extending the garbage collector to flatten the intervals (break into non-overlapping subintervals) is probably not a good idea. Extending to join intervals that are the same is easy enough for simple cases, but even for constant values contains some hidden complexity.

Exercise 19: Pure Containers

Generically, the problem of undefined conditions can be skirted by including an error value or, alternatively, a default value that is returned when required. For a stack of limited size, a put may be defined to lose, and a pop to duplicate, the datum at the bottom of the stack.

A two-dimensional stack can be constructed from a 2D semi-infinite square grid of cells, the upper left quadrant. We can put values on the left of any horizontal row or bottom of any vertical column. Thus, cput(i,x), puts value x onto the bottom of column i, and rput(i,x) puts value x onto the left of row i. The interaction between these can be quite complex, and are akin to some tile-pushing puzzles.

1. What are the axioms for a stack of limited size with an error value?

2. What are the axioms for a stack that duplicates its last element?

3. What axioms describe a two-dimensional stack?

4. What axioms describe a two-dimensional stack of limited size?

5. Implement a two-dimensional stack in C or Java.

A finite two-dimensional stack is easier to define if something is put at the other end when a pop occurs. This can be an error value, a default value, or the previous value in the cell. The idea generalises to a two-dimensional queue, with the possible dropping of values at either end. Require that the put and get operation be combined; we must put something at one end in order to get something at the other end. Call this **data shove(queue,int,data)**, on each axis.

6. Implement the two-dimensional queue with shove.

7. Can you do it in pure Haskell or Prolog?

8. Can you avoid constant array copying to do the shove?

Notion 154: Generic Maps

At the right abstract level, arrays, records, and functions are identical. Each is a rule for associating a value with an index. For a function the index is the tuple of arguments, for a record it is the field name, but the underlying principle is the same. That is, $f(x)$, $a[i]$, and $d.field$ are all ways of encapsulating an indexed family of variables. This is the generic map datatype. It is a container with a static cell structure.

The distinction is in the pragmatics. An array normally allows incremental modification; typically, $a[i] = x$ is allowed, while $f(x) = y$ is not. A record might store disparate types, while functions and arrays, typically do not. A function can be defined compactly on indefinitely large, even infinite, index sets. An array typically contains identically sized data stored in contiguous blocks of memory, using a fast random access lookup algorithm, but the index set is [0 .. n], for some integer n.

A sparse array, however, stores a list of (index,value) pairs, any index that is not listed is associated with the value 0 by default. An associative array works the same way, except that the index set is not restricted to integers. The associative array is a truly generic map type for finite index sets, but pays for this by an increase in code complexity and access time. A linear array has an order 1 lookup (see note 19) while an associative array has order $\log n$ at best. Every array has a *value space* of items stored, and an *index space* of keys for finding values.

Every array has a lookup algorithm. For a linear array, the original is $a[i] = *(a + i)$. For a 2D array, the standard $a[x, y] = *(a + x + r * y)$ is only one of an infinite number of options.

Another is $a[i][j] = *(*(a + i) + j)$.

Many arrays are implemented by defining an indexing function

$f : (x_1, .., x_n) \to z$, i.e., tuples onto a single integer,

so that $a[x_1, .., x_n] = *(a + f(x_1, .., x_n))$.

On a Von Neumann machine, the memory is one big hardware array, and so all arrays are implemented in some fashion within a linear array, using an indexing function. Both a function and an array have associated code that is executed to determine the value of an indexed reference. An array is typically implemented as an in-line function. Different code is inserted depending on whether the reference is being used as an l-value or an r-value.

A common special case (example, an undirected graph connection matrix) is the symmetric array, where $a[x, y] = a[y, x]$. In this case, we may be tempted to store the data twice, leading to greater use of memory, longer time to update, and possible inconsistencies. Instead, we can use a different type of addressing, mapping (x,y) to the same location as (y,x).

```
a[x+y+(x>y?x*x-x:y*y-y)/2]

 0   1   3   6  10  15  21  28
 1   2   4   7  11  16  22  29
 3   4   5   8  12  17  23  30
 6   7   8   9  13  18  24  31
10  11  12  13  14  19  25  32
15  16  17  18  19  20  26  33
21  22  23  24  25  26  27  34
28  29  30  31  32  33  34  35
```

The idea of incrementally updating a function, in analogy to $a[10] = 20$ is easy to define:

```
put(f,a,b)(x) = if x==a then b else f(x)
```

This is really just the axiom for array behaviour (see page 318) in disguise, but gives an explicit implementation that would work in Haskell, albeit inefficiently.

We can deal with infinite arrays with a mild change in syntax:

```
using a[i=1..100] = i*i
```

to mean `for(i=1;i<=100;i++) a[i] = i*i`,

and then `a[10]=20` is shorthand for `a[i=10..10]=20`

Polymorphic functions are examples of this type of extension. In C++ overloading + do matrix addition is an example of assigning to an already existing function to increase its domain.

Exercise 20: Generic Maps

Cylindrical chess is played, conceptually, on a cylinder, so that
moving horizontally off the left-
hand side of the board finds a
piece on the right-hand side on the
same rank. Diagonal moves must
be adjusted in rank.

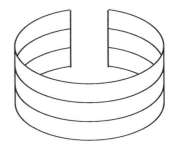

A Mobius board twists the board, as for a Mobius strip, before joining
the edge so that a piece finds itself on rank 7-n instead of n, where the
ranks are numbered 0 to 7. A double wraparound can produce a toroidal
surface or a pseudo-sphere, and wrapping to adjacent sides produces the
surface of a sphere. The index set for any wrapped axis must be all of
the int data type.

Implement the following:

1. A single direct wraparound, to produce a cylinder.

2. A double direct wraparound, to produce a torus.

3. A single twisted wraparound Mobius strip.

4. A double wraparound with one side twisted, Klein bottle.

5. A double adjacent wraparound, for a sphere.

6. A double twisted wraparound, Pseudo sphere.

A chessboard is an 8 × 8 square grid. The first four exercises are exercises in modular arithmetic. If you have trouble working out what
the numbers are, try making up a physical piece of paper that can be
wrapped around to check the numbers.

Warning, the sphere and pseudo sphere have some non-trivial traps to
them, not discussed here.

Notion 155: Showing That Infinite Lists Work

The following code defines an infinite list type in Scheme:

```
(define icar car)
(define (icdr l) (eval (cdr l)))
(define (icons a l) (list a (lambda () l)))
```

A particular list, the positive integers, is defined as follows:

```
(define (posif x) (list x posif (+ x 1)))
(define posi (list 1 posif 2))
```

A display function can also be defined:

```
(define
 (show l n)
 (if (= 0 n) '() (cons (icar l) (show (icdr l) (- n 1))))
)
```

Given that a list is (x f), where x is the first element on the list, and f evaluates to the rest of the list, the definitions of icar and icdr follow. The difficulty is icons. In particular, the following axioms are required.

```
(icar (icons a l)) == a
(icdr (icons a l)) == l
```

If we substitute (icons a l) = (x f), we get

(icar (x f)) == (car (x f)) == x, and thus $x == a$.

(icdr (x f)) == (eval (f)) == l, and thus f == (lambda () l)

Thus, (icons a l) = (list a (lambda () l)). But this is more than a proof. If we did not know what icons was, the above substitution procedure would have told us. So, we have derived the code by solving the axioms as equations.

Notion 156: Generic Lists

Sequences are a very useful and interesting container datatype, commonly known in orthodox mathematics, but treated rather differently in computing.

The first concept of a sequence introduced in orthodox mathematics courses is that of one-sided infinite sequence, such as 0, 1, 2 ...etc. To formalise this notion usually a sequence is defined as a map whose domain is the natural numbers. This can be generalised to include finite sequences, of length n+1, whose domain is the discrete interval [0 .. n]. Usually, the empty sequence, whose domain is [] is not considered, but it does satisfy the basic definitions.

In orthodox mathematics the sequence is a compound datatype built from sets, and rather difficult to manipulate abstractly. Generally an index notation is used like the index versus intrinsic concepts of tensors. In computing languages a sequence is usually called a list. But although there is a isomorphism of the abstract datatype, the difference in the operators used gives computer lists a completely different flavour from orthodox mathematics. Further, lists in computing are usually very primitive; we build things from list. We build sets as an equivalence class on lists. In orthodox mathematics we build lists from sets.

Since it uses indices, a mathematical sequence is really much more like an random-access array. Given a sequence x, we take it for granted that we may access x_i for any natural i, with impunity. In computer languages we use a mechanism in which the index of an entry, and the basic lookup x_i are compound, and typically not very efficient, operations.

From the point of view of orthodox mathematics, computer science is looking at sequences up to isomorphism of domains as ordered sets. There is no natural starting index in computer science lists. Given an ordering of a countable set, we may use it to index any list, by using the head and tail functions to remove the intervening element. Lists are defined from the cons, head, and tail functions.

In the same way that the reals miss the complexity of the computable reals, and that mathematics functions miss the complexity of computer programs, mathematics sequences miss the character of computer science lists.

Having defined basic lists, certain operations are useful:

```
head(x) = x(0)

tail(x)(i) = x(i+1)

cons(a,x)(1) = a
cons(a,x)(i) = x(i-1)

map(f,x)(i) = f(x(i))

iterate(f,a)(i) = f^i(a)

filter(f,x) = if f(x(0)) then cons(x(0),filter(f,tail(x)))
                         else filter(f,tail(x))

iterate(f,a) = cons(a,(map(f,(iterate(f,a)))))

map(f,x) = cons(f(head(x)),map(f,tail(x)))

rightFold f [a] = a
rightFold f (a:x) = f a (fold f x)

leftFold f [a] = a
leftFold f (a,b:x) = leftFold f (cons (f a b) x)
```

The generic idea of a fold operator is broader than just lists, for example we might very naturally fold a tree structure. One way of expressing the generic fold is that some operation other than the constructor is fitted in place of the constructor. Given a construction expression for some container, using only the put operations, change the definition of put; perhaps, changing cons to add.

Notion 157: Computing with Infinite Lists

It causes us no special problem to compute with infinite lists.

With some reservations (see page 93) we informally define natural numbers as N = (1,2,3, ...), even numbers as E = (2,4,6, ...), and compute the sum of these to be S = (3,6,9, ...), all without any conceptual difficulties.

We can do this on paper, why not in our programs?

The informality comes from the ellipsis. The computer can't guess what you mean.[40] In programming, the *and-so-on* must be replaced by an explicit statement. For N this means to keep incrementing. We define N by $n_1 = 1$ and $n_{i+1} = n_i + 1$.

Let $arith(s, d)$ mean the arithmetic sequence, starting at s, with common difference d. The sum of sequences is defined by $arith(s_1, d_1) + arith(s_2, d_2) = arith(s_1 + s_2, d_1 + d_2)$. This is a formal statement that the element-wise sum of two arithmetic sequences is an arithmetic sequence whose parameters are the sum of the original parameters. Although the sequences are infinite, the parameterisation and the algorithm are finite. Arithmetic sequences are not closed under termwise multiplication, so $arith(a_1, d_1) * arith(s_2, d_2)$ is not defined here, similarly to the square root of negative numbers. But we can define $c * arith(s, d) = arith(as, ad)$, where c is a constant. A similar development works for geometric sequences.

Arithmetic sequences are defined by the axiom $n_{i+1} = n_i + d$, and geometric sequences by $n_{i+1} = n_i \times r$. Generalise this to $n_{i+1} = f(n_i)$. Thus, store an infinite sequence as an ordered pair (s, f) of a starting value, and a rule for generation. However, such sequences are not closed under either element-wise addition, or multiplication, and so we cannot define a generic add or mul routine.

An arithmetic sequence may be defined either by $n_1 = s$ and $n_{i+1} = n_i + d$, or by the more explicit $n_i = s + (i - 1)d$. The second form has the advantage that we can now express the product of two arithmetic

---

[40] And should not try. AI would not solve this problem.

sequences as $(n * m)_i = n_i * m_i = (s + (i-1)d)(s' + (i-1)d')$. Moreover we can use a definition such as $n_i = f(i)$ to allow any expression for an element-wise combination of any finite collection of sequences. But, such an explicit expression for the ith element is not always available.

As an abstract type, lists require only the car, cdr, and cons operations. If we express a list as a starting value and method of generation, then $car(s, f) = s$ and $cdr(s, f) = (f(s), f)$. On the other hand, $cons$ is a bit trickier. In fact this type of list is not closed under the cons operation. Consider $cons(1,N) = (1,1,2,3,4,...)$; but that means that we have both $f(1) = 1$, for $i = 1$ and $f(1) = 2$ for $i = 2$, which means no such function will suffice. But if we let the function return a sequence, instead of an element, this problem can be resolved. Let the sequence be (s, f), then $car(s, f) = s$, and $cdr(s, f) = f(s)$, and $cons(a, (s, f)) = (a, g)$ where $g(a) = (s, f)$.

How do we handle the situation when x_{i+1} is not expressed as a function of x_i? For example, $x_1 = 1, x_2 = 1, x_{i+1} = x_i + x_{i+1}$ defines the Fibonacci sequence. It starts with $(1, 1, 2, ...)$ so there is no f that works as a generator. Instead, we must store enough $state$ information to be able to extend the sequence (extending it from the current element is just a special case). Thus, if we keep (x_{i-1}, x_i) of the Fibonacci sequence, we generate (x_i, x_{i+1}) by $(a, b) \rightarrow (b, a + b)$. We could store this as an ordered triple of two numbers and a function, but if we make the state the pair (x_{i-1}, x_i), then we just need to have an other function to tell us how to compute the current value.

The Fibonacci sequence is $((1, 1)$ $(\lambda(a, b).a)$ $(\lambda(a, b).(b, a + b)))$. More generally use (s, h, t) to represent an arbitrary sequence generated from some number of prior elements, plus any other state information that we want to throw in. Then we have $car(s, h, t) = h(s)$, $cdr(s, h, t) = t(s)$, and $cons(a, (s, h, t)) = (a, \lambda x.(s, h, t), \lambda x.x)$.

By these and other related techniques it is possible to build up provably correct implementations of a variety of infinite data structures. A number of algorithms are more naturally expressed using infinite data structures.

Notion 158: Sequence Builder

It is easier to compute with a datatype if there are reasonably generic methods for in-line construction. One very common and fundamental constructor for sets used in orthodox mathematics is the set-builder notation. The principle is to define a set as the image of a function of some other set (sometime implicit).

If we know what Z^+ is, then the set of squares is $\{x^2 | x \in Z^+\}$. For sets, multiplicity does not count, so the squares are also produced by $\{x^2 | x \in Z\}$. A more extreme case is $\{x\%2 | x \in Z\} == \{0, 1\}$. Functions can be explicitly constructed; the square function is $\{(x, x^2) | x \in Z^+\}$. But it can be difficult to know whether a function or a relation has been created, $\{(x^2, x) | x \in Z\}$. We can also use multiple sets: $\{x^2 + y^2 | x \in Z^+, y \in Z\}$ is the set of integers that are the sum of two squares. Finally, we can filter the set. $\{x^2 | x \in Z, x^2 > 100\}$ is the set of squares greater than 100.

The natural numbers are not just a set, they are also a foundational sequence, both in orthodox mathematics and in computer science. We can extend the idea of set building to sequence building. $[x^2 | x \in Z^+]$ is the sequence of squares, distinct, but not glaringly, from the set of squares. On the other hand, $[x\%2 | x \in Z]$ is $[0, 1, 0, 1, 0, 1, \ldots]$, which is an infinite sequence. Not only multiplicity but order in sequence counts. One particularly interesting exercise is trying to produce a sequence that contains each element of a set exactly once. If we construct a sequence of rationals in the naive manner, $[x/y | x \in Z, y \in Z^+]$, then not only do we get 1/2, but also 2/4, which is the same rational. The problem of removing the duplicates, skipped over in orthodox set construction, is often a difficult problem in programming.

Another bug in a sequence builder expression is pushing elements off past infinity.

$[(x, y) | x \in Z^+, y \in Z^+]$ is $[(1, 1), (1, 2), (1, 3), \ldots]$

That is (2,2), never occurs on the list. The problem is that, at least in programming, the longest list is the simple, countable list. There is a form of back-tracking here. If you squint at the list you might notice a

Prolog program hiding there. The elements for y are all tried first, and then the elements for x. Because there are an infinite number of options for y, the second option for x is never tried.

It is validly argued that the list is

$$[(1,1),(1,2),(1,3),\ldots,(2,1),(2,2),(2,3)\ldots,\ldots]$$

But since we can only process the list from the head, the second part of this would only be noticed after the universe had ended and begun again. Looking back at the definition of the rationals, we see that it too suffers from this problem.

The resolution of this, listing the pairs of positive integers, is also the solution to a variety of other listing problems on pairs of integers. One principle is to introduce an auxiliary variable, the sum of the two integers. The details are left as an exercise to the reader.

Apart from being analogous to a Prolog program, sequence builder notation also features strongly in Haskell, explicitly. The Haskell notation uses slightly different symbols, mainly because of the font limitations.

```
[(x^2)+(y^2) | x <- [1..] , y <- [1..] , (x^2)>100 ]
```

This is a powerful technique, and it can be combined with recursion. $s = 1 : (map \ (+1) \ s)$, Thus, $s = [1..]$ is the list of positive integers.

The factorial sequence, 1, 1, 2, 6, 24, ... has the property that if you multiply it element-wise by the integers (first element by 1, second by 2, and so on), this is the same as the tail of the sequence.

```
mul (a:b) (c:d) = (a*c) : (mul b d)
fact = 1 : (mul fact [1..])
```

The actual calculation only computes each required product once. With a bit of thought, manipulating lists as entire entities can produce short, efficient code.

Exercise 21: Sequence Builder

1. Enumerate the pairs of positive integers, so that each occurs exactly once.

   Hint: Look at the sum of the integers.

2. List the pairs of integers, so that each occurs exactly once.

   Hint: This is more complicated than the positive integers, one option is to think about a spiral on the integer grid in the plane.

3. Write a sequence-builder expression for the filter function.

   Hint: Very basic, filter takes a Boolean function and a list, and removes all those element from the list that the filter returns false for, but leaves everything else in its original order.

4. Write a sequence builder expression for the map function.

   Hint: The map function applies a function to each element of a list.

5. Write a sequence-builder expression that has one free integer parameter n, and returns the list of all positive square roots of n (it will contain either 1 or 0 elements.

6. Sequence builder expression for all the positive integers with neither 3 nor 5 as a factor.

7. The list of powers of 2, using only multiplication, and recursion.

8. Write the list of prime numbers, given set-builder basic arithmetic and the gcd function.

9. Write, using only list comprehension and equality, the list of factors of n.

10. The Fibonacci sequence.

    Hint: Use an auxiliary list of ordered pairs.

Notion 159: Infinite Lists in Haskell

To compute with infinite lists we need a constructive notation. In Haskell `[a,b .. c]` defines an arithmetic sequence by its first and second elements a and b, and a bound c. So `[1,3 .. 10]` = `[1,3,5,7,9]`. Both b and c are optional, the defaults being `succ(a)` and ∞, respectively. Thus, `P = [1 ..]` is the list of positive integers defined by the implicit assertion that $n_1 = 1$ and $n_{i+1} = n_i+1$. Make the rule explicit, $a_1 = x$ and $a_{i+1} = f(a_i)$, to produce `(x, f(x), f(f(x)), ...)`. In Haskell this is `(iterate f x)`.

This is valid Haskell, but it takes *forever* to print out.

More complex list generation is available in Haskell.

```
[a | (a,b)<-(iterate (\(x,y)->(y,x+y)) (1,1))]
```

is Haskell code for the entire infinite Fibonacci sequence.

Compare this with the Scheme code for the same thing (see page 334). You should be able to identify all the essential components, even though the format is slightly, but not essentially, different from the structure used in the Scheme example. In practice, there are many different ways to produce infinite lists.

We are generating the elements of the list *on the fly*. What if we do not know how to generate these elements? Really? We do not know how to generate the next element? We do not know how to generate the next element from all the previous elements together with any auxiliary data that we might provide? Most likely, we would have very great difficulty doing *any* computation on such a list.

Most infinite lists are non-computable. Any attempt to construct an infinite list abstract type will leave out the vast majority of lists. But we do not have to worry about this here; the non-computable infinite lists correspond to non-computable problems.

There is no way to solve them on a digital computer.

Notion 160: Infinite Lists in Scheme

Some infinite structures can be implemented on digital computers. To
do so they must be encoded in the finite structures directly available on a
computer. An integer function, as code, implements an infinite structure
of ordered pairs. Certain computations may be expressed neatly using
infinite structures.

The computation of the primes may be expressed as

```
1. Start with (2,3, ... )
2. Eliminate all the multiples of the head from the tail
3. Repeat from step 2 on the tail
4. The primes are the head and what is left of the tail
```

In a more formal notation:

```
primes    = (sieve (cdr natural))
(sieve X) = (cons (car X) (sieve (eliminate (car X) X))
```

The infinite structures required are inbuilt in Haskell.
In Scheme we may encode an infinite list as (data mycar mycdr).

The natural numbers are

```
(
 1
 (lambda (x) (car x))
 (lambda (x) (cons (+ (car x) 1) (cdr x))
)
```

However, the normal car and cdr will not recognise what we are trying
to do with the infinite lists, so we need our own icar and icdr,

```
icar = (lambda (x) ((cadr x) x))
icdr = (lambda (x) ((caddr x) x))
```

A generic method for creating infinite sequences:

```
(iterate f x) = (x (f x) (f (f x)) (f(f(f x))) ... )
```

However, Fibonacci is not of this form. How do we create the Fibonacci sequence? Recall how to compute Fibonacci in a tail-recursive manner (or with a loop), `(a,b) -> (b,a+b)`

```
(
  (1 1)
  (lambda (x) (caar x))
  (lambda (x)
         (cons
              (cons (cadar x) (+ (caar x) (cadar x)))
              (cdr x)
         )
  )
)
```

The elements of this look like those from the while-loop:

```
                       (
x=init               init
while true
print result(X)   (lambda (x) (result (car x)))
X = body(X)       (lambda (x) (cons (body (car x)) (cdr x)))
                       )
```

This encapsulates computation of the entire infinite Fibonacci sequence. Since the loop never terminates, the test is not relevant.

A generic while-loop computes the elements of the sequence

$$(data, body(data), body^2(data), body^3(data)\ldots)$$

and returns the first element of this list for which the test is false.

In Haskell we can do this explicitly:

```
while test body data =
                 head (dropWhile test (iterate body data))
```

computing naturally with infinite structures.

Notion 161: Primitive List Recursion

The simplest way to express a short list is to write its elements explicitly. In Haskell and Prolog this is [1,2,3,4], in Scheme this is (1 2 3 4). The basic constructor is the cons operation, which prepends an element to a list. In Scheme this is (cons 1 '(2 3)), in Haskell (1:[2,3]) and in Prolog [1|[2,3]]. All produce the equivalent of [1,2,3].

Inductively, we define the list type as containing [ ], and for each list s and element e, the list type contains cons(e,s).

Many operations on lists can be defined using at most one instance of the cons operation.

For example,

```
length([ ]) = 0
length(cons(e,s)) = 1 + length(s)
```

We can also generate lists in the same way:

```
iota(0) = [ ]
iota(n+1) = cons(n+1,iota(n))
```

and with this definition:

```
iota 5 = [5,4,3,2,1]
```

These are examples of primitive list recursion.

Sometimes it is difficult to define a list in this manner, due to dependencies that go deeper down the list, for example, given a list, find the list of sums of two consecutive elements. (This will be one element shorter than the original).

This code covers it, but uses a nesting of cons operators.

```
addTwo([ ]) = [ ]
addTwo([a]) = [ ]
addTwo(cons(a,(cons(b,c))) = cons(a+b,addTwo(b,c))
```

We can avoid this problem by ...

```
addTwo(cons(a,b)) = aux(a,b)
aux(a,[ ]) = [ ]
aux(a,cons(b,c)) = cons(a+b,aux(b,c))
```

In this case, the aux function can be viewed as a mechanism to hide the extra cons application, however, when dealing with deeper dependencies, such as the list of all partial sums of a list, there is no longer any constant depth that will cover the problem.

A basic map operation is

```
map(f,[ ]) = [ ]
map(f,cons(a,b)) = cons(f(a),map(f,b))
```

Map is the principle of applying a function to each element of the list, turning a_i into $f(a_i)$

A basic filter operation is

```
filter(f,[ ]) = [ ]
filter(f,cons(a,b)) = if f(a) then cons(a,filter(f,b))
                               else filter(f,b)
```

Filter is a selection principle. We obtain from the list the list (in order with multiplicities intact) of all those elements that satisfy the selection criterion.

A basic fold operation is

```
fold f [ ] = d
fold f cons(a,b) = f a (fold f b)
```

A fold is the principle of replacing the cons operation with the operation f, but we need a definition to take care of the singleton list situation.

These operations together can be used to build up other operations on lists rapidly. The principle is to construct small formulae using the lists as primitive entities, like integers, which we manipulate by standard operations.

Exercise 22: Primitive List Recursion in Haskell

There are many functions that can be neatly written in Haskell from what amounts to a mathematical definition, using only the list constructor, and the integer field operations. The exercises on this page are intended to give practice in this approach.

1. Write a primitive list recursion that increments each of the integers on an integer list. For example `inclist [1,2,0] = [2,3,1]`.

2. Write a primitive list recursion that eliminates all the zeros from a list, that is `delzero [1,2,0] = [1,2]`. This should be done with three clauses, one for the base case, one for zero and one for non-zero.

3. Write a primitive list recursion that produces the list of all partial sums of a list, e.g., `psum [1,3,4,2] = [1,4,8,10]`.

   Hint: write a function `paux n l` that has the number to add as its first argument. And define `psum` in terms of this.

   This is a typical situation. The routine that we want to write can't be written nicely, so we write a different routine with more arguments as an auxiliary function to assist us.

   In this case, we want to write something that produces the partial sums of a list, but instead we write something that produces the partial sums, given the sum so far.

4. Write a primitive list recursion that adds up the squares of the integers on a list.

5. Write a primitive list recursion that computes the list of the first n Fibonacci numbers.

   Hint: Compute the generalised Fibonacci sequence. Use the basic tail-recursive form of Fibonacci. `(a,b)->(b,a+b)`, passing the state explicitly as two arguments to the function.

Appendices

End notes 340

Bibliography 351

Glossary 353

End notes

Note 1

Programmer discipline is the programmer voluntarily restricting the syntax to a subset of the full syntax available. This admits other language concepts into the language being used. Most corporate directives to programmers about the minutiae of programming refer to such disciplines. They may include conventions for naming of variables, for commenting of programs, when dynamic memory may be used, and so fourth. When a construct can be produced by replacing each nonexistent piece of syntax by a compound fragment of code in the existing language, then the extensions are referred to as *syntactic sugar*; they reduce the self-discipline required of the programmer, but do not substantially change the manner in which the program is written. If, however, the discipline requires substantial utilities to be written elsewhere and then called in the body of the program, this is no longer just sugar, but an emulation, or implementation of the feature. Adding garbage collection is an example. It certainly can be done in C, but it requires of the programmer a substantial understanding of techniques not directly related to the task at hand. This is why the step from C to Java is, from a fundamental perspective, a larger step than from C to C++.

Note 2

Abraham Robinson [18] approaches calculus from the principle that the differential dx is a symbolic constant δ, which can be added, subtracted, multiplied, and divided, like the variable in a polynomial expression, something that I·personally, at least, was told not to do in high school.

Note 3

In mathematics the term *algebra* unqualified, usually refers to linear algebra; this is unfortunate since linear algebra is a special case of the more natural universal algebra [5], which is relegated to using the composite term. The essential element of study of universal algebra is any collection of sets with any collection of operations on them satisfying any collection of axioms.

Note 4

Ben-Ari [3] covers a lot of material on basic problems and solutions of a type relevant to networked programming, such as on the world wide web. As well as giving solutions and code it also gives a number of proofs of the results, and example to motivate the requirement for demanding a proof of a protocol, rather than relying on testing. Although the chance of a fault may be demonstrated to be small by testing, once millions of transactions are going on all over the world there is bound to be a failure somewhere if it is just a matter of an accident of timing. Further testing of concurrent processes often does not model the true real-time behaviour of a network of millions of humans and computers all with their own interests at stake. Present day models for network behaviour are typically mainly empirical in nature, and limited in scope. Nothing beats a live test for coming up with the bizarre accident scenario.

Note 5

See work by Pratt [16] Generically the memory store of a computer can be modelled as a map from identifiers to values. An explicitly state-based computation proceeds by incrementally modifying this map. In particular, the command x=6 is essentially an array update, memory['x']=6. (See also the notion on generalised arrays and maps.)

Note 6

As explained by Marvin Minsky [15], these models of computation are intended as models for pragmatic computation. While infinitely extensible memory (that is, no hard limit) is actually a better model than a specific limit in practice, if we supposed that this infinite memory contained (arbitrary) infinite information, we could just list the answer to every problem there. To put it differently, we are looking to make a computer that will usefully compute something; where is that infinite information coming from? If it comes from a human, then we do not have an autonomous computer; if it comes from another computer, then in the chain of descent of computers one will have to have finite information, so that we can program it in a finite time and then leave it to run. In principle, we can have a tape full of symbols that are generated by another machine. In this case we are better off modelling it as one machine taking the input from another, since we can't wait forever for the first machine to start, in practice this always would be a buffered producer/consumer situation.

Note 7

Niklaus Wirth wrote a classic of computer science [21]. On the first page of the first chapter, Wirth comments *"The data represent an abstraction of reality in the sense that certain properties and characteristics of the real objects are ignored because they are peripheral and irrelevant to the particular problem. An abstraction is thereby also a simplification of the facts."* One, and possibly the single most important, of the core matters in science in general is to know what to ignore. You can *never* take everything into account. Attempting to do so will only result in failure. This matter is logically prior to almost everything else in any systematic study.

Note 8

The Mathematical Games Column, by Martin Gardner Scientific American 223 (October 1970): 120–123. The fantastic combinations of John Conway's new solitaire game "life". Since 1970 this cellular automata has been subjected to enormous quantities of serious, speculative, or recreational research. There is a large body of material and many life programs available on the web, which the reader should have no trouble in finding rapidly with a few simple searches. Philosophical and technical questions, many still open, abound in relation to this automaton so simple to define. I am unaware of any studies on the effect of non-planar topologies on the global behaviour of the evolution.

Note 9

Dewdney [7] wrote a particularly cogent example of the theory of two-dimensional universes. There are others, such as the classic by Abbot [1], but it really only covers geometry. Hinton [9] attempts to cover aspects of two-dimensional life, but ignores all the gory details. Dewdney, on the other hand, considers problems such as digestion, breathing, transfer of bodily fluids, predation, computation, and quantum mechanics. His book includes an illustrative story line, as well as some technical appendices. However, we should also mention Burger [4], and to a lesser degree Rucker [19]. It all makes for deeply fascinating reading, but is almost entirely outside the scope of the present book.

Note 10

There is a technical complication in the definition of equality due to the possibility of quoting. We may have $x == y$, but $"x" \neq "y"$ does not follow. Similarly $x == y$ does not mean $\&x == \&y$. This is a matter of notation, and relates to levels of indirection (see page 50). It does not otherwise affect the point being made. If an expression has access to the names of its arguments, rather than its values, then its *real* arguments are the names, and not the values. In the expression $M(a, b)$, we assume that a and b are the *real* arguments to M, whatever they may be. In an opposite view, given an understanding of equality, we might say that an expression, M, with no side effects, is a quoting function if $A = B$ does not imply $M(A) = M(B)$.

Note 11

Dr Carter Bays [2] http://www.cse.sc.edu/ bays/ (as of Feb 2005), of the University of South Carolina Department of Computer Science and Engineering, has worked on a three-dimensional version of John Conway's life cellular automata. This was discussed by Dewdney [6]. Implementations of this are fairly easy to find on the web. There are multi-dimensional equivalents of blinkers, gliders, and so fourth.

Note 12

You do not have to subscribe to materialistic philosophy to appreciate the pragmatic intention here. I am not a materialist, but the philosophy is useful in technical discussions. Independent of metaphysics, I assert that the mind is software, possibly running on hardware other than the brain. There is subconscious processing, which the conscious mind can affect. Anything carried in the conscious mind eventually filters into the subconscious. If we do not keep a logically clear conscious mind, then we can't validly expect the subconscious to be able to think clearly either. Constant regurgitation of ideas from the subconscious to the conscious (a mental chewing of the cud) is required for the healthy rational mind.

Experimental neurophysiology supports this view, as does our theoretical understanding of large neural nets. Large nets typically need a smaller moderator net to be able to learn. Without this the larger net is vulnerable to catastrophic loss of accumulated learning. The conscious mind appears to serve this purpose. This is why the central portions of the brain have been promoted as the true seat of consciousness. Necrosis (or a bullet) in this region kills the manifestation of mind faster and more effectively than does damage to the frontal lobes, which often result in behavioural damage that looks more like an inability to process certain information, than a critical loss of mind.

Note 13

Written on a piece of paper, an expression is a partially ordered collection of symbols. It is possible to build up a theory of expressions by considering them to be no more or less than a string of symbols written on paper. However, a central problem in this development is the difficulty of grouping sections of the string, and insulating them from other sections. By admitting the power of parentheses to group terms in the standard nested fashion, we solve all these problems. In practice, developments that do not admit parentheses spend the first part working on simulating the effect. The fact that it can be done is important, and it is advisable to understand one or two methods. However, to begin at this point would be rather like starting a course on driving by taking about the combustion properties of petrol. Thus, the entry point to this material is chosen as expressions considered as nested sequences of symbols, structured by parentheses. This is equivalent mathematically to saying that an expression is a tree decorated by the symbol set.

Note 14

It is fundamental to the normal operation of Von Neumann machines that some form of indirection can occur. That is, an address of some data may be handed over instead of the data itself. In this context, problems arise if there are more registers than symbols. The standard way around this is to store the address in multiple registers. This also leads to the concept of an offset address, in which only the relative location of the required data from the current instruction is stored. Other problems arise when memory is not available at an address. This commonly occurs, since the address space of a processor may be greater than that currently purchased for the given computer. This requires the concept of a memory fault ...what to do when an address is not valid, or refers to no data. All of these matters complicate the simple picture of register indirection, but do not invalidate it. For illustrative purposes only a clean centre of the material has been expressed.

Note 15

Although the term *register* may generically be taken as a synonym for memory cell, which is where the term *register indirection language* came from, it is probably more common to see this referring to a small number of fast cells that might not even be on the standard memory-addressing range, requiring special assembler operations to refer to them. On the PDP11 series of computers, registers could also be addressed through normal addressing techniques, and some of PDP11 code looks rather like register indirection language. This distinction in the use of the term register will not be emphasised here.

Note 16

Technically, primitive recursion refers to the class of primitive recursive functions. These are functions for which the only operations allowed are integer increment, and pure recursion. From this we can define addition by repeated increments, multiplication by repeated addition, exponentiation by repeated multiplication, tetration by repeated exponentiation, and much more. In fact, any computable function can be rigged up in this manner.

A natural generalisation of this begins by noticing that the point is that the integers themselves are defined by the idea of beginning with 0 and repeatedly adding 1. This can be taken as a definition of the natural numbers. We can then say that a primitive recursion is one that uses only the inductive structure in the definition of the original datatype.

Lists are made from a base datatype, the empty list, and repeated cons operations. In this sense, a primitive list recursion is one that involves only pure recursion and the use of cons inside an argument.

Primitive integer recursion in more detail:

Increment is primitive recursive. If f is primitive recursive, and $E(n,f)$ is an expression using only primitive recursive functions, then $f(0)=a$, $f(n+1)=E(n,f)$ is a primitive recursive definition.

Define the function at 0, define the recursion $f(n+1) = E(n,f)$.

$id(0) = 0$
$id(n+1) = n+1$

$add(x,0) = x$
$add(x,y+1) = (add(x,y))+1$

$zero(0) = 1$
$zero(n+1) = n*zero(n)$

$if(x,y,z) = zero(x)*y + (1-zero(x))*z$

$fact(0) = 1$
$fact(n+1) = (n+1)*fact(n)$

In a similar way we can define primitive recursion in lists.

In a similar way we can define primitive tree recursion.

For example, () is a tree and (t1, a, t2) is a tree for any two trees, t1 and t2. We define the action on the empty tree, and then give a decomposition $f(t1, a, t2) = E(t1,a,t2,f)$.

Note 17

There are several concepts wrapped up in the idea of literate programming. However, the central matter that I am interested in here is that programming by humans should be a human enterprise. Knuth has suggested that a program should, first and foremost, be a literary work, to be read by humans. This is analogous to the approach in a mathematics book. The text of the book is like the comments in a program, and it is typically bigger than the formal development.

Note 18

Suppose we want to define in a formal manner the set of properly bracketed expressions. By this we mean the set of expressions (for simplicity with only brackets) in which the brackets are properly nested. We could try saying that () is a properly bracketed expression, and if A and B are properly bracketed, then (AB) is also. It might seem that we have a good inductive definition. The problem is that it does not strictly *exclude* the expression "(". The axioms are all *positive* axioms. But to exclude explicitly all the other expressions can be troublesome, leading to definitions that are awkward. A standard method for getting out of this is to state that the set we want is the *smallest* that satisfies the axioms, which is also stated as the intersection of all those sets that satisfy the axioms. Because of the positive nature of the axioms it is clear that the intersection of any set of sets that satisfies the axioms also satisfies the axioms.

Note 19

It is often asserted that array lookup in an orthodox language is constant time, no matter what the size of the array. This, however, is wrong. Any practical cpu has a limit to the size of the addressable memory, and a typical desktop machine does not even have this much memory. Beyond the cpu capcity access would have to be to a disk, or tape, or over a network to a file server, and so on.

In the limit to infinity, this will be an order (log n) operation, rather than just order (n). This is because resolving an address by multiply indirections takes time proportional to the length of the address. This is the exact same limitation that is on the more pure languages.

While in practice it is certainly significant, the point is that the contemporary desktop machine has hardware assistance for constant time lookup in an array up to a certain size. This improves performance for the small size of array that is usually used. But this is explicitly because of hardware assistance, just as a matrix multiply can be constant time, up to a given size, when we have a graphics card installed.

Similar hardware assistance would speed up the pure expression languages as well, and in practice, Haskell, for example, has an array class that uses the underlying machine to get this speedup.

A similar matter often overlooked is that arithmetic is not constant time, addition is (log n) as well.

A practical example is sorting a very big list, so big that it overflows onto large disk files that cannot be loaded into memory. It does not conform to the standard constraints on sorting that are based on the presumption of constant time lookup.

Note 20

Arthur Koestler [12] used the word *holon* to mean a part which is also a whole in itself. At first I thought this was needless, since a part is generally also a thing on its own. But, in trying to describe what each entry in this book is, I realised that I also wanted to emphasise, a part which is a viable whole in itself, without needing a reference to what it is a part of. So each entry is indeed a holon.

Note 21

Just to put this into context, the three R's of primary education are reading 'riting, and 'rithmetic. (It works better if you say it). And the phrase *the three R's* is often used to refer to the basics of any subject. Usually the words are picked to have some word play involved. My favourite is the three F's of biology, Feeding, Fighting, and Reproduction. However, when I came up with three R's of programming, they just fitted so naturally that no word-play presented itself. Maybe next time.

Note 22

The Hanoi sequence, named here from the puzzle *the Towers of Hanoi* is something of which all computer scientists should be aware. It can be defined in many ways, one direct method is $H_{n+1} = H_n, n + 1, H_n$ with H_0 being the empty string, and $H = \lim_{n \to \infty} H_n$. It is implicated in the solution to the Towers of Hanoi puzzle, but also in the incrementing of a

Gray's code number, and a variety of other computer-related problems. Many of the non-trivial puzzles, such as Chinese rings, also use this pattern in their solution. It is as ubiquitous as π.

Note 23

Reductions can define negative integers, rationals, and complex rationals (see page 223), but not real numbers. The limitation is not specific to reduction. It is a central issue in discrete computation that **there is no digital representation of real numbers**. It is an important general point. All digital computation is computation with integers. This has strong practical implications when dealing with continuous data (e.g., by using floating-point) on a digital computer. The interested reader could follow up with readings in lambda calculus, universal algebra, Peano arithmetic [8], the word problem in monoid theory, Markov machines, Post machines, and DNA computers. There is also work in general graph reduction and representation of recursive functions by finite graphs.

Bibliography

[1] *Flatland: A Romance in Many Dimensions* by Edwin Abbot Abbot, Dover Publications [1992], ISBN: 048627263X.

[2] *A New Candidate Rule for the Game of Three-Dimensional Life.* Carter Bays, Complex Systems 6 1992, pages 433–441.

Further Notes on the Game of Three Dimensional Life. Carter Bays, Complex Systems 8 1994, pages 67–73.

Cellular Automata in the Triangular Tessellation. Carter Bays, Complex Systems 8 1994, pages 127–150.

[3] *Principles of Concurrent and Distributed Programming* by M. Ben-Ari, Prentice Hall [1990] .

[4] *Sphereland* by Dionys Burger, Harper Resource [1994], ISBN: 0062732765.

[5] *A Course in Universal Algebra* by Stanley Burris and H.P. Sankappanavar. Out of print from Springer Verlag Graduate Texts in Mathematics [1981], this excellent book can at the time of writing (2005) be downloaded from http://www.thoralf.uwaterloo.ca/htdocs/ualg.html.

[6] *The Armchair Universe* by A.K. Dewdney, W.H. Freeman & Company [1988], ISBN: 0716719398.

[7] *The Planiverse* by A.K. Dewdney, Picador [1984].

[8] *Frege, Dedekind, and Peano on the Foundation of Arithmetic (Methodology and Science Foundation: No. 2)* by D.A. Gillies Longwood Pr Ltd (June 1, 1982) ISBN: 9023218884.

351

[9] *An Episode of Flatland* by Charles Hinton. (Hard to get, I have only a pdf copy of some pages.)

[10] *Communicating Sequential Processes*, by C.A.R Hoare. Prentice Hall, Series in Computer Science [1985], ISBN: 0131532715.

[11] *Denotational Semantics, The Scott-Strachey Approach to Programming Language Theory* by Joseph Stoy, Forward by Dana Scott, The MIT Press [1977].

[12] *The Ghost in the Machine* by Arthur Koestler, Arkana reprint edition [1990], ISBN: 0140191925.

[13] *Electronic Analogue Computers*, by Granino Korn and Theresa Korn, McGraw Hill Book Company, [1956].

[14] *Hilbert's Tenth Problem* by Y.V. Matiyasevich, MIT Press, [1993].

[15] *Computation: Finite and Infinite Machines* by Marvin Minksy, Prentice Hall International [1972].

[16] *Programming Languages, Design and Implementation* by Terrence W. Pratt & Marvin V. Zerlkowitz, Prentice Hall [2001], ISBN: 0130276782

[17] *The C Programming Language* by Kernighan and Ritchie, 2nd edition, Prentice Hall software series [1988], ISBN: 0131103628.

[18] *Non-Standard Analysis* by Abraham Robinson, originally published 1965, available from Princeton Press, series Landmarks in Mathematics [1996], ISBN: 0691044902

[19] *The Fourth Dimension* by Rudy Rucker. Houghton Mifflin, Reprint edition [1985], ISBN: 0395393884

[20] *What is The Name of This Book* by Raymond Smullyan, Touchstone, reissue edition [1986], ISBN: 0671628321.

[21] . *Algorithms + Data Structures = Programs* by Niklaus Wirth, Prentice Hall, series in Automatic Computation [1976], ISBM: 0130224189.

Glossary

Abstract: Taken in a pure sense as the subject of formal studies, and removed from practical considerations, simplified, made amenable to reason.

Algorithm: A method for computing with clear deterministic steps which is sure to get the right answer in a finite number of steps.

Analogue (computer): Technically meaning to compute by analogy, usually used to mean continuous rather than discrete, misapplied to most "analogue" watches, whose hands actually move in discrete steps.

Axiom: A explicit basic assumption to be used in reasoning about a system. If not stated explicitly it would be a hidden assumption, and should be made into an axiom.

Heuristic: A method for computing with clear steps, but which might generate the wrong answer or fail to terminate.

Infinite: A number unchanged by addition of 1. Informally, indefinitely large. More precisely, a set is infinite if it is the same size as some proper subset of itself.

Lambda Calculus: The study and use of expressions built up from $(\lambda x.xx)$ and similar, indicating the argument and code for a computation.

Natural Language: The type of language a human might like to communicate using. In particular, one that has appeared "naturally" in the general environment.

Polynomial: An expression of the form $x^n + 3x + 5$, or similar, a sum of powers of one or more variable symbols. May be taken to represent a real function, or a formal expression.

Recursive: Being defined in terms of itself. Strictly this makes its definition a non-trivial equation to solve.

Stochastic: A method for computing with some stochastic (random, non-deterministic) component in the steps, and possible non-zero chance of error.

Substitution: The process of replacing one thing for another in a bigger structure, especially the value of a variable for the variable itself.

Tuple: The generalisation of couple, being a list of items such as (a, b, c, d), the standard workhorse for construction and definition in mathematics, means roughly the same as the notion of a record in computer science.

Turing Machine: A simple computer that reads and writes a tape using a head with limited movement controlled by a finite state machine. Several variations are defined. Of theoretical rather than practical interest.

Uncountable: Being more numerous than the integers. The real numbers are uncountable, and so are the integer functions. But the computable integer functions are countable.

Unification: The process of finding out what variable substitutions will make two expressions equal. Is the implicit basis of most formal reasoning.

Von Neumann Machine: A computer with a linear random-access memory, and a finite state machine cpu similar to contemporary desktop hardware.

Index

Y-combinator, 86, 88, 90, 260, 262

Abstract, 2
Abstract datatypes, 54
Abstract machine, 18, 48
Abstract methods, 175
Algebraic, 115, 225
Algorithm, 48, 144
Analogue computer, 41
Analogue machine, 39
Applet, 209
Arithmetic, 58, 84, 115, 138, 205,
    215, 217, 219, 221, 223, 225
Array, 161
Artificial Intelligence, 149

Blocking, 306
Boole, George, 97
Boolean algebra, 99
Bracketing, 74
Bubble sort, 121

C, 70
C code, 155, 157, 159, 161, 163,
    165, 167
Cantor, 152
Casting, 171, 173, 185
Cauchy sequence, 115
Cellular automata, 40, 42
Checking, 185, 188
Churche's thesis, 143
Circle, 93
CODASYL, 181, 183

Code blocks, 200
Code derivation, 125
Combinators, 90
Complex numbers, 223
Complexity, 144
Computability, 140
Computable reals, 151
Conscious, 4
Control flow, 117
Conway's game of life, 42
Conway, John, 134
CPU, 44
Craft, 12

Database, 183
Dedekind, 115
Design, 190
Desktop, 44
Deterministic, 30
Differentiation, 81
Digital, 20
Digital machine, 46
Dijkstra, Edsger, 6
Discrete, 20
Documentation, 10

Ellipsis, 93
Equality, 66
Equations, 62, 68
Exact, 225
Expression, 74
Expressions, 66

Factor graph, 111, 113
Factorial, 119
Field, 174
Finite state machine, 132
Formal, 109, 119, 121, 123
Formal equation, 64
Formal logic, 99
Formal models, 102
Function, 163
Functions, 159, 167, 191

General machine, 46
Godel, Kurt, 138
Graph, 105
Grobner, 142
Guards, 300

Haskell, 77, 199
Heuristic, 48
Hexagonal grid, 40
Hidden state, 30
HTML, 209
Human error, 150
Hyper-link, 209
Hyperfactorial, 88
Hypertext, 209

Imperative, 195
Impure, 80
Infinite, 26, 30, 34, 36, 38, 44, 46, 132
Infinite lists, 204, 325, 328, 333, 334
Inheritance, 181
Integer, 115, 219
Interaction, 20

Jacobi, 60
Java, 18, 70, 76, 169, 173–175, 192, 203, 209, 258
JVM, 18

Karnaugh map, 99
Klein, Felix, 142
Knuth, Donald, 10

Lambda, 80, 82, 84, 86, 87
Lambda calculus, 136
Life, 42
Linked lists, 54
List, 193
Lists, 54
Literate, 10
Logic, 97, 101, 127, 138, 201
Logic programming, 76, 78

Markup, 209
Math induction, 125
Maths, 102, 134
Matiyasevich, 142
Meaning, 136
Mechanical computer, 41
Memory protection, 34
Meta logic, 207
Mind, 4
Models, 6
Modularity, 2
Modulo, 217
Mutex, 307, 309, 310
Mutual exclusion, 296, 298, 299
Mythos, 8, 161

n log n, 133
Natural language, 150
Naturals, 215
Negation, 78
Nesting, 200
Network, 105
Networks, 54
Non-deterministic, 30
NP, 148
NP complete, 148
Numeral, 58

Numerals, 60

Objects, 177, 179, 183

P, 148
P and NP, 30, 146
Paradoxes, 136
Peano arithmetic, 58
Peterson, 310
Petri nets, 107
Physical computer, 41
Pneumatic, 24
Pointers, 159, 171
Polynomials, 142
Post condition, 127
Powers, 244
Pragmatics, 8
Pre condition, 127
Predicate calculus, 76
Predicates, 101
Preprocessing, 166
Prime program, 117
Product graph, 113
Programming, 12
Prolog, 201, 203–205, 207, 208
Proof, 119, 121, 129, 308, 314
Propositions, 97
Protocols, 314
Psychology, 6, 93, 101, 166, 197
Pumping lemma, 132
Pure, 52

Quantifiers, 101
Quantum, 33
Quantum computing, 46

R's, the three, 12
Radicals, 142
Random, 129
Rational, 4, 14, 115
Rationals, 221

Reasoning, 123
Reduction, 58, 70, 74, 82, 88, 201
Reduction engine, 72
Reference, 173
Register language, 50
Register machine, 38
Russell's paradox, 134
Russell, Bertrand, 134

Satisfiability, 148
Scheme, 193
Semantics, 8
SK combinators, 90
Sorting, 133, 197, 199, 302, 304
Spaghetti, 41
Specification, 62
Stack, 38
Stack machine, 36
Stacks, 54
State, 30
State machine, 20, 22, 103, 110
Stochastic, 48
String reduction, 58
String substitution, 56
Substitution, 52, 54, 56, 62, 68, 197
Substitution computing, 61
Subtype, 189
Summation, 95
Swapping, 284
Symbolic, 22
Syntax, 8

Technical code, 2, 12, 14
Temporal, 107
Theories, 6
Threads, 192, 272, 274, 280, 284, 288, 296, 298, 299
Tree scan, 203
Tree search, 201
Truth table, 99

Tuple, 110
Turing, 149
Turing machine, 26, 28, 109
Turing test, 149
Type, 181, 183, 185, 187–190

Uncountable, 152
Unification, 62, 64, 66, 201
Unification reduction, 70
Universal machine, 46

Virtual machine, 18
Von Neumann bottle-neck, 34
Von Neumann machine, 34

Web-page, 209

Zebra, 97